l.a.
with kids

Travel Guides to Planet Earth!

CRITICAL ACCLAIM FOR
OPEN ROAD TRAVEL GUIDES!

Whether you're going abroad or planning a trip in the United States, take Open Road along on your journey. Our books have been praised by **Travel & Leisure, The Los Angeles Times, Newsday, Booklist, US News & World Report, Endless Vacation, American Bookseller, Coast to Coast**, and many other magazines and newspapers!

Don't just see the world – experience it with Open Road!

about the author

Elizabeth Arrighi Borsting is the former public relations manager for the Queen Mary in Long Beach, California. Currently, she is a free-lance writer and public relations consultant for the hospitality industry. In addition to *L.A. with Kids*, she has also authored three other books for Open Road Publishing: *Celebrity Weddings & Honeymoon Getaways, Southern California Guide,* and *California's Best B&Bs.*

Borsting has been a contributing editor for *Honeymoon Magazine,* and her work has also appeared in *National Geographic Traveler* and the *Los Angeles Times,* just to name a few. She resides with her husband, dog, and two young children in Long Beach, California, just south of Los Angeles.

Open Road - Travel Guides to Planet Earth!

Open Road Publishing has guide books to exciting, fun destinations on four continents. As veteran travelers, our goal is to bring you the best travel guides available anywhere!

No small task, but here's what we offer:

• All Open Road travel guides are written by authors with a distinct, opinionated point of view – not some sterile committee or team of writers. Our authors are experts in the areas covered and are polished writers.

• Our guides are geared to people who want to make their own travel choices. We'll show you how to discover the real destination – not just see some place from a tour bus window.

• We're strong on the basics, but we also provide terrific choices for those looking to get off the beaten path and experience the country or city – not just see it or pass through it.

• We give you the best, but we also tell you about the worst and what to avoid. Nobody should waste their time and money on their hard-earned vacation because of bad or inadequate travel advice.

• Our guides assume nothing. We tell you everything you need to know to have the trip of a lifetime – presented in a fun, literate, nononsense style.

• And, above all, we welcome your input, ideas, and suggestions to help us put out the best travel guides possible.

l.a.
with kids

Travel Guides to Planet Earth!

Elizabeth Arrighi Borsting

open road publishing

Open Road Publishing

We offer travel guides to American and foreign locales. Our books tell it like it is, often with an opinionated edge, and our experienced authors always give you all the information you need to have the trip of a lifetime. Write for your free catalog of all our titles.

Open Road Publishing
P.O. Box 284, Cold Spring Harbor, NY 11724
E-mail: Jopenroad@aol.com

1st Edition

Library of Congress Control No. 2002117522
ISBN 1-892975-85-8

Front cover photo courtesy of CalTour. Maps by James Ramage.
The author has made every effort to be as accurate as possible, but neither she nor the publisher assume responsibility for the services provided by any business listed in this guide; for any errors or omissions; or any loss, damage, or disruptions in your travels for any reason.

l.a. with kids

contents

8. which one is my room?   141

9. i'm hungry!   166

index   191

Maps

Chapter 1

Los Angeles is as much a playground for children as it is for adults. The never-ending stream of theme parks, sporting events, greenbelts, entertainment and offbeat attractions creates the idyllic setting for a family holiday.

Unlike other major cities, where the core of activity is isolated to a single location, L.A. is a sprawling metropolis with many unique pockets. The geography is as diverse as the people. Primarily a desert basin, the region is surrounded by the San Gabriel Mountain range and divided by the Santa Monica Mountains. Los Angeles County boasts 81 miles of coastline with altitudes fluctuating from nine feet below sea level at Wilmington to 10,080 feet above sea level atop Mt. San Antonio. The entire county, which spans 467 miles, is home to 88 incorporated cities ranging from Vernon (population 100) to Los Angeles (population 3.7 million). There are several unique and charming neighborhoods to be found, including the ethnic Eastside, trendy Westside, bustling Downtown, a pair of Valleys, one of which spawned the Valley Girl craze, and, of course, the glistening beach cities immortalized in both music and film. Los Angeles is both a creative and inventive city having given birth to the Internet, Barbie Doll, Mazda Miata, Space Shuttle, DC-3 and, of course, the lovable Mickey Mouse.

For children, Greater Los Angeles represents a land of perpetual fun and excitement. There's the major theme parks, such as Disneyland Resort, Universal Studios Hollywood, Six Flags Magic Mountain and Knott's Berry Farm, where looping rides and endless entertainment provide hours of mindless fun. Those mesmerized by movie making magic will enjoy touring some of Hollywood's major studios, strolling along Hollywood Boulevard and its Walk of

Fame, and visiting some famous and historic theaters. There's even a likely chance you'll catch a production in the making as many television shows and major motion pictures are filmed on the city's streets.

With an average of 329 days of sunshine each year, time spent among L.A.'s great outdoors is time spent well. There are plenty of parks, beachside bike trails, water parks and jutting piers to explore by day, as well as an array of outdoor venues to discover once the sun begins to set. And, while Los Angeles can be pricey, it is also extremely affordable. There are many ways for you and your family to enjoy yourselves without spending a dime, including prowling around selected museums, listening to a live outdoor concert, being part of a studio audience at a taping of television show, scouting legendary landmarks, matching your hand and footprints with those of a celebrity in front of Grauman's Chinese Theatre or taking a self-guided tour of the stars' homes.

Los Angeles has been called many things: Lost Angeles, City of Angeles, Tinseltown, La La Land. And, while it is probably best known as the entertainment capital of the world, it is also a city of many distinctions. There are more than 300 museums and, according to the National Register of Historic Places, the largest historical theater district in the world is located along Downtown's Broadway. Los Angeles is also the only city to play host to the Summer Olympics...twice...1932 and 1984. And, for the seafaring enthusiast, the only remaining wooden lighthouse in the world is located here as well. Politicos might find it interesting to learn that Downtown L.A. is the largest government center outside of Washington D.C. And, parents take note: Los Angeles County is home to 158 colleges and universities, including such prestigious institutions as Occidental, The University of Southern California (USC), Pepperdine University and UCLA, just to name a few.

With that said, be sure to arm yourself with some double-digit sunblock, a pair of dark shades, maybe an autograph book and this guide of course. Then set out to discover Los Angeles for yourself. Just like the thousands who have ventured here before you, you'll come to love L.A.

Chapter 2

From Reel to Real

Los Angeles wasn't always about glitz, glamour, close-ups and comebacks. It began as a sleepy pueblo whose first known inhabitants were the peaceful Gabrieleno Indians. These natives lived in dwellings from Orange County to Malibu with their main village, Yang-Na, located where City Hall stands today. Explorers, such as Juan Rodrieguez Cabrillo, began arriving as early as 1542, but it wasn't until 1769 when Gaspar de Portola conducted land exploration that the real Spanish settlement took hold. Soon after, the San Gabriel and San Fernando Missions, which still stand today, were established and Franciscan fathers and Spanish soldiers were summoned to settle the area. The Indians provided the labor, while the missionaries took it upon themselves to convert the natives to their Christian faith.

Los Angeles's official birthday is September 4, 1781, which marks when 44 "vecinos pobladores" —village set-tlers from the Mexican provinces of Sonora and Sinaloa—made what is now Downtown Los Angeles their new home. Only two of the original settlers were Spaniards, the rest were Indians, Blacks and Mestizos, all of whom were greeted by the tribe of Yangna Indians. The Spaniards named their new settlement "El Pueblo de Nuestra Senora la Reina de Los Angeles," better known as the Queen of the Angels. In 1835, when the territory was passed from Spain to Mexico, Los Angeles was declared an official city. Eleven years later American soldiers entered Los Angeles and Old Glory has flown above the city ever since.

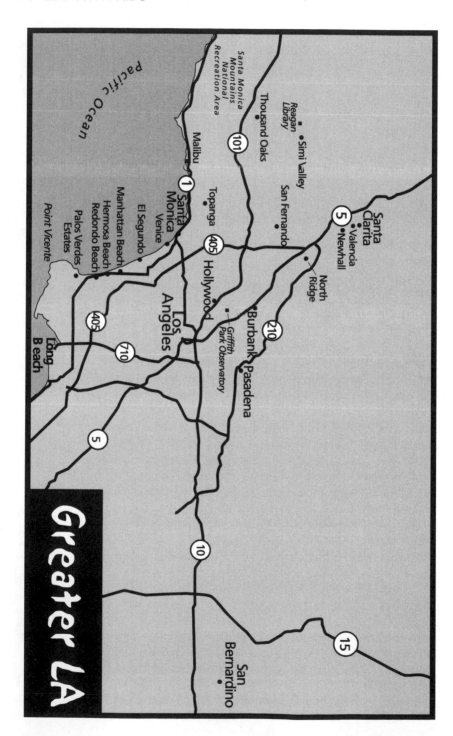

Less than 100 years later, Los Angeles would become fraught with would-be filmmakers and struggling actors looking to make their mark on the silver screen. It all began when Chicago filmmaker Col. William Selig, frustrated by the weather conditions of his native Windy City, eyed some promotional material from the Los Angeles Chamber of Commerce stating that the area boasted 350 days of sunshine a year. A skeptic, Selig sent two of his men west to investigate, both of whom spent most of their time bronzing themselves beneath swaying palms before summoning their boss to join them. In 1908 Selig completed the first full-length feature film in California, *The Count of Monte Cristo*, and thus an entire industry was born.

Today, Los Angeles is a sprawling city comprised of a number of remarkable facets. From Hollywood to Santa Monica, Downtown to Malibu, parents quickly discover there is never a dull moment. Along with the lights and cameras, there is plenty of action taking place within L.A.'s city limits.

Traveling with Kids

Traveling with children can be both trying and triumphant, depending on their moods and yours, of course. The old adage *Be Prepared* has never had as much impact as on a family vacation. You know your children best, so try to anticipate their needs before you find yourself 30,000 feet in the air or at a standstill during a typical L.A. traffic jam.

This book contains a number of attractions and venues that are appealing to both children and adults. There are **Parent Tips** to guide you along the way, as well as **Fun Facts** to make those trying moments a bit more tolerable.

In the meantime here are some tips to keep your sanity in check:

En Route

Whether traveling by plane, train or automobile, make sure you have all the essentials needed. If you're traveling with an **infant,** you'll want to have a diaper bag on hand filled with plenty of nappies, wipes, pacifiers (especially true when flying as this lessens the pressure on tiny ears), formula/juice/water, finger foods such as Cheerios, toys, and at least one change of clothes. To eliminate the need for refrigeration, pre-measure water into bottles then add powder formula at feeding time.

Toddlers and pre-schoolers have shorter attention spans, but the excitement of traveling, especially by plane or train, can keep little ones mesmerized for hours. Be sure to have a stash of toys (avoid ones with several pieces as they will most likely get lost), plus diapers or disposable underwear as accidents can happen to those who are potty trained, favorite foods and sippy cups. For **older children,** especially teenagers, you may want to share with them maps and brochures, provide them with disposable cameras, and also take along some of their favorite snacks.

As for parents, be sure to have handy a change of clothes in case you're spit up on or spilled on, whichare common occurrences when traveling with young children. Also, make sure you carry a recent photo of your children in case you should become separated at anytime during your trip.

Parent Tip

California law requires all children under six years or 60 pounds traveling in automobiles to ride restrained in a safety seat. Drivers and parents can be fined up to $250 for not complying. Rental car companies provide car seats for an additional charge, but cannot guarantee one will be available. If flying, you can still bring along your own. At check in, the airline will consider it one piece of baggage, place it in a secured plastic bag, and send it on its way with the rest of your luggage.

Hotels

While many hotels provide cribs, I have found that unless I'm staying at a four-star hotel, the quality of the crib can be unpredictable. Also, some hotels will charge extra for this service. You may want to consider bringing along a portable playpen, which can double as a crib (don't forget the bedding). Most hotels also have a policy where kids stay free. This typically applies if the child is under 18 years of age and shares the same room as their parents or guardians. If your brood is large, you may want to consider booking adjoining rooms or checking in at a suite-style hotel, such as the Embassy Suites, where rates include breakfast as well.

Also, if traveling with toddlers, don't forget to baby proof the room. Bring outlet protectors, and make a sweep of the balcony and bathroom for potential hazards. Put away small objects and be sure to teach your children to never open the hotel door to ANYONE.

This applies to both young children and teenagers.

Note on tipping: this is generally an uncomfortable subject. Did I tip too much? Not enough? Should I tip at all? Generally bellhops receive 50¢ to $1 a bag, daily maid service requires $1-$2 a day left at the end of your stay, and parking valets usually receive $2. When it comes to tipping restaurant servers, simply double the sales tax.

Involve the Kids

As parents, we're accustomed to telling our kids what to do and when to do it. But try to remember this is their vacation, too. Involve them in the decision making by letting them help plan the itinerary.

What do they want to see and do while in Los Angeles? Do they want to hit every theme park? Hang out in front of Brad Pitt's house? Or, if you have teenage daughters, are they wanting to prowl around the mall? Remember, kids mean well but can be self centered. Before you flat out refuse, be willing to teach them the importance of compromise. Every theme park may be out of the question, but a visit to their top two favorites is doable. Squatting in front of Brad Pitt's home for the day is simply not an option, but an organized tour of the stars' homes is.

Remember to allow for some down time so that everyone has an opportunity to pursue their own interests, and don't attempt to do everything together. Maybe one parent takes the kids for the afternoon, while the other lounges at the swimming pool. Older children should be allowed to do some exploring on their own as well. A little separation for all is the key in reducing crankiness. Be sure to consider optional activities; in other words, have a "Plan B" in place.

Keep it Simple

You've been planning this trip for months and have probably spent a lot of time and money just getting to Los Angeles. So it's only natural that you want to do and see as much as humanly possible. But sometimes kids, especially younger children, don't necessarily share that sentiment. Here are some tips that might be of help:

The Art of Traveling

Seek out **museums and historical sites that offer something for families**. The California Science Center, Getty Museum, and the Petersen Automotive Museum all offer family programs. The sheer size of the Queen Mary in Long Beach never ceases to amaze young ones, and the ship's history is fascinating to both children and parents.

It also helps to think outside the box. Both Grauman's Chinese Theater and the El Capitan are beautiful Hollywood landmarks with ties to Hollywood's Golden Age, but they are also functional in that they are still operating as movie theaters. Before going into either (they're located on opposite sides of Hollywood Boulevard), spend some time at the Forecourt of the Stars, which fronts Grauman's, to see if your hand and footprints match any of the celebrity casts.

And Action!

If your kids are movie buffs, prior to your visit rent some films in which Los Angeles serves as the backdrop. A few good ones are *Double Indemnity, Fast Times at Ridgemont High, The Rocketeer, L.A. Confidential, Nick of Time, Sunset Boulevard, Earthquake* and *Chinatown*. Of course, you'll want to be sure they're age appropriate before popping one into the DVD player. Then hunt for some of the landmarks featured in the film. Also, a stroll down Hollywood's Walk of Fame always makes for an interesting afternoon. As for museums, there are a few in town that specialize in nothing but Hollywood lore.

Making History

Add an educational element to your travels by visiting one of the 21 **California Missions** established by Father Junipero Serra during the 18th century. Los Angeles County is home to **Mission San Gabriel Arcangel** and **Mission San Fernando Rey de Espana**, while Orange County is home to the breathtaking **Mission San Juan Capistrano.** To learn more about the California Missions, log onto to these informative websites:

• *http://missions.bgmm.com*
• *www.ca-missions.org*
• *www.rawbw.com/~cmi*
• *www.californiamissions.com*

Long Beach has two ranchos, Los Cerritos and Los Alamitos, shows what life was like in these parts during the early 19th century. Both ranchos originated from Rancho Santa Gertrudes, the largest land grant ever bestowed in Southern California, and offer tours, picnics and special events year round.

Travel the Globe

Los Angeles is probably one of the most diverse cities in the world. In one afternoon you can travel the globe just by visiting one of the city's ethnic neighborhoods. Perhaps your child has studied about China, Mexico or Japan in a world history or geography class. Well, if they can't get to these countries personally then at least they can get a flavor for these and many other cultures while in Los Angeles. There is Little Toyko, Chinatown, and Olvera Street, just to name a few. Most of these destinations have cultural centers, as well as plenty of shops and restaurants.

Keeping to a Routine of Sorts

There is nothing better than hitting the open road. But no matter how fabulous the trip, kids still seem to yearn for some kind of routine. One summer when we were vacationing at a great resort on the Big Island of Hawaii, our five-year-old son insisted that he begin his day by watching the latest episode of his favorite cartoon. It was part of his routine at home and, thankfully it came on rather early in the morning so it really didn't impact our day. But these "routines" of sorts are important to children, so if you can still keep some sort of schedule (i.e. eating at regular times, going to bed near the regular hour, and so on), then it makes life that much easier.

Fun Facts

Since you're visiting California, you might be interested to know that the state is home to the 14, 494-feet Mt. Whitney, the highest peak in the Continental United States, as well as the lowest point, Death Valley at 282 feet below sea level. Ironically, the two are geographically and visibly close to one another. Here are some interesting facts about the nation's 31st state.

State Flower: The Golden Poppy has been the official state flower since 1903, beating out such competitors for the title as the white poppy and the Mariposa lily.

State Dance: What else? The West Coast Swing, which came into fashion during the 1930s when a new form of music swept the nation.

State Animal: Since 1953 it has been the California grizzly bear.

Largest City: Los Angeles

State Motto: "Eureka, " a Greek term for "I have found it." It refers to the discovery of gold and the subsequent frenzy that ensued during the mid-19th century.

Origin of Name: California was named by the Spanish after Califia, a mythical paradise written by Montalvo in 1510 and featured in his Spanish romance. California's nickname is the Golden State.

State Song: *I Love You California*, written by F. B. Silverwood and A.F. Frankenstin, was adopted as the state song in 1951, but didn't get the official stamp of approval until 1988.

State Tree: The majestic California Redwood was named the official state tree in 1937.

State Flag: California's historic Bear Flag was raised in Sonoma, California, on June 14, 1846, by a clan of American settlers revolting against Mexican rule. Designed by William Todd on a piece of un-bleached cotton, its single crimson star mirrored the lone star of Texas. The image of a grizzly bear represented the state's population of such beasts, and the words *California Republic* were written beneath both images. The design was adopted by the 1911 Legislature as the official State Flag.

Play Time

If running around town from place to place can be tiring on adults, just imagine how taxing it is on little ones? Once when we were traveling through California's Wine Country our son, who was three at the time, eyed a playground in the middle of Sonoma's town square. That day we had dragged him through vineyards, gourmet markets, shops and every other place that holds no interest for children. Now it was his turn. So, instead of dining at one of the area's great restaurants, we grabbed sandwiches from a nearby deli, picnicked in the park and let him play until it was dark. The down time did his dad and I some good, too.

Chapter 3

planning your trip

Climate & Weather

Is there ever a bad time to visit Los Angeles? Hardly. L.A. enjoys an enviable climate, which accounts for the many transplants that now call it home. Though the region has been accused of having only one season—Idyllic—temperatures definitely dip once summer comes to an end, evenings tend to be cool year round and humidity is rarely an issue.

Summer

While Los Angeles can be enjoyed all year long, the influx of visitors arrive during the summer months. This is the peak season when accommodations and crowds, especially families and students, reach a crescendo. The theme parks are at their busiest and remain open until late in the night. June typically remains cool, but temperatures tend to rise dramatically during July and August, hovering somewhere around the low- to mid-80s.

Spring

While the calendar may say otherwise, Los Angeles and most of Southern California really begins its spring in February. You'll find flowers beginning to bloom, the days growing slightly longer and average temperatures in the mid 60s. It's not unusual to see small crowds gathering at the beach in the hope of getting a head start on their tans. You'll also see hotels and attractions lower their prices, especially if you take advantage of the mid-week bargains.

Fall & Winter

This is one of the nicest times to experience Los Angeles. The weather is still warm; in fact, September is typically a hot month. As the temperatures begin to drop, so do hotel prices, and the crowds begin to vanish as well. Winter is a snowless wonderland, and at holiday time it's especially festive with Santa arriving to various areas via surf board, helicopter, skis, boat and bungee. You'll also find that most every beach community hosts an annual boat parade where everything from a kayak to a luxury yacht is draped in holiday lights.

If you enjoy theme parks, Disneyland Resort goes all out during the holidays with a cleverly orchestrated parade, free shopping along Main Street, and an ice-skating rink located within their resort hotel. The winter is also a great time to participate in a whale watching expedition or take a day trip to Catalina Island. The average daytime temperatures remain in the mid- to high-60s and, although this is typically considered the rainy season, in 2002 the region experienced its lowest rainfall in decades.

Parent Tip

Along the ocean and the coastal regions, the weather boasts a Mediterranean climate year round. Temperatures rarely drop below 40 degrees in the winter, and never reaches much beyond 80 degrees during the summer months. A thick marine layer, or fog, often hangs over the beach cities in the mornings and usually burns off by the early afternoon. While it creates plenty of bad hair days for residents, it also serves as a natural cooling device and a form of insulation. You'll discover the hottest months to be August and September with average temperatures ranging from the mid-70s to the low 80s. Move a bit inland, and the temperatures begin to rise.

In fact, the Los Angeles valleys can often be 10-degrees hotter than the coastal communities and, because they are surrounded by mountains, they are conducive to smog. December and January are the chilliest months, when it's not unusual for temperatures to fluctuate in the 50s along the coast. For many, these "frigid" conditions will feel like paradise to those who hail from much harsher climates. At any rate, weather conditions should always play a factor when planning a trip.

With all this perpetual sunshine Angelenos have developed thin skins when it comes to fluctuating weather patterns. Should the temperatures climb near the three-digit mark, you'll hear plenty of complaints as residents flock to the beach or hole up in air-conditioned buildings. Should a winter storm sweep in from the north, it will inevitably be the lead story in local news. Though Los Angeles has some of the nicest weather on earth, when it does rain it tends to pour. Malibu, one of the region's most affluent areas, is subject to mudslides and flooding, as well as fires. An annual weather phenomenon is the Santa Ana winds. Unlike the name implies, they don't originate from the Orange County suburbs, instead they blow in from the desert creating hot, dry conditions. This is when the area's fire fighters are busy trying to control flames in an attempt to save homes, businesses and forests. Again, the residents of Malibu and those living in the canyon areas are the most vulnerable to these conditions and are often evacuated when a blaze erupts.

Still, with the occasional mudslide, flood, brush fire or earthquake, you can't beat the climate of Los Angeles.

What to Pack

Before we had children, packing for my husband and I usually consisted of one suitcase and a separate bag for toiletries. Oh, those were the days. Still, I find that overpacking is one of the easiest ways to ruin a trip, so I attempt to keep it light. Try to mix and match clothes, pack enough underwear plus two extra pairs for each day of your trip (same rule applies for socks), and since it's unlikely you'll be dining at any five-star restaurants with the kids, try to avoid packing anything too dressy. After all, what's the point? The last time I checked, McDonald's didn't require a tie and jacket. You may also want to consider the following advise when you're faced with the duty of packing for you and your kids:

Tip 1: **Better than a ribbon around your finger!** Make a list or an inventory of everything you'll need aside from clothes: toothpaste, tooth-brushes, makeup, razor, hair products, contact lens solution, etc. Yes, you can buy much of this stuff if you forget it, but why cut into your vacation budget? Of special importance are any prescription drugs you might need. MAKE A LIST!

Tip 2: **No more wardrobe dilemmas!** Coordinate your children's outfits for them ahead of time by putting the essentials—underwear, socks, shirt and shorts or pants—in plastic bags marked for each day you'll be gone. The best kind of bags are the huge freezer storage bags with a ziplock that you can pick up at any grocery store. This will save you not only space in your suitcase, but a lot of time in the morning when you're trying to get out the door.

Tip 3: **Shoe fetish!** Pack at least two pair of comfortable shoes and a pair of slippers or flip flops. The slippers or flip flops are for walking around in the hotel room as you never know what microscopic crud may be lurking in the carpet or on the bathroom floor.

Tip 4: **Don't be left in the dark!** Be sure to bring a small flashlight along with you and extra batteries. I never knew how handy this could be until we found ourselves traveling down a two-lane road from Dublin to Northern Ireland on the opposite side of the road at dark. There were no street lights to speak of, the rental car's interior light was burned out, and we needed to study the map frequently. Thankfully, we had a flashlight.

Tip 5: **Be prepared!** Even though it hardly ever rains in Southern California, chances are it will if you don't have an umbrella. I remember spending a week in London carrying around my umbrella even though the sun was shining every day. Finally, on my last day, I decided to leave it in the hotel room, and guess what? It began to pour as I was waiting outside to enter an attraction. Lesson learned the hard way. A compact umbrella will easily fit in the side of a suitcase. Also, evenings in Los Angeles can be cool so be sure you have a light jacket or sweatshirt with you. If your travels include other parts of the state, such as the Central Coast or the Bay Area, keep in mind the climate is drastically cooler than Southern California.

Tip 6: **Have seat will travel!** California law requires that children under six years of age or 60 pounds must travel in a car seat. I've always preferred to bring along my own car seat if I plan on renting a vehicle for two reasons: 1.) Car rental companies cannot guarantee that a car seat will be available at the time of your pick up, and 2.) Kids tend to spit, throw up, spill and do other things while bouncing along on the open road. How clean can a rented car seat really be? Also, car rental companies tack on a daily fee when using one of their car seats, so you can also save money by bringing your own. The airline will put it in a secure plastic bag and check it with the rest of your luggage. Keep in mind, however, that it does count as one piece of baggage.

Tip 7: **Portable Toy Chests!** Make sure each child has his or her own backpack filled with things to keep them busy on the plane or in the car. The items will also come in handy once you've settled in to your hotel. Some ideas include coloring books, plush toys, hand-held video games, and books. A change of clothes, along with a toothbrush and toothpaste, is also a good idea in case you miss a connecting flight or you arrive before your luggage does.

Tip 8: **California Casual!** Though Los Angeles is a sophisticated city with a sense of style, it's also extremely casual when it comes to apparel. Unless you plan on going to a trendy restaurant or nightclub, which is unlikely unless you hire a sitter, you can pretty much get away with shorts, t-shirts, jeans, sandals and athletic shoes. Make sure you pack a few nice slacks and collared polo-style shirts, plus a pair of casual shoes for more upscale dining. One color that works well in L.A. is black, which seems to be the basic hue of fashion. And, since Los Angeles is known for its beaches, don't forget a swimsuit, hat and sunscreen.

Strollers & Baby Carriages

When it comes to strollers and baby carriers, it's a matter of convenience. For newborns and infants, you definitely need one or the other if you have any expectations of an enjoyable vacation. For toddlers and pre-schoolers, it can be tough call. Our son is five now, and we rarely have a need for a stroller. However, on long journeys or outings I still carry along a collapsible, umbrella-style stroller just in case his little legs give out. These types of strollers are relatively inexpensive (I picked one up at Sears for under $15) and extremely lightweight. If you're flying, they'll fit in the overhead compartment or you can check them with your baggage. Just make sure when packing that you are counting the stroller as one item. Jogger strollers are another option as you can sometimes fit two children in them and they tend to be a bit more durable.

Parent Tip

If you forget to bring either a stroller or a carrier, you can always pick up an inexpensive one at a discount or department store. Also, most theme parks rent strollers at an additional charge, and many of L.A.'s upscale shopping centers allow shoppers to borrow strollers complimentary or for a minimal charge. These are usually available at the Concierge Desk.

International Visitors

Before leaving home, **international visitors** should allow ample time to obtain a passport and any visas that are required. It is also wise to contact the nearest U.S. Embassy or Consulate office as to what health requirements are needed before entering the United States. Customs and immigration formalities are conducted at the first point of arrival in the United States, regardless of whether or not it is your final destination. You are also advised to purchase travel and health insurance in case of emergency, as there is no government plan to assist you.

For a modest fee, most major banks and several independent bureaus are available to exchange foreign currency, and the major airports also house offices in the international arrival terminals. Traveler's checks issued in U.S.

dollars and major credit cards are widely accepted throughout Southern California.

Arrivals & Departures
Making Plane Reservations
While it use to be the best airfare deals were those made in advance, these days you can find some decent bargains at the last minute - especially on the Internet. Traveling in the off season also provides extra money in your pocket but, unless your children attend year-round school, you'll probably want to travel during the traditional holiday breaks with everyone else.

Once you settle on an arrival and departure date, start researching for the best fare. You can use the services of a travel agent, especially if you want a package deal (air/hotel/car), or you can go it alone on the Internet. If you have some flexibility, you might save money by traveling on a day of the week that is typically less busy or take a red-eye flight to save money. The children might actually snooze while en route. Each airline determines whether or not they'll offer a special rate for children; however, I find such rates to be the exception rather than the norm. Typically children 2 years and younger fly free, that is as long as a parent is willing to allow them to sit on their lap for the duration of the journey. For specific information and regulations regarding children, check with a travel agent or the airline directly.

By Air
Los Angeles is primarily served by **Los Angeles International Airport** (LAX) and is part of Los Angeles World Airports (LAWA). Ranked third in the world for the number of passengers it handles, the airport averages more than 67.6 million travelers annually and is responsible for routing more than 2.2 million tons of freight. Be aware when arriving and departing that LAX's daily travel peak periods are from 11 a.m. to 2 p.m. and 7 p.m. to 11 p.m. (PST).

The airport is actually located near the coast in Inglewood, just south of Downtown. LAX is served by approximately 100 airline carriers grouped in eight terminals which are housed in the central terminal area. Also in this complex is the **Tom Bradley International Terminal.** Departing passengers enter their designated terminal from the upper level roadway to check-in for flights, while arriving passengers claim their baggage and exit their terminal from the lower level. There are easy to read overhead signs on both the upper and lower roadways, which list the airlines that serve each terminal.

The central vehicle lots are used for short-term parking, and rates run from $1 hour to $16 for 24 hours; Lots B and C are for long-term parking ($5-$7 for 24 hours), and offer free shuttle service to and from the terminals.

Ontario International Airport, also part of LAWA, is located 35 miles east of Downtown Los Angeles in the west end of San Bernardino County. The airport is serviced by AeroMexico, Alaska, American, America West, Continental, Delta, Frontier, Hawaiian, JetBlue, Northwest, Southwest, United Airlines and United Express.

Other Los Angeles-area airports, some of which may be more convenient to your hotel, include **Burbank-Glendale-Pasadena Airport**, the closest airport to Downtown Los Angeles, Hollywood, the San Fernando Valley, and Pasadena. The airport is serviced by **Alaska, Aloha, American, American West, Southwest** and **United Airlines.** If you're staying along the coast, **Long Beach Airport,** which straddles the Los Angeles/Orange County line, offers limited commercial service with four carriers: **America West, American Airlines, JetBlue Airways** and **Horizon Air.**

Visitors coming from New York City, Washington D.C., Oakland, Las Vegas, Dallas, Chicago, Phoenix, Seattle and Salt Lake City can fly non stop into Long Beach. The fact that service is limited to only a quartet of carriers is a major plus. If you are arriving from any of these areas, I strongly recommend flying into Long Beach - you'll save a lot of time getting in and out, plus the car rental agencies and their vehicles are located on the premises.

If you plan on staying mostly near or around Disneyland Resort in Anaheim, which is in neighboring Orange County, **John Wayne/Orange County Airport** is another option. Noted as the 15th busiest airport in the world for takeoffs and landings averaging an estimated 7.7 million passengers a year, the airport is located 11 miles from Disneyland Resort and 35 miles south of Los Angeles. The airport is served by 11 carriers, including **Alaska, Aloha, America West, American, Continental, Delta, Northwest, Southwest, United and USAirways.**

Ground Transportation
From LAX

Outbound buses, shuttles, hotel and rental car courtesy vans are available on the Lower/Arrival Level Islands in front of each terminal under the sign designating the particular transportation desired: Shuttle Vans, LAX Shuttle, Bus Stop, or Courtesy Tram.

Metropolitan Express, *Tel. 800/338-3898*, travels to Downtown Los Angeles and to Union Station (Amtrak Service), located about 19 miles northeast of LAX.

Prime Time Shuttle, *Tel. 800/262-7433*, and **SuperShuttle,***Tel. 323/ 775-6600*, both operate from LAX and are authorized to serve all Southern California Counties.

Taxis can be found curbside, and drivers will present a ticket stating typical fares to major destinations. Only authorized taxis with an official seal issued by the City of Los Angeles Department of Transportation displayed on each vehicle are allowed to conduct business in the airport.

Airport Bus, *Tel. 800/772-5299*, travels to Anaheim (Disneyland) and Buena Park, where Knott's Berry Farm is located. Both locations are approximately 30 miles southeast of LAX.

Public Transportation, including Culver City Bus Lines, Santa Monica Big Blue Bus, and Torrance Transit, pick up passengers at the LA County Metropolitan Transportation Authority Bus Center located in Lot C. The "C" Shuttle will bring you to this area, and other city buses serving the Los Angeles area also stop in Lot C. Passengers can obtain local transit information by calling, *Tel. 800/266-6883*.

More than **40 car rental agencies** operate out of LAX with vehicle rental sites located off airport property. Many of these companies provide phone links inside or near the baggage claim areas, so travelers can request a free shuttle pick up to reach the rental car sites. Then, you'll need to gather your bags and wait for the appropriate rental car company shuttle on the Lower/Arrival Level Islands located in front of each terminal under the purple sign reading **Rental Car Shuttles**.

Parent Tip
Still not sure how to get to where you are going? Once you arrive at LAX look for a QuickAid machine located in each terminal. These machines are easy to operate by touching the symbol of category on the screen that pertains to your interest.

From Ontario International Airport
Assuming you are staying in Los Angeles or one of its surrounding communities, the best bet from Ontario is to either use a **shuttle van**, which retrieves travelers from the island curbs outside of baggage claim, or rent a car. Both **Prime Time**, *Tel. 800/733-8267*, and **SuperShuttle**, *Tel. 909/984-0040*, serve Ontario International Airport along with a few other companies. There are a half dozen **car rental companies** located within the airport complex, and a free airport shuttle links the terminals with the Ground Transportation Center where the car rental agencies are located.

From Burbank-Glendale-Pasadena Airport
Shuttles and cabs are available on the islands in front of the terminal, and car rental counters are located in Terminal B. The airport is also a stop for a number of Metro Transit Authority bus lines. For information and schedules: *Tel. 800/COMMUTE*.

From Long Beach Airport

There are five car rental agencies located in the parking lot directly across from the terminal. Vehicles are located in adjacent parking lots, so you simply have to walk to your car. Taxis also line up outside the terminal, but if you're staying anywhere besides Long Beach, the fare can get quite expensive. Both **Prime Time Shuttle**, *Tel. 800/262-7433*, and **SuperShuttle**,*Tel. 323/775-6600*, serve Long Beach Airport, and arrangements should be made prior to your arrival

From John Wayne/Orange County Airport

The Ground Transportation Center (GTC) houses all ground transportation services including buses, taxis, shuttles and car rentals. The GTC is located in the center of the East Parking Structure directly across from the Thomas F. Riley Terminal. The Orange County Transportation Authority bus stop is on the Upper Level Roadway (Departure Level) between Terminals A and B. Unless you're staying in Orange County, taking a taxi from this area to Los Angeles would be costly. Again, your best bet from here into L.A. is either a rental car or shuttle service.

By Car

All roads may lead to Rome, but all freeways manage to weave their way through Los Angeles. As you approach the city, you may experience a slow down in traffic. Once predictable traffic patterns are quickly becoming a thing of the past due to the area's rising population, roadside accidents, merging lanes, road work, or the growing sport of high-speed police pursuits.

If you are approaching Los Angeles from the northern part of the state, **Route 5**, the **Golden State Freeway**, will take you south into the core of the city, where it undergoes a name change to the **Santa Ana Freeway**. If you are arriving north along the coast, you'll most likely be traveling along **Highway 101**, the **Ventura Freeway**, which weaves along the coast before heading inland around Oxnard. The freeway eventually veers southeast towards Downtown becoming the **Hollywood Freeway**. If you're arriving from the southwest, you'll be traveling on **I-15,** which leads down to the San Diego area. You can veer west on either **Route 10** or **Route 60,** both of which will take you toward Downtown Los Angeles.

The **405 Freeway**, fondly known as the **San Diego Freeway**, runs through the San Fernando Valley, the Westside, down through Long Beach and out to Orange County. The **Santa Monica/San Bernardino Freeway, Route 10**, cuts across Los Angeles beginning near the pier in Santa Monica taking you through Downtown Los Angeles then out to San Bernardino County.

Helpful Hints for Driving & Parking

To keep you moving, LA Inc., The Convention & Visitors Bureau offers these helpful tips for driving and parking.

1. If there are no signs posted, the maximum speed is 25 miles per hour on city streets and 65 miles per hour on freeways.

2. You must wear a seat belt in a private vehicle.

3. You may turn right after stopping at a red light unless a posted sign indicates otherwise.

4. Pedestrians have the right-of-way.

5. Drunken driving laws are strictly enforced, and open containers of alcoholic beverages are not permitted in vehicles.

6. Be sure to carefully read all signs stating what days and hours you may park. Illegally parked vehicles will be ticketed and may be towed away. Be especially cautious when parking in West Los Angeles, as many side streets require a resident permit.

7. A red curb means no parking, while a green curb means parking for a very limited time (typically 10-20 minutes). A white curb is for loading and unloading passengers only.

8. Parking is generally available in lots or garages. Prices vary, and some places, such as retail centers, offer discount or free parking with validation.

9. Many restaurants offer valet parking for a nominal fee.

Fun Fact

Next time you're sitting on the freeway and barely moving consider this: The freeway system of Los Angeles encompasses 510 miles of highway, linking suburbia to the urban core. More than 23.9 million vehicle trips are made in an average 24-hour weekday. And you wonder why traffic is an issue?

By Train

Union Station, located in Downtown at **800 North Alameda Street,** is once again buzzing with activity. Built in 1939 and considered to be "The last of America's great rail stations," Union Station continues to enjoy a renaissance and is often used as a backdrop in major motion pictures - especially period pieces.

Amtrak provides service to Los Angeles via Union Station aboard the San Diegan (San Diego -Los Angeles/Los Angeles - Santa Barbara); the San Joaquin (Los Angeles-Bakersfield, and via Amtrak Thruway Bus from Fresno and Oakland); the Southwest Chief (Los Angeles - Kansas City - Chicago); the

Sunset Limited (Los Angeles - New Orleans - Miami); and the Coast Starlight (Los Angeles - Oakland - Portland -Seattle). Fares vary, *Tel. 800/USA-RAIL.*

From Union Station, you can connect to various parts of the city and county using Metro Rail, the county's emerging light rail system. The **Red Line** stops at Union Station's Gateway Transit Center, from here you can travel as far north as North Hollywood in the San Fernando Valley, or connect at the 7th Street Metro Station and go as far south as Long Beach on the **Blue Line**. The Blue Line also intersects with the **Green Line** south of Watts Tower, which will take you to the Redondo Beach area. For assistance, call 1-800-Commute. You may also want to stop by the staffed information desk inside Union Station for any additional assistance.

By Bus

Greyhound Bus Lines, *Tel. 800/231-2222,* provides service to the Los Angeles area from virtually every nook of the country. The main terminal for Los Angeles is located Downtown at **1716 East 7th Street,** *Tel. 213/629-8400.* If at all possible, arrive during the day as this is no place you want to encounter after dark. Other depots include **Hollywood,** 1409 North Vine Street, *Tel. 323/466-6381;* **Pasadena** at 645 East Walnut Street, *Tel. 626/792-5116;* and **North Hollywood** at 11239 Magnolia Boulevard, *Tel. 818/761-5119.* The same rule applies: avoid nighttime arrivals.

Public Holidays

With such great weather and places to visit, it's a shame that every day can't be a holiday. Just because most people have the day off, you can still expect traffic jams along the freeways as everyone else is out to make the most of their time away from the office. Expect government offices, schools and banks to be shut, as well as many businesses with the exception of retailers, restaurants, theme parks and major attractions. Closing days and times are noted in the *Where Are We Going Now?* chapter.

• January 1	New Year's Day
• Third Monday in January	Martin Luther King, Jr. Day
• Third Monday in February	President's Day
• Last Monday in May	Memorial Day
• July 4	Independence Day
• First Monday in September	Labor Day
• Second Monday in October	Columbus Day
• November 11	Veteran's Day
• Fourth Thursday in November	Thanksgiving Day
• December 25	Christmas Day

Special Events

Each month Los Angeles packs its calendar with some fun and often unusual events. Whether its the doughy smell of fresh-baked funnel cake being torn apart at the county fair, or lederhosen-clad crowds celebrating Oktoberfest, a weekend rarely goes by without some kind of fanfare or celebration. The events listed below, held throughout Greater Los Angeles, are ones deemed appropriate for children. A phone number is provided for additional information and, when available, a web address is also listed. For more events, visit the Los Angeles Almanac at www.losangelesalmanac.com

January

Tournament of Roses Parade/Pasadena
Tel. 626/449-4100, www.tournamentofroses.com
January 1 or 2 if January 1 falls on a Sunday

February

Golden Dragon Parade/Chinatown in Downtown L.A.
Tel. 213/617-0396, www.lachinesechamber.org
Mid-February

Queen Mary Scottish Festival/Long Beach
Tel. 562/435-3511, www.queenmary.com
President's Day Weekend

March

City of Los Angeles Marathon/Downtown L.A.
Tel. 310/473-8105, www.lamarathon.com
First Sunday in March

Los Angeles Bach Festival/Downtown
Tel. 213/385-1341, www.fccla.org
Mid-March

St. Patrick's Day Parade & Festival/Hermosa Beach
Tel. 310/374-1365, www.stpatricksday.org
The Saturday before March 17th

Sierra Madre Wisteria Festival/Sierra Madre
Tel. 626/306-1150, www.sierramadrevillage.com
Late March

April

Toyota Grand Prix of Long Beach

Tel. 562/436-9953, www.longbeachgp.com
Typically the first or second weekend in April

Blessing of the Animals/Downtown Los Angeles
Tel. 213/625-5045, www.olvera-street.com
The Saturday before Easter

Los Angeles Times Festival of Books/UCLA Campus
Tel. 800/528-4637 ext. 72665, www.latimes.com
Last weekend in April

May
Cince de Mayo at El Pueblo de Los Angeles/Downtown
Tel. 213/625-5045, www.olvera-street.com
First weekend in May

Renaissance Pleasure Faire/Devore
Tel. 909/880-0122, www.renfair.com
Early May through late June

FunFest & Children's Day Celebration/Downtown
Tel. 213/628 2725, www.jaccc.org
Mid-May

June
San Fernando Valley Fair/Lakeview Terrace
Tel. 818/557-1600, www.sfvalleyfair.org
Early June

Sawdust Festival/Laguna Beach
Tel. 949/494-3030, www.sawdustartfestival.org
Runs From June till the end of August

July
Twilight Dance Series/Santa Monica Pier
Tel. 310/458-8900, www.santa-monica.org
July through end of August

Orange County Fair/Costa Mesa
Tel. 714/708-3247, www.ocfair.com
Two Weeks starting Mid-July

Lotus Festival/Mid-City
Tel. 213/485-1310, www.laparks.org
Mid-July

August
Ojai Shakespeare Festival/Ojai
Tel. 805/646-9455, www.ojaishakespeare.org
Typically the first three weeks in August

September
Alpine Village Oktoberfest/Torrance
Tel. 310/327-4384, www.alpinevillage.net
Second Week of September through end of October

Manhattan Beach Arts Festival/Manhattan Beach
Tel. 310/802-5417
Mid-September

Los Angeles County Fair/Pomona
Tel. 909/623-3111, www.fairplex.com
Last two weeks of September

Taste of Newport/Newport Beach
Tel. 949/729-4400, www.newportbeach.com
Mid-September

October
Port of Los Angeles Lobster Festival/San Pedro
Tel. 310/366-6472, www.lobsterfest.com
First Weekend in October

Day of the Dead/Hollywood
Tel. 877/844-2827, www.forevernetwork.com
Last Saturday in October

Queen Mary Shipwreck Halloween Terror Fest/Long Beach
Tel. 562/435-3511, www.queenmary.com
Month of October

November
Doo Dah Parade/Pasadena
Tel. 626/440-7379
Mid-November

Hollywood Christmas Parade/Hollywood
Tel. 323/469-2337, www.hollywoodchristmas.com
Last Sunday in November
December
Marina Del Rey Holiday Boat Parade/Marina del Rey
Tel. 310/822-9455, www.mdrlights.org
Mid-December

Los Posadas/ Downtown Los Angeles
Tel. 213/625-5045, www.olvera-street.com
Mid-to-late December

Getting Around Los Angeles

The expression *nobody walks in L.A.* is no cliche. Unlike other cities, L.A. is a huge, sprawling metropolis, and sometimes getting around can be a production all its own. To make the most of you're time, especially where children are involved, I strongly urge you to rent a car. Otherwise, you'll have to rely the city's slow, but improving, public transportation system. Taxis are another option, but they're much more scarce in L.A. than other major cities and, of course, they can be costly.

If you're going to drive, it's a good idea to familiarize yourself with L.A.'s freeway system. Conquering the intricate network of roads can be easy, and it's important to know that freeways have both a number and name. The name is supposed to indicate the road's final destination from Downtown Los Angeles but, just to shake your confidence a bit, this is not always the case. The San Diego Freeway, also known as the 405, doesn't end in San Diego, but rather merges with the Interstate 5 Freeway in Orange County, also known as the Santa Ana Freeway. It is the 5 Freeway, the Santa Ana Freeway, that leads you into San Diego. Confused yet? Read on.

When approaching the exit to the northbound San Diego or Golden State freeway from one of the east/west freeways, the signs say *Sacramento*, which is another 400 miles away. The moral of the story in both cases is this: signs often indicate a larger city in the general direction of traffic.

The name rule does apply to the Interstate 10, which when traveling between Downtown and Santa Monica it is known as the Santa Monica Freeway; when heading east from Downtown it is referred to as the San Bernardino Freeway because that's where the roadway once ended. When traveling from Downtown south on the 110, the freeway is known as the Harbor Freeway because its route concludes at the Port of Los Angeles; when heading north from Downtown it becomes the Pasadena Freeway, named so for its final destination. The 101 Freeway is known as the Hollywood Freeway as it heads north out of Downtown, only to become the Ventura Freeway once it curves West. Other freeways that follow this rule of thumb include the 2/

Glendale Freeway, 210/Foothill Freeway, the 105/Century Freeway (which runs east and west from Los Angeles International Airport to the 605/San Gabriel Freeway), the 605/San Gabriel Freeway, the 710/Long Beach Freeway, and Highway 1/Pacific Coast Highway simply referred to as PCH.

Look for the Diamond Lane or Carpool Lane when traveling on freeways. This lane, located to the far left, caters to vehicles with two or more passengers - a plus for the nuclear family. A break in the double line allows you to enter and exit - don't break this law, or travel alone, as both will cost you in hefty fines. Call boxes with free phones are placed every half mile along the freeways for emergencies, and it's wise to tune in to the traffic reports on the radio while en route - KNX 1070 and KFWB 980, both on the AM dial, give traffic reports every five minutes.

The following chart are the **freeways** that run in and around Los Angeles County. They are first listed by their official number and then by name. Those going east and west have even numbers, and north-south roads have odd numbers. Ask for both when getting directions. To further confuse you, some share the same name. If you are a member of AAA, you can call the auto club member services line *(Tel. 800/222-4357)* to get specific directions - weekends included.

2	Glendale	10	Santa Monica/San Bernadino
22	Garden Grove	57	Orange
71	Corona Expressway	91	Riverside/Artesia
105	Century	118	SimiValley/San Fernando Valley
170	Hollywood	405	San Diego
710	Long Beach	5	Golden State/Santa Ana
14	Antelope Valley	30	Foothill
60	Pomona	90	Marina
101	Ventura/Hollywood	110	Pasadena/Harbor
134	Ventura	210	Foothill
605	San Gabriel		

By Car

Traveling along L.A.'s surface streets is, for the most part, simple, but it's wise to consult an area map. As is typical with most city's, L.A.'s streets are a grid of roadways running north and south, east and west. Sunset Boulevard stretches all the way from Downtown to the beach near Santa Monica, as does Wilshire Boulevard. Pacific Coast Highway is a picturesque stretch of highway running mostly along California's coastline, occasionally veering inland. La Cienega Boulevard travels from Hollywood all the way south near Los Angeles International Airport. While for the most part these avenues are safe, it's wise to consult a map when traveling on surface streets. The landscape, in terms of safety, can change dramatically within a few blocks.

By Bus

The Metropolitan Transit Authority (MTA) offers bus service that criss-crosses through town and to outlying areas. It's a slow haul, but you can travel throughout the city for $1.35 one-way plus an additional 25 cents for a transfer. As this book goes to press there are talks of a minimal fee increase.

To find out which bus will take you to where you're going, call the MTA information line, *Tel. 213/626-4455*. Let them know your point of origin, where you want to go, and at what time. They will be able to provide you with accurate instructions to help expedite your travels.

Many of the outlying cities in the Greater Los Angeles areas also have their own inner city transportation including Culver City, Long Beach, Pasadena, Santa Monica and Torrance, all of which the MTA is able to provide assistance. Orange County has its own public transportation system, Orange County Transit Authority (MTA), which serves the entire county with a Northern County System and a Southern County System plus transfer links between the two.

Parent Tip

Looking to travel from Los Angeles to Disneyland sans automobile? Though I don't recommend it, it is possible to take the bus from Downtown Los Angeles to Disneyland. Bus #460 travels east along Sixth Street en route to Disneyland, or you can catch the #460 at Wilshire Boulevard and Flower Street in Downtown. You can also connect to Downtown from other parts of the city via the Metro Rail or the bus. Typically, if you were driving, the one-way trip would take 30-40 minutes. On the bus it will take you approximately 2 hours. Be sure to find out when the last bus leaves Disneyland so you're not stranded in Anaheim.

By Foot

In order to stroll about the city, you'll need to already be in your designated area (i.e. you can't walk from Downtown to West Hollywood nor would you want to). While most areas are rather safe, some become questionable after dark. Others are not pedestrian-friendly at all and should be viewed from within the confines of a vehicle.

By Metro Rail

The Metro Rail is a barrier-free system consisting of electric trains that ferry passengers within town and to county suburbs. Should you be staying in Los Angeles and want to venture beyond the city proper, this would be the fastest way to get there. Each rail makes several stops along the way. The **Metro Blue Line** goes from Downtown Los Angeles to Downtown Long Beach; the **Metro Green Line** runs from the suburb of Norwalk to the seaside community of Redondo Beach; the **Metro Red Line** transports people from Union Station in Downtown out to mid-Wilshire and the museum area, as well as further to the north to Hollywood Boulevard and Vine Street; Universal City; and the community of North Hollywood in the San Fernando Valley. Fares vary greatly depending on where you're going. And while there are no conductors collecting tickets, frequent police checks ensure no one rides for free. For information and a list of schedules: *Tel. 213/626-4455, www.mta.net.*

Metrolink is the rail system serving commuters throughout Southern California, providing service between Union Station in Downtown and beyond, including Orange County. Most trains typically operate Monday through Friday. No service on major holidays. For a personalized itinerary to get you where you want to go: *Tel. 800/371-LINK.*

There are eight commuter rail stations currently serving **Orange County** with one located at Anaheim Stadium, just a short distance away from Disneyland. OCTA offers free connecting bus service from the stations. From Union Station in Downtown L.A. to Anaheim, trains depart as early as 6:44 a.m. and the ride lasts approximately 40 minutes. From here, you can connect to Bus #50, which will take you to the intersection of Harbor and Katella Boulevards. Once you get off the bus, you'll need to walk about a half-mile north to the Disneyland entrance. For trip planning information, contact OCTA: *Tel. 714/626-RIDE, www.octa.net.*

By Shuttle

The **DASH** shuttle is the quickest way to get around Downtown and other various business districts. For just 25¢, you can hop on one of five routes that will take you to Chinatown, Little Tokyo, the Fashion District, Olvera Street, the Music Center, and the University of Southern California, just to name a few. Look for the white and purple DASH signs, which indicate stops. Most hotels have DASH maps, and many of the shuttles carry maps as well.

Santa Monica, San Pedro, and Long Beach have similar people movers in and around their Downtown areas.

By Taxi

Unlike New York, Chicago or Washington, DC, taxis in Los Angeles are not only expensive, they're uncommon. Typically taxis line up in front of the major hotels and some of the more swank eateries, but don't expect to stand on a street corner bellowing "Yo taxi," while in town. If you need a cab, you'll most likely need to call ahead and request that one be dispatched to you. Don't get

taken for a ride—literally—by a "bandit cab;" be sure to look for the Official City Taxicab Seal, which should be prominently displayed. A few of the more established taxi companies include:
- **Checker Cab Co.**, *Tel. 323/938-8294*
- **LA Taxi Co-Op/Yellow Cab. Co.**, *Tel. 800/200-1085*
- **Independent Cab Co.**, *Tel. 213/385-8294*
- **United Independent Taxi**, *Tel. 323/653-5050*

Getting Around By Organized Tour

There are many organized tours available in and around Los Angeles, from the fundamental to the downright funky. While you'll find traditional bus tours that travel past all the usual suspects, there are also some rather offbeat options that expose L.A.'s more innovative side.

Architectural Tours

Architours, *Tel. 323/294-5821, www.architours.com*, takes you to L.A.'s collection of notable architectural and cultural sites, including the works of legendary architects Frank Lloyd Wright and Richard Neutra. There are also restaurant design tours that take you behind the kitchen doors of some of L.A.'s most notable eateries, as well as garden tours and public art walking tours. What's even more unique is that each itinerary is conducted by the architects, artists, chefs or owners. Fees vary.

Bicycle Tours

L.A. Bike Tours, *Tel., 434/466-5890, www.labiketours.com*, shows you how to get around in L.A. on two wheels. The docent-led pedal tours cruise past both well-known and obscure landmarks, from the Hollywood Walk of Fame to Marilyn Monroe's childhood orphanage. Tours for all ages and levels. Prices start at $20 per person excluding bike rental.

Celebrity Interests

Starline Tours, *Tel. 800/959-3131, www.starlinetours.com*, gives you a peek into both L.A.'s glamorous side and macabre existence with its STARS' Homes and Celebrity Grave Sites tour. Air-conditioned mini-buses travel down the palm-lined streets of Beverly Hills pointing out the mansions that belong to the stars, such as Nicolas Cage, Harrison Ford and Barbra Streisand. Former homes of Hollywood legends, such as Lucille Bal, are also included. You'll also visit the final resting places of the stars, from Rudolph Valentino to Marilyn Monroe, with stops to some of L.A.'s celebrity-laden cemeteries. Adults are $42, children $30.

City Tours

LA Tours, *Tel. 323/993-0093, www.la-tours.com*, offers an all-day City Tour that includes the beach areas and shopping. The tour covers Downtown Los Angeles, Hollywood, Beverly Hills, Marina del Rey, Venice Beach and shopping along Santa Monica's Third Street Promenade. Adults are $63, children $40.

Red Line Tours, *Tel. 323/402-1074, www.redlinetours.com*, offers a unique Inside Historic Hollywood walking tour that covers Tinseltown's famous and infamous landmarks, including Grauman's Chinese Theatre, the Walk of Fame, and the Hollywood Sign, just to name a few. This tour is better suited for older children. Adults are $20, children ages 9-15 are $15.

Cultural Tours

Beyond the Glitz Tours, *Tel. 323/658-7920, www.beyondtheglitz.com*, lets you see L.A. either via foot or in a chauffeured-driven car. The more culturally inclined can choose from tours that explore the Hollywood sign and Lake Hollywood, the modern-style residential architecture of Silverlake, or the Victorian homes of West Adams near the USC campus. Walking tours are $20 per person including snack; half-day chauffeured tours vary in price. Call for information.

Personal Guided Tours

Take My Mother Please, *Tel. 323/737-2200, www.takemymotherplease.com*, is a unique tour company offering customized agendas. Owner-led tours are conducted by Anne Block, a flaming-haired southern transplant who knows the city inside and out, and is eager to introduce visitors to what she calls the "real' L.A. The trek takes place from within the confines of Ms. Block's silver Cadillac, and she'll plan the itinerary according to your interests. Though the agenda is thoughtfully orchestrated, plans can easily veer off track often taking a turn for the unusual - depending on what is taking place on the streets of L.A. Innovation comes with a price - half-day tours are $400 for a group of five.

L. A. Neighborhoods

As I've mentioned, Los Angeles is extremely spread out. The neighborhoods and regions below are the area's that have the most to offer travelers. Instead of trying to take in everything all at once, may I recommend spending one day exploring one or two areas then conquering another neighborhood the next day? Trying to do it all at once may leave you feeling highly frustrated and, more than likely, stranded in traffic.

Downtown

Downtown essentially is the birthplace of Los Angeles. Surprisingly, many locals have yet to discover its pleasures. Yet with the recent blessing and dedication of The Cathedral of Our Lady of the Angels, the new Catholic cathedral, and the pending opening of the new Walt Disney Concert Hall at the Music Center, that could easily change.

There are sunrise visits to the flower market, nine-cent cups of coffee at a local eatery, and strolls along Broadway where classic movie palaces await restoration. During weekdays, you'll find executives en route to high-rise offices buildings atop **Bunker Hill**. At the same time, in a less swanky part of town, you'll see rolling racks noisily pushed from the factories to the showrooms throughout the **Fashion District**. Along **Olvera Street** merchants are displaying their wares of Mexican pottery, while the scent of fresh herbs waft from storefronts in neighboring **Chinatown**. Adding to all this is the new multi-million dollar **Staples Center**, where the **Los Angeles Clippers, Lakers** and **Kings** compete during their respective seasons.

Hollywood

La La Land, as its often been called, has helped revitalize many a sagging career and now, after a major revitalization, it's making a major comeback of its own. Hollywood Boulevard, the town's main drag, is often referred to as the "Boulevard of Broken Dreams," but it's slowly picking up the pieces and reimagining itself as a place not to be missed.

Recent attractions, such as the **Hollywood Entertainment Museum** and the newly renovated **Egyptian Theatre**, are complementing such boulevard landmarks as **Grauman's Chinese Theatre** and the pink terrazzo and brass stars, which grace the **Hollywood Walk of Fame**. In 2001, the new **Hollywood & Highland** complex, located at the intersection of the same name, opened to great fanfare. Though it's touted as the permanent home of the annual Academy Award presentation, the complex itself, though aesthetically appealing, is really a glorified mall anchored by the **Kodak Theater** and the new **Renaissance Hollywood Hotel**.

Across the street is the historic **El Capitan**, where Disney movies are exclusively shown. **Hollywood & Vine**, one of the town's most famous crossroads, is also expected to get a face lift. Plans call for a mixed-use transit-oriented development that would include hotel rooms, residential dwellings and more than 30,000 square feet of ground level retail space.

Nearby are the **Los Feliz** and **Silver Lake** districts, which are strewn with some great restaurants and one-of-a-kind funky shops.

West Hollywood

The city of West Hollywood, also known as WeHo, is often described as The Creative City. It's considered the west coast version of New York City's SoHo district only with perpetual sunshine. This area has a large and accepting gay population, and is overcrowded with young, beautiful people of all types, genders and sexual preferences. A tiny principality of sorts, West Hollywood is big on style. This is where you'll find the chic shops of **Sunset Plaza**; celebrity-laden restaurants such as **Morton's** and **Le Dome**; the trendiest night clubs and bars; and countless showrooms, including the gigantic **Pacific Design Center**, which caters to the interior design industry.

Beverly Hills and the Westside

If West Hollywood is the epicenter of creativity, than its neighbor to the west, **Beverly Hills**, can only be regarded as the lap of luxury. Multi-million dollar homes, posh hotels and ultra-expensive boutiques are as common for this town as tract homes and strip malls are in more modest communities. Beverly Hills is where many of the movie industry's elite reside, and you're likely to see a celebrity or two sauntering down Rodeo Drive.

Neighboring districts on Los Angeles' Westside include **Century City**, the former backlot of 20th Century Fox; **Bel-Air,** a residential enclave even more exclusive than Beverly Hills; **Westwood**, home of the UCLA Bruins; and **Brentwood**, made famous—or infamous— by former resident O.J. Simpson.

The Valleys

Except for a few attractions, L.A's valley areas are fraught with bedroom communities. The San Fernando Valley lies west of Downtown Los Angeles and further west is the **Simi Valley** where the **Ronald Reagan Presidential Library** is located. To the north is the **Santa Clarita Valley**, home of **Six Flags Magic Mountain.**

The **San Gabriel Valley**, located to the east of Downtown, is home to **Pasadena** and its **Tournament of Roses Parade**. The town of **Arcadia** is home to **Santa Anita Race Track**, where the ponies run December through April, and again during the month of October.

Beach Cities

Los Angeles' beach cities offer perfect waves, unbeatable weather and a bevy of hard bodies. More than 70 miles make up the coastal communities, stretching from Malibu to the north all the way south down to Long Beach. Each town shares the obvious—surf, sand and sun—but each offers its own individuality. The beach communities are divided into two distinct areas: those north of Los Angeles International Airport (LAX) and those south.

North of LAX

Malibu is home to **The Colony** where movie moguls and stars live in beachfront mansions, and the nearby canyons promote an almost bohemian lifestyle. **Santa Monica** also has its share of celebrity citizens, but is somewhat less pretentious with inviting shops, restaurants and lounges. When it comes to offbeat and quirky, **Venice** wrote the book. Home for years to the working class citizens of L.A., recently celebrities, such as Anjelica Huston and Julia

Roberts have purchased homes here and are changing the neighborhood demographics. Still, there is no need to pay for entertainment when you can get it for free along the boardwalk, where a parade of street entertainers (some talented, some not) put on the zaniest show on earth. And nearby canals, dredged during the turn-of-the-century to create an American version of Venice, Italy, almost go unnoticed as they wind their way through the town's more quieter neighborhoods.

You'll find one of the largest man-made marinas in **Marina del Rey**, the least appealing of the seaside towns. Void of any culture, but sporting plenty of luxury water craft, Marina del Rey is filled with mostly cookie-cutter condos and pricey restaurants. **Playa del Rey** on the other hand also offers little to do or see. But where Marina del Rey is somewhat overdeveloped, this tiny community offers one of the last remaining wetlands habitats in Southern California.

South of LAX

The **South Bay,** which includes the towns of **Manhattan Beach, Hermosa Beach, Redondo Beach**, and the **Palos Verdes Peninsula**, is the epitome of California dreamin'. Aside from a few unusual attractions, mostly in Palos Verdes and the inland town of Wilmington, there isn't much to do or see here. These towns are best enjoyed from the sand or atop a surf board. **San Pedro** on the other hand is a real seaside, blue-collar town with lots of interesting sights—mostly of the maritime variety—but with little verve or style. With a number of respected restaurants and the restoration of a 1931 movie house, Old Town San Pedro struggles to recapture some of the charm it once enjoyed. San Pedro is also home to the Port of Los Angeles where a number of cruise ships depart for exotic locales.

The Vincent Thomas Bridge connects San Pedro to **Long Beach**, where the famed Queen Mary ocean liner is permanently berthed. While San Pedro continues to chip away at a revitalization, a renaissance is in full swing in Long Beach's Downtown district. Along Pine Avenue and Ocean Boulevard you'll find a bustling streetscape unfolding with upscale bistros, swanky nightclubs and various retailers. Taking a cue from Baltimore, the city completed the first phase of a $600-million waterfront harbor, which includes the Aquarium of the Pacific. The second-phase, which has been delayed by several years, is finally underway and, when completed, will feature even more shops, restaurants and entertainment venues.

Parks, Playgrounds & Recreation

Stretching more than 70 miles, Los Angeles is home to one of the largest sandboxes; a place commonly referred to as the beach. It's possible to enjoy the beach all year round, and many have their own playgrounds and bike trails, as well as designated areas for volleyball and basketball. While there is no admission, there is usually a fee to park in city-owned lots. The beaches below are listed from north to south.

Malibu

LEO CARRILLO STATE BEACH, adjacent to the Ventura County line along Pacific Coast Highway. Named for the late actor who played Pancho in the television series *The Cisco Kid*, this beach conceals a natural tunnel, caves and tide pools. To the north folks opt to don birthday suits rather than bathing suits, and those caught with their pants down—or in this case, off—are fined. Still, it doesn't stop some daring folks from taking it all off.

ZUMA BEACH, six miles west of Malibu on Highway 1. This beach is often the backdrop in cheesy movies immortalizing the California surf scene. A hybrid of sun worshippers flock to various areas of the sand, staking claim to their territory. One area belongs to Hispanics, another is overrun with mall rats from the San Fernando Valley, one section belongs to nuclear families, and yet another is popular with co-eds from Pepperdine University. The beach is kept up nicely thanks to the high property taxes bestowed on Malibu residents.

POINT DUME COUNTY BEACH, entrance to the south of Zuma Beach. This is a great location for surfing and swimming, and along the far side is a secluded stretch known as **Pirate's Cove**, where nude sunbathing was once the order of the day.

ROBERT H. MEYER MEMORIAL STATE BEACHES, On route 1 about 11 miles west of Malibu. This area if often referred to as Pocket Beaches because of its triad of small sandy coves — **El Pescador, La Piedra**, and **El Matador**. Together their waning bluffs and velvety sands create a nice beach province. Pay careful attention to the surf conditions as there are no lifeguards on duty.

MALIBU LAGOON STATE BEACH, Pacific Coast Highway at Cross Creek Road. It's the end of the trail for Malibu Creek, which empties into this tidal area. With a wetlands area, there is plenty of marine life to observe. You'll find the waves manageable if you're a swimmer, and the swell disappointing if you're a surfer.

LAS TUNAS STATE BEACH, between Tuna Canyon Road and Big Rock Drive. The Spanish name refers to the fruit of the prickly pear cactus. What that has to do with surf and sand remains a mystery at this slice of California coastline.

Santa Monica

WILL ROGERS STATE BEACH, at the south end of Sunset Boulevard and Pacific Coast Highway. This is the land of the beautiful people, but families will feel right at home here too. There is a playground, volleyball courts and picnic spots available. If your stomach starts growling, the ever festive Gladstones 4 Fish is also located here.

SANTA MONICA STATE BEACH, north and south of Santa Monica Pier. Be as active or inactive as you want along one of the widest stretches of sand the Pacific Coast has to offer. Jogging, swimming, surfing, skating, biking and volleyball keep things in constant motion.

MUSCLE BEACH, south of Santa Monica Pier. Pecks and abs still ripple at this former Jack LaLane haunt, but not quite the way they did during the beach's heyday. This was the place to pump iron during the '50s and '60s, and efforts are being made to return this area to its body building glory days.

Venice

VENICE BEACH, adjacent to the south end of Santa Monica State Beach. Spend a couple of zany hours here, and you'll agree that this is the wackiest place on earth. It's constant chaos with skaters, street performers and countless sidewalk vendors. You can take part, or watch the whole scene unfold from the safety of your towel.

Playa del Rey

DOCKWEILER STATE BEACH, fronting Vista del Mar Boulevard at the foot of Imperial Highway. If you think the surf sounds louder here, it's not the crashing of pounding waves. What you're hearing is the reverberating sound of airplanes taking off from Los Angeles International Airport just a few miles down the coast. If the noise doesn't bother you, you'll find the swimming and surfing conditions to be rather good. Fishing is done from the rock jetties, and fire pits provide for a great weenie roast at night.

Manhattan Beach

MANHATTAN STATE BEACH, located at the foot of Manhattan Beach Boulevard. This is where California Dreamin' was born, immortalized in song by a group of young local musicians known as **The Beach Boys**. During their youth, members of the band, most of whom lived a few miles inland, would spend their days swimming and strutting along. The Strand, a esplanade that parallels the beach. Million-dollar homes sit perched on the bluff, overlooking the sand and surf. This beach is ideal for swimming and surfing.

Hermosa Beach

HERMOSA CITY BEACH, at the foot of Pier Avenue. Where Manhattan State Beach to the north draws a classy crowd, Hermosa City Beach is your typical surf ghetto. Aging beach bums take to The Strand alongside the wrinkle-less crowd. The beach itself is extremely wide with grains of sand that are almost alabaster in color. Surf conditions are always good here.

Redondo Beach

REDONDO STATE BEACH, Located along the Esplanade. Surfers enjoy this area as do swimmers, bicyclists, joggers and sun worshippers. Volleyball courts are rarely without players, and a number of eateries are within walking distance.

Torrance
TORRANCE COUNTY BEACH, located off Paseo de la Playa. Sandwiched between the beauty of the Palos Verdes Peninsula and the ugliness of a manmade industrial complex complete with smokestacks, this extensive stretch of beach has nothing more to offer than sand and water. While fisherman find this beach suitable, the surfers are hanging 10 at nearby **Malaga Cove**, a more scenic continuation of the county beach.

Palos Verdes Peninsula
ALBONE COVE CITY BEACH, Off Palos Verdes Drive South. Palos Verdes is a beautiful area boasting million-dollar views and a bevy of estates to match. The shoreline is craggy and hard to reach, and reminds me of the beaches in the northern part of the state. This alcove is not without its rugged rock formations and pounding surf. Tide pools, fishing and swimming are all activities to be enjoyed with caution, and surfers seem to favor the east end of the beach.

San Pedro
CABRILLO STATE BEACH, Steven M. White Drive. Cabrillo State Beach stretches just a mile below the bluffs and is popular with grunion which emerge from the water twice a month to lay their eggs.

Parent Tip
The Cabrillo Marine Museum in San Pedro conducts grunion hunts twice a month for $1. After audiences see a short film on the subject, they are then taken out to the beach to observe the phenomenon by moonlight. *Tel. 310/548-7562*, for information, or watch the grunion run on your own at any of the public beaches.

ROYAL PALMS STATE BEACH, located along Paseo del Mar near the south end of Western Avenue. At one time this beach had its own hotel, but a 1920s storm put an end to San Pedro's seaside lodging. This beach is flanked by swaying palm trees and gigantic boulders, and is filled with both surfers and tide pool observers.

Long Beach

LONG BEACH CITY BEACH, stretching from Alamitos Boulevard down to 72nd Place. There is a reason they call this town Long Beach: it's got a looooong beach. But the city beach is my least favorite. Depending on where you sprawl, the closer you get towards Downtown the more undesirable the element. Also, because Long Beach is at the end of the Los Angeles basin, debris seems to collect in parts of the Downtown marina, often overflowing into the ocean.

On the palisade there are a number of quaint beach apartments and modern high-rise condominiums, creating an eclectic landscape. You'll find metered parking off Shoreline Drive; at the foot of Junipero; near the Belmont Plaza Pool; and at the foot of Bay Shore Drive. If you want to hang with the locals, try **Alamitos Bay** (a.k.a. Horny Corner) or the **Peninsula's** bayside strand.

ALAMITOS BAY, between Second Street and Ocean Boulevard on Bay Shore Drive in Belmont Shore. This is the respectable name given to this stretch of sand, but it's more commonly known among residents as *Horny Corner*. Not that any lewd acts are taking place in broad daylight, but it's a popular beach among young hormonally-charged singles and, more recently, former singles with families. Since it is a bayside beach, the water is always calm. Beyond the buoys is where passing windsurfers cause an occasional ripple.

MOTHER'S BEACH, located near Marine Stadium just off Second Street on Naples Island. The lack of waves seems to be the reason young mothers flock to this marina beach with their kids. A grassy park and lots of shade make for a relaxing day.

THE PENINSULA, located along Ocean Boulevard past Bay Shore Drive. A skinny strip of land, covered every inch with beach cottages and stucco apartment buildings, features a bayside beach on one side and an oceanfront beach on the other. The bayside, which looks across to the million-dollar homes on Naples Island, is my personal sanctuary and is rarely crowded. The beachside, part of the city beach, is also enjoyable, and the stretch of sand ends at a stone jetty where Alamitos Bay begins. Parking is at a premium along the Peninsula, but it's not impossible to find a spot.

PARKS & GARDENS
Hollywood/Los Feliz

GRIFFITH PARK, 4730 Crystal Springs Drive, *Tel. 323/661-7212,* Free admission. In 1896 Colonel Griffith donated more than 4,000 acres of land northeast of Hollywood to the city of Los Angeles. For more than a century, Los Angeles families have been flocking to Griffith Park for picnics, concerts, train rides and more.

The park is divided into two main areas which include the flatlands and the more mountainous terrain. The flatlands, which contain the entertainment venues, include two **golf courses, picnic areas, pony and train rides, tennis courts,** a historic **carousel,** the famed **Los Angeles Zoo,** the **Gene Autrey Museum** and the **Museum of Transportation,** the legendary **observatory** (currently closed until 2005 for renovations), and the world-famous **Greek Theatre.** The mountainous terrains in the central and western regions of the park are mostly undeveloped except for a few hiking paths and horse trails.

The **Visitors' Center** is located at the **Ranger Station** at 4730 Crystal Springs Drive near Los Feliz Boulevard and Riverside Drive, *Tel. 323/665-5188,* and is open daily until 10pm. Free information is available including road and hiking maps.

The 1926 **Merry-Go-Round** is located at the Park Center Picnic Area off Griffith Park Drive, *Tel. 323/665-3051,* and will be recognizable to movie buffs having appeared in dozens of celluloid productions. The **Pony Rides** are conducted on a safe, small track, and the miniature **Train Ride** may be small in size, but is big on fun. Kids and adults of all ages are welcome to climb aboard.

The 75-acre **Los Angeles Zoo** (see Animal Attractions in the *Where Are We Going Now?* chapter) opened in 1966 and is home to more than 2,000 animals. Four-legged residents reside with or near other animals from their original continent and are housed in their natural habitat. Of special interest is the two-headed snake as well as the **Koala House** and the **Animal Nursery,** where the newest arrivals are kept. There are picnic tables available and tram tours, too. The easiest way to reach the zoo is to take the I-5/Golden State Freeway to Zoo Drive. *Tel. 323/666-4090.*

Just north of the Greek Theatre is the **Bird Sanctuary,** where rangers harvest foliage to protect and encourage the birds to nest. The wooded canyon is home to serene ponds and streams, and you can picnic here while you keep your eyes peeled for a sparrow or hawk. Open dusk till dawn.

LAKE HOLLYWOOD, Take Highland north and turn right on Franklin. Take Franklin to Beechwood and turn left. Stay on Beechwood, passing through the stone gates of Hollywoodland and turn left on Ledgewood. Ledgewood will wind up through the hills, past gracious homes, eventually taking you to the top. As you begin to descend down the other side, you'll follow Canyon Lake Drive to Lake Hollywood. Free admission.

Nestled in the Hollywood Hills, this unique reservoir is surrounded by a chain link fence, but joggers can run around the scenic perimeter which features a secluded jogging trail. In the 1970s disaster movie *Earthquake,* you might remember a scene in which a dam collapses and a gush of water sweeps away a litter of people and buildings in its path; part of that scene was filmed here. There is a dog park located nearby with a playground on the premises.

From Lake Hollywood you can also get a good look at the infamous **Hollywood Sign,** as well as **Castillo Del Lago** at 6342 Mulholland Highway. This nine-story home was mobster **Bugsy Siegel's** gambling parlor during the 1930s. It gained more notoriety when **Madonna** lived here during the early

1990s. To the dismay of her neighbors, the Material Girl's blonde ambition got the best of her when she had the exterior painted a stripe motif.

Long Beach

BURNS MILLER JAPANESE GARDENS, on the campus of California State University Long Beach at 1250 Bellflower Boulevard, *Tel. 562/985-8885.* Hours: Tuesday-Friday 8am-3:30pm, Sunday 12pm-4pm, Free admission. When I was a student living in the dormitories at Long Beach State, I would spend many afternoons here in order to escape the chaos of dorm life. Arched bridges link the tiny garden plots together, and multitudes of koi swim freely in the many ponds. This is also a popular site for weddings and one of the area's best-kept secrets.

EL DORADO PARK NATURE CENTER, 2800 North Studebaker Road, *Tel. 562/570-3145,* Free admission. Hidden in this sprawling public park, which is also home to numerous playgrounds, picnic areas and duck ponds, is an 85-acre refuge for birds, foxes, weasels and other wild species who consider this sanctuary home. There are countless trees and plant life to discover throughout, as well as serene ponds. Night tours are also available, and specially trained guides will introduce you to a plethora of resident owls, coyotes, foxes and other nocturnal creatures.

Malibu

TOPANGA STATE PARK, 20835 Entrada Road. *Tel. 310/455-2465,* Hours: Sunrise to sunset. Free admission. $5 per vehicle. Located in a sprawling 10,000-acre refuge, there are grassy meadows for picnics, hiking and simply experiencing nature at its best. The highest peaks yeild views of the ocean and San Fernado Valley, and a self-guided trail details the region's ecology.

Pasadena Area/Arcadia

ARBORETUM OF LOS ANGELES COUNTY, 301 North Baldwin Avenue. *Tel. 626/821-3222, www.arboretum.org.* Hours: Open daily 9am-4:30pm, Admission: $5 adults, $3 seniors and students, $1 ages 5-12, under 5 free. Located across from Santa Anita Race Track, this sprawling arboretum contains 127-acres of botanical gardens, free roaming peacocks, and an historic preservation area. You'll discover more than 30,000 exotic plants from all reaches of the globe, and the gracious Queen Anne cottage may be recognizable from the opening of *Fantasy Island.* The home has also appeared in such films as *The African Queen* and nearly a dozen *Tarzan* movies.

Pasadena Area/La Canada-Flintridge

DESCANSO GARDENS, 1418 Descanso Drive. *Tel. 626/952-4401, www.descanso.com.* Hours: 9am-5pm daily, Admission: $5 adults, $3 seniors and students, $1 children, under 5 free. Located on 160 acres, this public garden is nestled in the San Rafael hills and features a 35-acre camellia forest scattered with more than 50,000 resplendent shrubs. Here you can take tea every weekend at the Japanese Tea House, an appropriate setting for such a divine ritual since the camellia originates from Japan.

While strolling through the grounds, you'll also discover a five-acre International Rosarium arranged in 20-themed gardens boasting antique and contemporary roses, a bird sanctuary and more than 1,500 varieties of irises, lilacs and other fragrant flora. The **Hospitality House** plays host to indoor beauty with its collection of fine art.

Rancho Palos Verdes

SOUTH COAST BOTANICAL GARDEN, 26300 Crenshaw Boulevard. *Tel. 310/544-6815*. Hours: Open daily 9am-5pm, Admission: $5 adults, $3 seniors and students, $1 ages 5-12, under 5 free. Discover more than 2,000 plant and tree species collected from around the world on the grounds of this 87-acre park. Ironically, the land on which the garden sits was an experiment in landfill until 1957, but has now become an archetype on reclaiming lands used for such purposes. Tram tours are available on weekends, but the best way to view the gardens is on foot.

San Pedro

POINT FERMIN PARK, 807 Paseo Del Mar. *Tel. 310/548-7756*. Free admission. Spanning 37 acres on an ocean bluff, you can bring a picnic lunch and graze under sheltered pergolas at the edge of the palisade. Monarch butterflies find the area so appealing they flock here during the winter months.

Hailing from the 19th-century, the **Fermin Lighthouse,** the park's focal point, is a typical clapboard structure complete with crow's nest and beacon.

Parent Tip

One pastime our five-year-old seems to love is a walk along any one of L.A.'s piers. Most every seaside town has one, and Californians take pride in their wooden and concrete landings. Many are historic landmarks having withstood countless lashings from the wind, rain, fires and pounding surf. Some have been destroyed and rebuilt only to be destroyed again.

There are seven Los Angeles County piers stretching from Malibu to Long Beach: the **Malibu Pier,** built in 1929; the **Santa Monica Pier**, built in 1916 and framed by a vintage neon sign; the condemned **Venice Pier**; the reconstructed **Manhattan Beach Municipal Pier**; the **Hermosa Beach Pier**; the 1969 **Cabrillo Beach Pier** in San Pedro; and Long Beach's **Belmont Pier**.

Sadly, it's not open to the public but the panoramic vistas, as once viewed from this maritime relic, are just as breathtaking today as they were decades before.

Santa Monica
PALISADES PARK, Ocean Avenue between San Vicente Boulevard and Colorado Avenue. Overlooking the beach below, this is the town's most famous and scenic greenbelt. Swaying palms, lush foliage, scattered park benches and a walkway that hugs the curve of Santa Monica Bay makes for a lazy California afternoon.

San Fernando Valley/Agoura
PARAMOUNT RANCH, 2813 Cornell Road, *Tel. 818/597-1036.* Hours: Open daily dawn till dusk. Free admission. The Old West is alive and well in the heart of the San Fernando Valley. This was a premiere location for filming westerns beginning in the 1920s when Paramount Studios practically staked their claim here. Movie moments include scenes from *Broken Lullaby* with Lionel Barrymore and *Thunder Below* with Tallulah Bankhead. In the 1950s, television westerns, such as *The Cisco Kid* and *Have Gun Will Travel*, also used the property for filming. The site has also doubled as Tombstone, Arizona, and Dodge City, Kansas, throughout its career. It has also been a stand-in for the Ozark Mountains, Albuquerque, New Mexico, and Tom Sawyer's Missouri.

Today the old sets are history with the exception of "Western Town" where such television shows as *Dr. Quinn Medicine Woman* were filmed. Escape civilization with a hike along the hilly meadows, across the tree-lined streams or spend the afternoon lounging under a willow tree. If you're in town during the months of July and August, you can watch a silent film beneath the stars on hot, balmy nights.

BIKING
If you're going to bike, head to the beach and the **South Bay Bicycle**

Parent Tip
You'll likely hear about or spot signs for **Macarthur** and **Echo Parks**, but I don't endorse bringing the family to either for an outing. MacArthur Park is located in a high-crime area along Wilshire Boulevard and bordered by Alvarado and Park View Streets, and is a haven for drug dealers. Echo Park, though not quite as seedy as MacCarthur Park, is located at Park Avenue between Glendale Avenue and Echo Park Boulevard just north of the 101/Hollywood Freeway and the 110/Pasadena Freeway. Though the lake, with its spouting fountains, looks inviting it also gets its share of undesirables.

Trail, which stretches 20-miles along the coast from Will Rogers State Beach to the north all the way to Torrance Beach down south. Along the way you'll encounter in-line skaters, joggers and leisurely strollers, as well as snack shacks.

Long Beach also has its own bike path that goes from the city's Peninsula neighborhood all the way to Shoreline Village in Downtown. Bicycle rentals, including surrey cycles, are available at Marina Bike Rentals in Redondo Beach, 505 North Harbor Drive, *Tel. 310/318-2453* or Alfredo's Beach Rentals in Long Beach, 5411 Ocean Boulevard, *Tel. 562/434-6121.*

HORSEBACK RIDING

The Hollywood/Los Feliz area offers two places to trot: Riverside Drive and Main Street in Griffith Park, *Tel. 818/840-8401*; and **Sunset Stables,** 300 Beachwood Drive, *Tel. 323/469-5450.* The former features 43 miles of horse trails within Griffith Park, and several commercial stables surround the park making hourly horse rentals convenient. Sunset Stables offers a popular **Moonlight Ride**, which takes riders over the Hollywood Hills to a Burbank cantina and then back again. Offered Friday nights: No riding experience is required.

DOWNHILL SKIING & SNOWBOARDING:

With near-perfect weather conditions almost year 'round, skiing in Los Angeles County seems almost unlikely. But believe it or not, some great resorts are found less than an hour away. The season usually begins around Thanksgiving weekend and concludes sometime near Easter. The following resorts are located in the San Gabriel Mountains and cater to both skiers and snowboarders. Most of the resorts are within a one-hour drive from Downtown Los Angeles.

MT. BALDY. Take the San Bernardino (I-10) Freeway east to the Mountain Avenue off ramp and head north. *Tel. 909/982-0800, www.mtbaldy.com.* Hours: 8am-4:30pm, Lift tickets: $40/all day adults; $10 all-day children under nine. Top elevation is 8,600 feet with its base at 6,500 feet. More than half the terrain is dedicated to advanced skiers, while beginners and intermediates share the rest of the mountain.

MOUNTAIN HIGH. Located in Wrightwood, take the I-10 Freeway east to the I-15 Freeway north to the Highway 138 west to Highway 2. There is no mountain driving, which makes this resort a favorite among skiers. *Tel. 760/249-5808,www.mthigh.com.* Hours: 8am-4:30pm, night skiing 5pm-10pm, Lift tickets: $43 daytime, $25 nightime for adults; $15 either time for kids 7-12. Mt. High consists of two separate mountains offering a wide array of lifts and landscapes. Each base area offers its own ticket window, snack area, rentals, ski school and more. East Mountain offers a peak of 8,200 feet and a base of 6,600 feet; West Mountain's peak is 8,000 feet and its base is 6,800 feet. The longest run is **Gold Rush**, which measures 1.6 miles, and 40% of the mountain caters to advanced skiers.

MT. WATERMAN. Take the 210 Freeway to Highway 2. *Tel. 818/840-1041, www.aminews.com/waterman.* Hours: 8:30am-4:30pm, Lift tickets: $25/all day. While others are heading to the bigger mountain resorts, locals know that the lines at Mt. Waterman are never long. This is one of the area's best-kept secrets for downhill skiing, and one of the most affordable too. Covering more than 150 acres, this vintage resort has a top elevation of 8,030 feet and a bottom elevation of 7,000 feet. More than 60 percent of the mountain is geared towards advanced skiers.

PROFESSIONAL & SPECTATOR SPORTS
Baseball

The **Los Angeles Dodgers** play at Dodger Stadium in Elysian Park near Downtown, perhaps one of the country's most idyllic ballpark settings. The regular season runs April-October. *Tel. 323/224-1500, www.dodgers.com.*

The **Anaheim Angels**, 2002 World Champions, play at Orange County's Edison Field in Anaheim. Their regular season also runs April-October, *Tel. 714/940-2074.*

Basketball

Both the **Los Angeles Lakers** and the **Los Angeles Clippers** now play at the new **Staples Center** in Downtown Los Angeles from October-April. Tickets are available at the box office, and it is not recommended that you walk around this area at night. For Laker information, *Tel. 310/419-3100;* for Clipper information, *Tel. 213/748-8000.*

College teams play at various facilities around town. The **UCLA Bruins** play at **Polly Pavilion** on the UCLA Campus in Westwood, **USC Trojans** play at the **Sports Arena** in Downtown, **Cal State Northridge** play at their campus arena in the **San Fernando Valley**, and **Cal State Los Angeles** play at their campus facility just east of Downtown.

Football

Since both the Los Angeles Rams and Los Angeles Raiders made the exodus from Southern California, Angelenos have been without a professional football team. It's still possible to get a football fix from college PAC 10 teams **UCLA** and **USC** from August to December. The **UCLA Bruins** play at the **Rose Bowl** in Pasadena, and the **USC Trojans** play at the **Coliseum** in Downtown. Every season, the two cross-town rivals play one another, and the week leading up to the big game is always teeming with traditional college pranks. On January 1, following the annual Tournament of Roses Parade, the two best NCAA teams compete against one another at the **Rose Bowl** in Pasadena.

Hockey

The **Los Angeles Kings** also play at the **Staples Center** in Downtown. The **season** begins around the first week of **November** and continues through **mid-April**. Tickets are available at the box office or at TicketMaster locations.

Although not as famous as the L.A. Kings, the **Long Beach Ice Dogs** take a decent bite out of the sport. Part of the **International Hockey League**, the team plays their home games at the **Long Beach Arena** from October through April. *Tel. 562/423-3647* for tickets and information.

Horse Racing

Los Angeles offers two tracks where you can enjoy a day at the races. Generally, the first race begins around 1pm and there are typically nine races per day. The eighth race is usually the featured race.

Santa Anita Park, set against the majestic San Gabriel Mountains in Arcadia, opened in 1935. Opening day is December 26 with the season concluding in mid-April. The **Oak Tree Meeting** runs October and November, and enthusiasts can enjoy morning workouts during race months at no charge. The infield is ideal for picnics, and there are swingsets and entertainment for the kids. Santa Anita Park is located at 285 W. Huntington Drive in Arcadia just of the 210 Freeway. *Tel. 626/574-7223.*

Across town in Inglewood is **Hollywood Park** at 1050 South Prarie Avenue, *Tel. 310/419-1500.* Although Hollywood Park opened in 1938 under the chairmanship of movie mogul Harry Warner and scores of celebrity share holders such as Walt Disney, Bing Crosby and Joan Blondell, it lacks the class and character of Santa Anita. Race season runs from mid-April to July, and an autumn meet is held mid-November to mid-December.

Soccer

While professional soccer may not rank high among American spectators, it's extremely popular with the Latino community. The **LA Galaxy,** the town's only professional team, plays from March through October at the **Rose Bowl** in **Pasadena**. For tickets and information, *Tel. 310/445-1260.*

Tennis

Ever since **Arthur Ashe** dominated this sport as a student, UCLA has hosted many tournaments. Spectators can enjoy free collegiate matches at the campus's **L.A. Tennis Center** from **October through May**. For a schedule: *Tel. 310/206-6831.*

Also taking place on campus in **May** are the **NCAA championship matches**. *Tel. 310/UCLAWIN* for tickets and information; and the **Infiniti Open** happens here every **July**. *Tel. 310/824-1010* for tickets and informaiton.

CULTURAL EVENTS
In a city this size, culture blooms with every season. From opera to symphony to drama, Los Angeles is well rounded in the arts.

MUSICAL PERFORMANCES & VENUES
Beverly Hills
BEVERLY HILLS SUMMER CONCERT SERIES, various locations, *Tel. 310/285-2537.* Numerous concerts are held throughout the city at such breathtaking locales as the Greystone Mansion Courtyard. Performances, held June through August, run the gamut to include jazz, opera, theater and more.

Downtown
LOS ANGELES MASTER CHORALE, at the Music Center's Dorothy Chandler Pavilion, 135 North Grand Avenue, *Tel. 213/972-7211, www.lamc.org.*

L.A. OPERA, at the Music Center's Dorothy Chandler Pavilion, 135 North Grand Avenue, *Tel. 213/972-8001, www.losangelesopera.com.* Principal conductor **Placido Domingo,** one of the world's most respected tenors, oversees the country's fifth largest opera company.

LOS ANGELES PHILHARMONIC, at the Music Center's Dorothy Chandler Pavilion, 135 North Grand Avenue, *Tel. 323/850-2040, www.laphil.org, Tickets: $9-$65.* During the summer months the Los Angeles Philharmonic moves outdoors to the Hollywood Bowl.

Concerts for the Grown-ups!
The **Music Center**, 717 West Temple Street, *Tel. 213/972-7200,* is a mecca for cultural happenings with music, opera and theater all under one roof. The **Dorothy Chandler Pavilion,** the site of the 1999 Academy Awards, is the backdrop for musical performances while the **Mark Taper Forum** and **Ahmanson Theater** present an array of award-winning plays.

The new **Walt Disney Concert Hall,** whose inaugural season gets underway October 2003, is no Mickey Mouse operation. It will be the new home of the **Los Angeles Philharmonic** as well as local and international arts organizations. The new venue will include nearly 2,400 seats, a restaurant, cafe, bookstore, gift shop and an outdoor public garden.

Hollywood

HOLLYWOOD BOWL, 2301 North Highland Avenue, *Tel. 323/850-2000, www.hollywood.bowl.org*. Admission: $1-$100. When the Hollywood Bowl opened on July 11, 1922, audiences had to endure performances while seated on hard wooden benches scattered about the rolling hillside. More than 75 years later, the wooden benches remain but theater-style seating along with cushy box seats have been added for those willing to pay a higher premium for comfort. Summers at the Hollywood Bowl are legendary and the outdoor amphitheater, with its dramatic shell-like stage, is where the **Los Angeles Philharmonic** and the **Hollywood Bowl Orchestra** perform July-September. Picnic areas and tables abound, but get here early to stake your claim. Or, just bring a bottle of wine, a loaf of baguette and celebrate from your seats.

A word of warning: parking at the Bowl is expensive and chaotic with stacked parking only. Designated buses leave from various points throughout Los Angeles County, and the cost is about the same as it would be to park. Call the Hollywood Bowl for more information.

GREEK THEATRE, 2700 North Vermont, *Tel. 323/665-1927*. Tickets: $20-$60. Located in Griffith Park, this outdoor amphitheater opened in September 1930 and its original mission of combining contemporary and classical music hasn't changed in more than 70 years. The setting is spectacular and the acoustics are superb for its season of spring and summer concerts. While outdoor tables and expansive lawn areas are ideal for picnicking, you must purchase your meal from vendors; no outside food or drink is permitted.

Stacked parking, which runs about $6 a car, makes leaving a hassle. Quickpark, which gets you on your way in a flash; reservations must be made in advance. For information: *Tel. 213/665-5857*.

JOHN ANSON FORD THEATRE, 2580 North Cahuenga Boulevard, *Tel. 323/461-3673*. Tickets: $20-$50. Various musical concerts are presented al fresco on summer evenings.

UNIVERSAL AMPHITHEATER, 100 Universal City Plaza, *Tel. 818/777-1000, www.universalstudios.com*. Tickets: $30-$75.

Parent Tip

Younger audiences, who may not be quite as taken with *Evita* or *The Producers*, might enjoy a trip to the **Bob Baker Marionette Theater**, *Tel. 213/250-9995*. It is one of the oldest marionette theaters in the country and ticket prices include both refreshments and a backstage tour.

LIVE THEATRE
Beverly Hills
BEVERLY HILLS PLAYHOUSE, 254 South Robertson Boulevard, *Tel. 310/855-1556*
CANON THEATRE, 205 North Canon Drive, *Tel. 310/859-8001*
WILSHIRE THEATRE, 8440 Wilshire Boulevard, *Tel. 323/468-1700*

Downtown
THE AHMANSON THEATER, *717 West Temple Street, Tel. 213/972-7200*

JAPAN AMERICA THEATRE, 244 South San Pedro Street, *Tel. 213/680-3700*
MARK TAPER FORUM, 717 West Temple Street, *Tel. 213/972-7200*

Hollywood
HENRY FONDA THEATRE, 6126 Hollywood Boulevard, *Tel. 323/468-1761*
JAMES A. DOOLITTLE THEATRE, 1615 Vine Street, *Tel. 213/480-3232*
PANTAGES THEATRE, 6233 Hollywood Boulevard, *Tel. 213/480-3232*.
Alexander Pantages opened his namesake theater on June 4, 1930, as part of the Fox Theatre chain. For decades, it was one of the town's most coveted movie houses, and during the late 1940s and '50s was owned by Howard Hughes.

After Hughes' reign, the theater continued to operate as a movie house for several more years. But in January 1977 its silver screen went dark for the final time, and reopened a month later as a venue for live theatrical productions. Recent productions include *Annie, Cirque Ingenieux* and *Evita.* Perhaps creating the biggest roar among audiences was *The Lion King*, which closed December 2002, in order to make room for *The Producers.*

Parent Tip
Unlike London's Leicester Square or NYC's Time Square, which offer half-price tickets to selected theatrical performances, expect to pay full price for most of L.A.'s sporting and entertainment events. Aside from visiting each box offices personally, the best way to obtain tickets to productions is through Ticket Master. Charge by phone: *Tel. 213/365-3500*, or visit one of Ticket Master's many outlets found inside Tower Records, Robinsons-May Department Stores and Wherehouse Music. You can also purchase tickets on-line at *www.ticketmaster.com.*

Pasadena
THE PASADENA PLAYHOUSE, 39 South El Molino, *Tel. 626/792-8672*

West Hollywood
TIFFANY THEATERS, 8532 Sunset Boulevard, *Tel. 323/289-2999*

West Los Angeles
GEFFEN PLAYHOUSE, 10896 La Conte Ave. *Tel. 310/208-6500*

WHALE WATCHING

Follow the plight of the grey whale as they make their way from Mexico to Alaska. Tours available during migrating season (December-April). Some companies guarantee you'll see a whale, or you get to return free to scout again. Hours of operation vary, call for a schedule.

Redondo Beach
REDONDO SPORT FISHING, 233 North Harbor, *Tel. 310/372-2111*

San Pedro
SPIRIT CRUISES, Ports O'Call Village at Berth 77, *Tel. 310/548-8080*

Parent Tip

If you have a child with an interest in the culinary arts, consider enrolling him or her in one of L.A.'s cooking classes for kids. Not only will you get some time to yourself, but you might unknowingly be grooming the next Emeril Lagasse or Julia Child. Most classes are available to children six to 16 and are divided by age. Curriculum varies, from simple baking to extravagant four-course meals. The best part of all is that you might have an afternoon all to yourselves!

Bristol Farms, 1570 Rosecrans Avenue, Manhattan Beach, *Tel. 310/726-1350*

Epicurean, 8759 Melrose Avenue, Los Angeles, *Tel. 659-5990*

New School of Cooking, 8690 Washington Blvd., Culver City, *Tel. 310/842-9702*

Ritz Carlton, 1410 S. Oak Knoll Ave., Pasadena, *Tel. 626/585-6240*

Sur La Table at The Grove, 6333 W. 3rd Street, Los Angeles, *Tel. 323/954-9190*

Sur La Table, 301 Wilshire Blvd., Santa Monica, *Tel. 310/395-9712*

Long Beach
   SHORELINE VILLAGE CRUISES, 429 Shoreline Village Drive, *Tel. 562/495-5884*

Tourism Information

This book should answer most, if not all, of your questions. But you may also want to use some other resources when planning your trip. The **California Division of Tourism,** *Tel. 916/322-2881 or 800/862-2543*, produces many free publications and maps for the entire state, and LA Inc, The Convention & Visitors Bureau, as well as other city tourist offices that represent areas mentioned in this book, (see list below) can also assist with planning. Most of these bureaus are membership driven and heavily promote those businesses that support the bureau through annual dues.

Not that this is a bad thing, it's just the way it works. But you'll find most reputable hotels, inns, restaurants and attractions are members of these various bureaus and rely on cooperative advertising and promotion to attract visitors to their establishments.

   Anaheim/Orange County Convention and Visitors Bureau, *Tel. 714/999-8999; www.anaheimoc.org*
   Long Beach Convention and Visitors Bureau, *Tel. 562/436-3645; www.golongbeach.org*
   LA Inc., The Convention and Visitors Bureau, *Tel. 213/689-9922, www.lacvb.com*
   San Diego Convention and Visitors Bureau, *Tel. 619/232-3101; www.sandiego.org*

Major Hotel Chains Operating in Los Angeles
• Best Western Hotels, *Tel. 800/248-7234, www.bestwestern.com*
• Days Inn of America, *Tel. 800/DAYS-INN, www.daysinn.com*
• DoubleTree Hotels, *Tel. 800/222-TREE, www.doubletreehotels.com*
• Hilton Hotels, *Tel. 800/HILTONS, www.hilton.com*
• Holiday Inn, *Tel. 800/HOLIDAY, www.holiday-inn.com*
• Hyatt Hotels, *Tel. 800/HYATT-CA, www.hyatt.com*
• Marriott, *Tel. 800/839-7000, www.marriott.com*
• Ramada Hotels, *Tel. 800/2-RAMADA, www.ramada.com*
• Sheraton Hotels & Resorts, *Tel. 800/325-3535, www.sheraton.com*
• Travelodge Hotel, *Tel. 800/578-7878*

b
a
s
i
c

i
n
f
o
r
m
a
t
i
o
n

Chapter 4

Things you should know when visiting Los Angeles.

Agricultural Inspections

While it may seemed hard-pressed to find even a vegetable patch in Los Angeles, agriculture ranks first as the state's number one industry. The state's Department of Food and Agriculture conducts random inspections at the state's borders to control unwanted pests that would threaten the industry. State and federal quarantines prohibit importing certain plants, vegetables and fruits.

Area Codes

Communicating via telephone can be confusing in Los Angeles. In the last two decades, the 213 area code, which once served the entire county, has been split, divided and subdivided. Even residents find the system somewhat confusing with more than a half-dozen area codes now in use.

To help ease the dialing dilemma, the following area codes have been assigned to the various regions:

213: Primarily Downtown Los Angeles

310: West Hollywood, Beverly Hills, West Los Angeles and the beach communities (excluding Long Beach)

323: Hollywood and part of West Hollywood

562: Long Beach and surrounding towns

626: Pasadena/San Gabriel Valley

661: Santa Clarita Valley

818: San Fernando Valley

There are talks that certain area codes are slated to split again. Once the change is made, the old area code can still be accessed for up to one year. When in doubt, dial zero for operator assistance.

Babysitting Services

Most of the hotels listed in the *Which Room is Mine?* chapter offer babysitting services or can make recommendations. However, if you wish to make arrangements on your own the **Baby-Sitting Guild**, *Tel. 818/552-2229*, is L.A.'s oldest and largest such service. The office operates Monday-Saturday and is closed on Sundays; however, sitters are available seven days a week.

Bank Hours

Traditional bank hours are Monday-Friday 9am-4pm with limited hours on Saturday. Automated Teller Machines (ATM) are well lit and located outside most every banking institution. You'll also find ATMs at most grocery stores and at major attractions as well as in the lobby of selected restaurants.

Business Hours

These hours vary greatly depending on how you define "business." Services, such as dry cleaners and automotive repair shops, generally operate a standard 9 to 5 day Monday-Saturday. Retail stores and shopping malls are generally open seven days a week from 10am-9pm Monday-Friday, till 7pm on Saturday, and from 11am-6pm on Sunday. You'll find many major grocery stores and pharmacy chains, such as Sav-On and Rite Aid, operate around the clock.

Currency Exchange

• **American Express Travel Service**, Santa Monica at 1250 Fourth Street, *Tel. 310/395-9588*
• **Associated Foreign Exchange,** Beverly Hills at North Beverly Drive, *Tel. 310/274-7610*
• **1st Business Bank**, Downtown at 601 West Fifth Street, *Tel. 213/489-1000*
• **Foreign Exchange Limited**, Hollywood at 6757 Hollywood Boulevard, *Tel. 800/437-6611*

Dentists

In the event you or your kids have a dental emergency, **Dental Referral Service**, *Tel. 800/422-8338,* can provide you with a recommendation.

Disabled Services

• **Los Angeles County Commission on Disabilities**, *Tel. 213/974-1053*
• **California Relay Service for the Hearing Impaired**, *Tel. 800/735-2922 (voice)* or *800/735-2929 (TDD/TTY)*

Driving Laws & Tips

No matter where you travel in Southern California you should do fine if you follow these rules of the road as advised by L.A. Inc., The Convention and Visitors Bureau and the California Highway Patrol.

- You must carry a valid driver's license from your home state or country. The minimum age for drivers is 16 with training, 18 without.
- California right allows motorists to make a right-hand turn after coming to a full stop at a red light. Conditions must be safe, and there can be no signs prohibiting this maneuver.
- You can get a ticket for becoming stuck in a busy intersection after the signal turns red. It's wise that you feel confident that you can clear the intersection entirely before taking this risk.
- Seat belt laws and car seats for children under six or weighing less than 60 pounds are required. Failing to oblige can result in hefty fines.
- Open bottles or cans containing alcohol located in the car's cabin can get you arrested, even if the cork or top is secured. Store such items in the trunk if necessary.
- Pedestrians in crosswalks have the right of way, and vehicles should yield to such individuals.
- Call boxes are located every quarter mile on the freeway, and operators can connect you to the Auto Club of America, a family member or your insurance company. Face traffic, and be aware of oncoming vehicles when making such calls.
- Avoid rush-hour traffic, which runs from 6am-10am, 4pm-7pm weekdays. If a big sporting event is taking place, you can figure the freeways in the vicinity of the stadium(s) will be tied up as well.
- Freeway carpool lanes, usually marked with a diamond symbol, and metered on-ramps are generally open to any vehicle with more than a solo driver. Pay attention as there are a few exceptions.
- If your vehicle stalls in a traffic lane, turn on your emergency flashers immediately. If your car is still able to move, steer it to the freeway shoulder and remain inside with seat belts fastened while you wait for help.
- In the event you have a collision with another vehicle, state law requires you to show your drivers license to the other driver. Do not block traffic to do so, pull to the side of the road first.
- For an update on traffic and weather conditions, listen to either KNX-AM 1070 or KFWB-AM 980 on your radio. The stations' signals are strongest in Los Angeles and Orange Counties.

Electricity

The standard electrical current for Southern California and the entire United States is 110 volts.

Emergency Contacts

In life-threatening situations, **emergency assistance** for police, fire or medical needs is 911 toll-free call from any public phone. You may be required to dial "9" first from a hotel room, or you can just press zero and ask the hotel operator to assist you. Do not dial 911 in non-emergency situations.

Health

Should you find yourself in need of medical attention, such as a doctor, dentist, chiropractor or board-certified specialist, **Travelmed, Inc**, *Tel. 800/878-3627*, can assist 24 hours a day, seven days a week with house calls, hotel or doctor's office visits within 30 minutes. They also provide physically-challenged travelers with wheelchairs, oxygen and other such needs. Payment is rendered at the time of service, so you may want to check with your health care provider to see if such an emergency service is reimbursable to you. Major credit cards are accepted.

Hospitals

- **Cedars Sinai Medical Center**, Westside, *Tel. 310/855-5000*
- **Good Samaritan**, Downtown, *Tel. 213/977-2121*
- **Long Beach Memorial Medical Center**, Long Beach, *Tel. 562/933-200*
- **Santa Monica/UCLA Medical Center**, Santa Monica, *Tel. 310/319-4000*
- **Saint John's Health Center,** Santa Monica, *Tel. 310/829-5511*

Liquor Laws

The legal drinking age in California is 21 and, unless you look 50 years or older, you might be asked to show picture identification such as a drivers license or passport. Alcohol is sold throughout the state, but it is not sold or served between the hours of 2am and 6am. At bars, the last call for alcohol is 1:30am.

Pharmacies

Sav-On and **Rite-Aid** drugstores are located in most every city and suburb of Los Angeles. Most are open 24 hours with a pharmacist on duty.

Publications

There are a number of weekly and monthly publications you may want to pick up at a newsstand once you arrive.

Los Angeles Magazine and *L.A. Weekly* are both good sources for what's going on in the City of Angels. Orange County is home to the monthly *Orange Coast Magazine* and the free *O.C. Weekly*, both contain decent information about the area and what's happening. Most hotels have their share of in-room publications with *Where Magazine* and *Guest Informant* being among the most popular.

Most daily newspapers produce an extensive entertainment section either on Thursday, Friday or Sunday, detailing all that is available for the upcoming week. *L.A. Parent* and *OC Parent* are also extremely informative.

Sales Tax

A state and county sales tax is imposed on food and merchandise. Sales tax in Los Angeles County is the highest at 8.25%. Orange and San Diego Counties are both 7.75%.

Smoking

Smoking is prohibited on public transportation, in public buildings as well as in most restaurants and bars. Many restaurants now offer outdoor dining to accommodate smokers, but definitely ask before you light up. Businesses that advertise themselves as a smoking establishment, such as cigar bars, are able to get around these ordinances. Also be prepared to show picture identification proving your are at least 18 years old if purchasing tobacco products.

Telephones

Public telephones can be found throughout city streets and are usually always at gas stations, in front of grocery or convenience stores, and in hotel lobbies. **Directory assistance** for the entire United States is 411. This once free service will now cost you, and fees vary. Toll-free directory assistance is still, surprisingly, toll free - dial 800/555-1212 for assistance.

Time Zone

Los Angeles, as well as the entire state of California, operates on Pacific Standard Time (Greenwich Mean Time minus eight hours) and trails three hours behind the East Coast. Daylight Savings Time is observed.

Visitor Resources

Correct Time
Tel. 853-1212 (from any area code)

Visitor Information
• **Automobile Club of Southern California,** *Tel. 213/741-3111*

- **Beverly Hills Visitors Bureau,** *Tel. 310/248-1015, www.bhvb.org*
- **Hollywood Chamber of Commerce,** *Tel. 323/469-8311, chamber.hollywood.com*
- **Long Beach Convention & Visitors Center,** *Tel. 562/436-3645, www.golongbeach.org*
- **LA Inc., The Convention & Visitors Bureau,** *Tel. 213/624-7300, www.visitlanow.com*
- **Pasadena Convention & Visitors Bureau,** *Tel. 626/795-9311, www.pasadenacal.com*
- **Santa Monica Convention & Visitors Bureau,** *Tel. 310/319-6263, www.santamonica.com*
- **West Hollywood Convention & Visitors Bureau,** *Tel. 310/289-2525, www.visitwesthollywood.com*

SAT

Beach/Final4

SUN

Hollywood
& studios
Northridge & LoveSack

MON

Malibu &
PC Highway

TUE

Beach (AM)
Ellen
2:30 - 7pm
Getty or Tar Pits

WED

Catalina Island
Dodgers Game?
UCLA

THUR

DR PHIL Tan-Noon

Lakers Game Pol

FRI

DISNEYLAND

Chapter 5

So you've arrived to Los Angeles. Now what? Do you take the city by storm trying to cover every inch of pavement and palm trees? Probably not. In fact, the best way to explore Los Angeles is by interest, then neighborhood. Keep in mind that your interests may not always coincide with your children's, so compromise is essential when planning your day.

If you're a movie buff or enjoy celebrity lore, than Hollywood would be a great place to start. If you want to take in the museums, the Mid-Wilshire area has a collection to keep you occupied for most of the day. Of course a trip to one of the area's theme parks is likely already part of your agenda. You can also mix it up a bit by spending the morning in one area and the afternoon in another.

If there is one thing I've learned as a parent it's this: The key to a successful family vacation is *flexibility*. Make daily plans to see the city, but be prepared for some changes in the agenda. Impromptu naps, whiny voices and an overall disinterest can put a damper on an otherwise good time. And, when it comes to driving in Los Angeles, frequent traffic jams will always prompt the kids to ask, "Are we there yet?"

Here are some itinerary suggestions to make the ride a bit smoother. Hopefully, everyone will have a heavenly time while in the City of Angels.

Three Day Itinerary

DAY 1

Morning: Begin your day by seeing the display of stars along Hollywood Boulevard's Walk of Fame. Be sure to visit the Forecourt of Stars in front of Grauman's Chinese

Theater and try to match your hands and feet with the impressions left by movie stars past and present. Tour the Hollywood Entertainment Museum and see the set of Cheers! and other movie and television memorabilia. Take a peek inside the Hollywood Roosevelt Hotel, where the Mezzanine level features a unique display of Hollywood's history. Try lunching in the shadow of the Hollywood Sign at the new Hollywood and Highland entertainment complex. There is a California Pizza Kitchen on site, as well as a number of eateries in and around Babylon Court. Pretend to walk the red carpet in front of the Kodak Theatre (tours of the facility are also available daily from 10am to 2:30 p.m.), now the permanent home of the Academy Awards.

Afternoon and Evening: Hop aboard the Metro at Hollywood and Highland for a speedy ride to Universal Studios (or get in the car and head north on the 101 Freeway). Spend the afternoon at the famed theme park, then stroll around Universal CityWalk where a number of restaurants and eateries are located.

DAY 2

Morning: Begin your day by having breakfast Downtown at The Pantry, a restaurant that has remained open 24/7 since 1924 and is currently owned by Richard Riordan, the former Mayor of Los Angeles. Tour Exposition Park, home to a number of museums including the kid-friendly California Science Center and Natural History Museum. Consider taking in a show at the seven-story high IMAX Theatre also located on the premises. College-bound children may want to visit the nearby campus of USC. Head back towards the heart of Downtown and dine at Philippe's, another dining landmark where the French dip was invented or eat at one of the restaurants along Olvera Street.

Afternoon: Continue your afternoon in Downtown with a stop inside Union Station where many films have been shot. Next, take a short walk to Chinatown. Hop in the car, or take the Metro Red Line, to the La Brea Tarpits or opt for an afternoon at the Petersen Automotive Museum - both are located along Wilshire Boulevard.

Evening: Head to Pink's, a hot-dog shack near La Brea and Melrose favored by most every celebrity. Next see what's playing at the recently restored Cinerama Dome, one of Hollywood's mid-century movie palaces.

DAY 3

Get an early start by hopping on the freeway en route to Disneyland. Once you arrive at the Magic Kingdom, head to Goofy's Kitchen for breakfast at the Disneyland Hotel where a cast of Disney characters are on hand to greet you. Then spend the day at Disneyland Resort, home to Disneyland, California Adventure and Downtown Disney.

Parent Tip

When it's time to eat, head to one of the restaurants at Downtown Disney or at one of Disneyland Resort's hotels. The selection and food are much better than what you'll find inside the park – and not all that much more expensive.

Five Day Itinerary

Use days one through three on the previous page, followed by:

DAY 4

Morning: Begin your day with breakfast at Patrick's Roadhouse in Malibu, a favorite celebrity haunt. Then spend the next few hours enjoying a morning walk through Paramount Ranch in Topanga Canyon.

Afternoon: Lunch at one of Malibu's oceanfront restaurants along Pacific Coast Highway (Pierview Cafe, Duke's and Gladstone's are good choices). Then head to the historic Santa Monica Pier for a spin on the antique Looff Carousel and have some fun on the rides at Pacific Park located at the end of the pier.

Evening: Stroll along Santa Monica's Third Street Promenade, home to a number of restaurants as well as some innovative street performers.

DAY 5

In the mood for a road trip? Consider taking a cruise to Santa Catalina Island. Boats depart daily from Long Beach and San Pedro. Or head down the coast to San Diego County, home of LegoLand, SeaWorld, and the World-Famous San Diego Zoo. Amtrak travels from Union Station in Downtown L.A. to San Diego daily.

Seven Day Itinerary

Use days one through five above, followed by:

DAY 6

Morning: If possible, let this day fall on a Sunday and begin your day by having an elaborate brunch aboard the Queen Mary in Long Beach. Included with your meal is a self-guided tour of the ship, which chronicles the heyday of ocean liner travel.

Afternoon: Spend the later part of the day at the Long Beach Aquarium of the Pacific, located just across the harbor from the Queen Mary. Kids will especially enjoy the touch tanks and shark exhibit.

Evening: Stroll over to Shoreline Village, a turn-of-the-century style shopping and dining complex. Dine at the Yard House, Tequila Jack's or Parkers' Lighthouse; then treat the kids to some arcade games and a spin on the carousel.

DAY 7
Get a thrill out of one of the area's theme parks such as Six Flags Magic Mountain, Universal Studios Hollywood or Knott's Berry Farm. If you have tiny tots, you may want to combine a visit to Knott's Berry Farm with one to Adventure City, an amusement park geared towards younger children. Both parks are located within a few miles of each other.

Seeing the Sights
ANIMAL PARKS
Los Feliz
   LOS ANGELES ZOO, 5300 Zoo Drive, *Tel. 323/644-6400, www.lazoo.org,* Hours: Open daily 10am-5pm, Admission: $8.25 adults, $5.25 seniors, $3.25 ages 2-12, and under 2 free. Boasting a menagerie of 1,500 animals and reptiles, the LA Zoo offers an amazing glimpse into the animal kingdom. Within its confines are animals from five continents including Africa, Australia, Asia, North and South America. Special attractions include the Red Ape Rain Forest, a state-of-the-art habitat for the zoo's resident orangutans. Flanked by bamboo and rubber trees, along with three inter-linking tent-like enclosures, families can view these amazing creatures up close in their 6,000-square-foot fortress. An exotic exhibit of Komodo dragons, the world's largest living lizards stretching more than 10 feet in length, adds to the overall excitement.

Fun Fact
Actress Sharon Stone surprised her husband, San Francisco Chronicle editor Phil Bronstein, by arranging for a private tour of the LA Zoo for Father's Day 2001. Bronstein got the shock of his life when he was invited to see a Komodo dragon up close. Upon entering the lizard's cage, a zookeeper asked him to remove his white athletic shoes to prevent the five-foot-long reptile from mistaking the shoes for his diet of white rats. With shoes removed the lizard's basic instincts went into high gear as he attempted to gobble the editor's foot. Bronstein managed to pry the reptile's mouth open and escape through a small feeding door. He was rushed to the hospital where he had surgery to reattach severed tendons.

The Winnick Family Children's Zoo brings storybook animals to life. Designed to create unique learning experiences, children's senses are awoken as they see, smell, hear and touch domestic animals. There are dairy goats, potbelly pigs, fuzzy rabbits, shaggy alpacas and miniature horses, just to name a few.

Parent Tip

Animal magnetism abounds in Los Angeles. Alternatives to the traditional zoo includes **The Gentle Barn** in Tarzana, 6050 Corbin Avenue, San Fernando Valley, *Tel. 818/705-5477*. More of a refuge for abused and neglected animals, visitors are introduced to the menagerie of some 80 creatures. Located on the campus of Cal Poly Pomona in the San Gabriel Valley, *Tel. 909/869-2224*, is the **W.K. Kellogg Arabian Horse Center**. Begun in 1926 by cereal mogul W.K. Kellog, to promote interest in Arabian horse breed, this ranch is now part of the Cal Poly campus. On the first Sunday of the month from October through June an equestrian show is presented to the public. Afterwards, guests are invited to visit the foals.

AQUARIUMS/SEA CENTERS
Long Beach
LONG BEACH AQUARIUM OF THE PACIFIC, 100 Aquarium Way. *Tel. 562/590-3100: www.aquariumofpacific.org*. Hours: Open daily 9am-6pm, Admission: $18.75 adults, $14.95 seniors, $9.95 children 3-11, under 3 free. The 12,000 ocean animals that call this 150,000 square-foot facility home could only be described as underwater masterpieces. One of the largest and most technologically advanced marine exhibitions ever conceived, the Long Beach Aquarium of the Pacific opened in June 1998 and is the world's only aquarium dedicated to the riches of the Pacific Ocean.

Once inside, you'll travel to the temperate waters of Southern California and Baja; the icy conditions found in the Northern Pacific; and the rainbow-splashed region of the Tropical Pacific. In addition to the three main galleries, the Aquarium features additional exhibitions including *Shark Lagoon* and *Lorikeet Forest*, as well as *Jellies: Phantoms of the Deep*. Stick around long enough and you're bound to see divers hand-feeding the fish.

There are numerous interactive displays for kids to enjoy, and the life-sized Blue Whale that suspends from the atrium lobby is a definite conversation piece. The entire experience lasts about 2-3 hours, and leads you outdoors as well. There is a restaurant and gift shop on the premises, and volunteers are available at various posts to answer any questions.

San Pedro
CABRILLO MARINE AQUARIUM, 3720 Stephen White Drive. *Tel. 310/ 548-7562: www.cabrilloaq.org.* Hours: Tuesday-Friday 12pm-5pm, Saturday and Sunday 10am-5pm, closed Monday. Admission: $5 adults, $1 seniors and children. This aquarium is an inexpensive way to meet, greet and interact with Southern California sealife. This facility has been providing marine education for more than 60 years along the shore of Cabrillo Beach. Here you'll discover tide pools, a man-made salt marsh and cliffs rich with fossil. Live exhibits include a touch tank and an interactive jellyfish lab.

MARINE MAMMAL CARE CENTER, 3601 South Gaffey Street. *Tel. 310/ 548-5677, www.mar3ine.org.* Hours: Open daily 8am-4pm, Free admission.. Sick and injured seals and sea lions are rehabilitated at this facility, where the public is welcome to observe their progress. At times you'll find as many as 40-50 animals being treated, and the facility also features exhibits and educational information pertaining to the plight of marine mammals.

ETHNIC NEIGHBORHOODS & HISTORIC DISTRICTS
Downtown
CHINATOWN, 600 block of North Spring Street and surrounding avenues. Chinatown has been around since the 1870s, when the Chinese were brought here to help build the railroads. At that time there was no official "Chinatown," but a district southeast of the original plaza was where most of the Chinese population lived. Present-day Chinatown was established after the old neighborhood was demolished to build Union Station during the 1930s. This area was originally the city's Little Italy district, but the Italians moved on years ago. They did leave behind **Little Joe's**, an authentic ristorante that opened more than a century ago. Sadly, Little Joe's closed its doors in December 1998 to the dismay of thousands of loyal customers. Any trace of Little Italy vanished with it.

These days **Chinatown Plaza** is the pulse of this bustling community. Here you can stroll by a variety of gift shops stocked with expensive imported items and fine artwork. The **600 block of North Spring Street** is always fun to traipse up and down, and you're bound to see a flock of roast ducks dangling from shopkeepers' window. This is where residents go to stock their pantries with herbs, fresh fish and produce.

LITTLE TOKYO, Bounded by 1st and 3rd Streets, Los Angeles Street and Central Avenue. While the architecture and cultural influences are still evident in this neighborhood, only about 700 Japanese-Americans still call this district home. However, it remains the center for Japanese traditions and is where the Japanese-American Cultural and Community Center is located along with a Buddhist Temple, plenty of shopping and authentic restaurants.

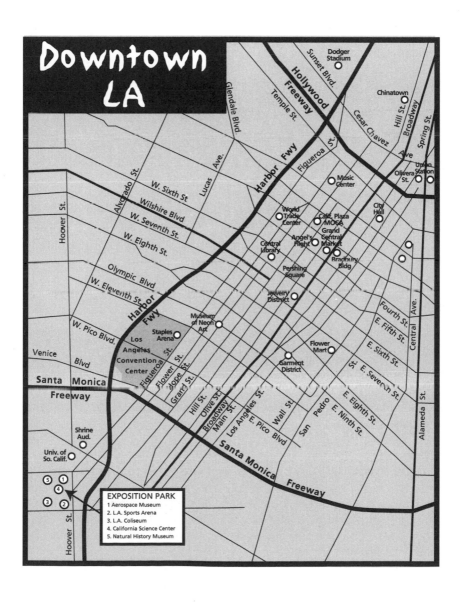

Hancock Park/Mid-Wilshire

HANCOCK PARK, bounded by Wilshire and Melrose Avenues, and Highland and Larchmont Boulevards. The grand mansions that line the streets of this upscale neighborhood are as every bit as magnificent as those found in Beverly Hills. Captain G. Allan Hancock created this exclusive residential neighborhood in 1910, and past and present residents include Nat King Cole, Whitney Houston, Cameron Diaz, Francis Ford Coppola, Anne Heche, Ellen DeGeneres, and many others. The Mayor of Los Angeles' official home is located at **605 South Irving Boulevard** just north of Wilshire; the estate was donated by the Getty Oil Company. While the homes are spectacular, the surrounding area leaves little to be desired.

MIRACLE MILE, Wilshire Boulevard between La Brea and Fairfax Avenues. In 1920, A. W. Ross purchased 18-acres along Wilshire Boulevard and developed a fashionable business and shopping district. All the big-name department stores could be found here: Bullock's Wilshire, The May Company, I. Magnum and others. It was dubbed Miracle Mile, and for many years this is where Angelenos shopped.

The area started going downhill during the 1960s, when shopping malls became a way of life. Many of the Art Deco buildings here have been torn down, but preservation groups have done their best to save as many as possible. All of the fine department stores have long since vacated.

WILSHIRE NEON, near MacArthur Park around the vicinity of Wilshire Boulevard and Alvarado. For years the classic neon signs that once illuminated this elegant corridor were dark. An effort to restore the glowing works of art got underway, and Wilshire Boulevard is once again glowing with neon lights.

The 1926 **Westlake Theatre,** a former movie palace overlooking MacArthur Park, is just one of the many signs worth noting. Take a drive through here in the evening, but be sure to keep your car doors locked. The Museum of Neon Lights (see Museums & Galleries in this chapter) conducts after-dark tours as well.

Hollywood

HOLLYWOOD WALK OF FAME, along Hollywood Boulevard between Sycamore Avenue and Gower Street, and Vine Street between Sunset Boulevard and Yucca Street. More than 2,000 terrazzo stars grace the streets sporting such names as Marilyn Monroe, Barbra Streisand, Nicolas Cage, Groucho Marx and countless others. Usually a fan club or a publicist rallies on behalf of a star for the honor.

Criteria for receiving a star includes professional achievement, longevity of five or more years, contributions to the community, a $10,000 fee upon selection, plus the guarantee that the celebrity will attend the ceremony. To locate a particular star or to find out about an upcoming induction ceremony,

Fun Fact

Joanne Woodward was the first celebrity to be inducted with a star along Hollywood Boulevard on February 9, 1960, when the concept was first introduced.

call the Hollywood Chamber of Commerce, *Tel. 323/469-8311.* Or visit their website: *http://chamber.hollywood.com/walkoffame.*

West Los Angeles

THE FAIRFAX DISTRICT, along Fairfax Avenue between Melrose Avenue and Wilshire Boulevards. This area became the hub of L.A.'s Jewish community during the height of World War II. Here you'll find Canter's Deli along with an array of kosher restaurants, shops and places of worship. The majority of established Jews now reside in more affluent areas, such as West Los Angeles and the San Fernando Valley. Taking their place are a new flux of Jewish immigrants arriving from Eastern Europe.

HISTORIC SITES & ARCHITECTURAL LANDMARKS
Beverly Hills/Century City

THE WITCH'S HOUSE, 516 N. Walden Drive, Not open to the public. Known locally by this moniker because of its Hansel and Gretal-esque facade, this home has a unique history. It was a former movie studio set during the era of silent films, and also served as offices for Irvin C. Willat Productions in Culver City. When the studio was sold in the mid-1920s, the house was relocated to this site where it has become a major attraction in its own right.

ACADEMY OF MOTIONS PICTURES, ARTS AND SCIENCES, 8949 Wilshire Boulevard. *Tel. 310/247-3000.* Call for hours, Free admission. Located in a refurbished and expanded building of Spanish-Romanesque design, this was the former location of the city of Beverly Hills' Water Treatment Plant No. 1. Built in 1927, the building was vacated in 1976 when the city began purchasing its water from the L.A. Metropolitan Water District.

Since 1991, the Academy has been headquartered here and the **Margaret Herrick Library**, located on the second floor, is open to the public Monday, Tuesday, Thursday and Friday from 10am-6pm. This research library includes some 20,000 books, 1,400 periodical titles, 600,000 screenplays, 200,000 clipping files and more than six-million photographs. You can actually request to look at press clipping files from celebrities past and present. Many of the older stars' clippings included their home addresses in feature articles.

Downtown

THE BRADBURY BUILDING, 304 South Broadway, *Tel. 213/626-1893, Call for hours and tours.* A building like no other, this five-story brick structure has graced the silver screen many times appearing in such films as *Blade Runner.* Built in 1893 by real estate and mining tycoon Louis L. Bradbury, the interiors are a work of art. Natural light beams in from the glass canopy roof casting a sepia glow on the iron balustrades, winding staircases, exposed hallways and open-cage elevator. Enhanced with coatings of marble and brick, this office building is truly spectacular once inside.

CATHEDRAL OF OUR LADY OF THE ANGELS, 555 West Temple Street, *Tel. 213/680-5273, www.cathedral.la-archidiocese.org.* Complimentary tours are available Monday-Friday 1pm and 3pm; Saturday 11:30am and 2pm; and Sunday at 11:30am. Deisgned by Pritzker prize-winning architect Jose Rafael Moneo of Spain, the City of Angels has been blessed with this new spiritual landmark. Situated on more than five urban acres in the heart of Downtown Los Angeles, the Cathedral is as much a museum as it is a place of worship.

Fun Fact

At 65,000 square feet, the Cathedral of Our Lady of the Angels is a foot larger than St. Patrick's Cathedral in New York City, making it the largest in the United States.

EL PUEBLO DE LOS ANGELES STATE HISTORIC PARK, bounded by Los Angeles Street and Main Street. *Tel. 213/628-1274.* Hours: Open daily 10am-9pm. Free admission. Most people refer to this area as Olvera Street, and the beginning of Los Angeles can be traced back to this very location. It is the oldest section of the city, and its cluster of 27 buildings create a colorful and historic mosaic.

In 1781 the first pueblo was established under the rule of King Carlos II of Spain. As the town prospered, retired soldiers were granted large portions of land for farming. In 1821, Mexico became independent of Spain and additional land grants were given to new immigrants. In 1846, Los Angeles became American territory as a result of the Mexican-American War and dramatic changes soon took place. Plaza landowners moved away, new buildings were erected, and farming was replaced by industry. New opportunities attracted such ethnic groups as the Chinese, French and Italians.

The area began to rapidly decline, and it wasn't until 1930 that a restoration effort was proposed. Preservationist Christine Sterling recognized the historic value this district offered, and she helped to establish **Olvera Street**. Soon the Mexican-style marketplace was thriving, and several historic buildings were rescued from demolition. The **Avila Adobe**, built circa 1818 by former mayor Francisco Avila, is the plaza's focal point and city's oldest landmark. Other notable structures include the **Pelanconi House**, the city's oldest brick house dating back to 1855, and the 1887 **Sepulveda House,** an Eastlake Victorian-style structure.

While there is no argument that Olvera Street caters to tourists, it remains a sentimental favorite among natives. The best tacos can be found at a tiny stand located at the entrance near Alameda Street, and the annual **Blessing of the Animals** is a cherished Easter event.

GRAND CENTRAL MARKET, 317 S. Broadway. *Tel. 213/624-2378,* Hours: Monday-Saturday 9am-6pm, Sunday 10am-5pm, Free admission. In operation since 1917, the Grand Central Market features more than 50 food stalls offering everything from fresh produce to pig snouts to herbal remedies. Although most items may turn your stomach, it's definitely worth traipsing through, and it's worth it just to see the authentic tortilla factory.

LOS ANGELES CITY HALL, 200 N. Spring Street. *Tel. 213/485-4423.* Call for tour schedule, Free admission. This white streamlined building has more film credits than most actors, and has aged better too. Superman soared above it in the 1950s television series when it served as the exterior for the *Daily Planet*, it was also seen nearly every week on the Jack Webb series

Fun Fact

Public art is as much a part of Los Angeles' landscape as are the Hollywood sign and studio gates. There are literally hundreds of brightly colored murals splashed on freeways, storefronts and historic buildings.

One of the more notable works is by muralist Eloy Torrez entitled *The Pope of Broadway*, which features Anthony Quinn dancing à la *Zorba the Greek*. The 1985 artwork graces the Victor Clothing Company building in Downtown Los Angeles at 240 South Broadway between 2nd and 3rd Streets.

Legends of Hollywood, which featured colossal portraits of Marilyn Monroe, Humphrey Bogart, Clark Gable, Bette Davis, Fred Astaire and James Dean, is perhaps Torrez's most recognized work having appeared in countless magazines and films. Sadly, the mural was destroyed during the 1994 Northridge earthquake. The Mural Conservancy of Los Angeles and the Hollywood Arts Council have assisted the artist in retrieving fragments of the mural, and a modified version is planned for a new location.

The MCLA provides mural bus tours throughout the city. *Tel. 310/470-8864 or 213/257-4544; www.lamurals.org.*

Dragnet. Free tours include stops at the central rotunda, the press room and council chambers.

RICHARD J. RIORDAN CENTRAL LIBRARY, 630 West Fifth Street. *Tel. 213/228-7000.* Hours: Monday-Thursday 10am-8pm, Friday-Saturday till 6pm, Sunday 1pm-5pm. It's not often you find tourists seeking out the local library, but the historic Central Library is definitely worth a visit. Built in 1926 by architect Bertrum Goodhue, the unique design includes a rooftop pyramid and imposing sphinxes. In 1993 the high-tech Bradley Wing opened, creating much needed space. It too offers a unique design with an eight-story atrium and whimsical chandeliers. Of course, there is always the vast selection of books, magazine, audio and videotapes to browse through, or you can check your e-mail on one of the new computers. Free docent tours are conducted daily, call for information.

LOS ANGELES TIMES, 202 West First Street. *Tel. 213/237-5757.* Free tours, call for reservations one week in advance. Children must be 10 years or older. Designed by Gordon Kaufman in 1935, a modern addition of steel and glass was added in the early '70s. Housed here is one of the largest daily newspapers in the country, and aspiring journalists can tour the facility and see the making of a newspaper from start to finish.

SHRINE AUDITORIUM, 649 West Jefferson Boulevard. *Tel. 213/749-5123.* Not open to the public. The Moroccan-style building was built in 1926 for the Shriners, and remains the largest theater in the United States. When the new Music Center was erected atop fashionable Bunker Hill, this was discarded as just another old building. It has since been restored and has been the site of numerous award ceremonies including the Academy Awards, the Emmys and the MTV Awards. Frank Sinatra's 80th birthday bash was televised from this location, and Michael Jackson's mane caught fire on stage during the taping of a 1984 Pepsi commercial.

Fun Fact

If you want to witness the **Emmy Awards** up-close, the Academy of Television Arts and Sciences now invites the public to attend. Tickets become available in the spring on a first come, first-served basis. All you need to do is call the Academy directly, *Tel. 818/754-2800*, or visit their website at *www.emmys.org*. Children who are able to sit in their seats are welcome to attend.

UNION STATION, 800 N. Alameda Street, Free admission. When Union Station was completed in 1939, it was the last of the magnificent train depots to be built in the country. With the onset of World War II, the station was flanked with young soldiers passing through Los Angeles on their way to foreign lands. When air travel became the preferred mode of transportation, Union Station resembled a ghost town. But with the return of commuter trains to Los Angeles, and folks yearning to travel by rail to San Diego, Santa Barbara or beyond, Union Station is once again thriving.

The Spanish Colonial Revival building is blended with streamline touches, reflecting the Art Deco era in which it was built. The soaring clock tower and arched entryways are complemented with a landscape of fig trees, Mexican fan palms, birds of paradise and so on. This is a favorite location for period-style films in which Los Angeles is featured. The station appeared in *Bugsy* and *L.A. Confidential*, as well as more contemporary movies such as *Nick of Time*.

Time to Eat:

Just across from Union Station at 1001 North Alameda is **Philippe's, The Original**, where the French dip sandwich was born. This landmark offers a no frills setting with communal tables, a sawdust-laden floor and counter service. While there is no kids menu, children can order a beef dip or simple cheese sandwich. There are also plenty of salads, 40-cent lemonade and dessert. Cash only - ATM on the premises.

Time to Shop

You can visit both China and Mexico within a two-block stroll of Union Station. Across the street is **Olvera Street**, the birthplace of Los Angeles, and home to an **outdoor mercado** filled with merchandise imported from South-of-the-Border. While it's a little kitschy, it brings back fond memories for any child who grew up in and around Los Angeles. Chinatown, located just a few blocks north, is a bit more authentic with a number of herb and specialty shops. Both are fun distractions.

Parent Tip

The Los Angeles Conservancy, *Tel. 213/623-2489*, a grassroots organization dedicated to preserving the city's historic buildings, offers walking tours of Broadway's historic movie palaces every Saturday. The ensemble of preservationists also give tours of other historic buildings that have played a significant role in the city's history.

Hollywood

The architecture of **FRANK LLOYD WRIGHT** is evident at three homes he designed in this area. The **Ennis-Brown House**, 2655 Glendower Avenue, *Tel. 323/668-0234*, was built in 1924, and its interiors were used in Ridley Scott's movie *Blade Runner* as Dr. Tyrrel's apartment. Situated in the Hollywood Hills,

Wright used hand-crafted Mayan-style block to create a most stunning facade. Hourly docent tours are conducted the second Saturday of odd numbered months, and reservations are required. Call for information.

The **Hollyhock House,** at Barnsdall Art Park is located at 4808 Hollywood Boulevard, *Tel. 323/913-4157*, was completed in 1921 for oil heiress Aline Barnsdall and is Wright's second California structure. The name *Hollyhock* comes from a stylized version of the flower by the same name, and is a decorative pattern that is repeated throughout the house's design. While it's hard to pigeon-hole this particular style of architecture, Wright himself referred to it as California Romana or the freedom to make one's own form. Rudolf Schindler, who assisted Wright on many projects, saw to the house's completion after Wright was fired from Barnsdall. Hourly tours are expected to resume sometime in spring 2004 after the house completes a substantial renovation. (Another FLW design is the 1928 Samuels-Navarro House located at 5609 Valley Oak Drive, which is a private residence).

The **Samuel & Harriet Freeman House**, 1962 Glencoe Way, *Tel. 323/ 851-0671*, was built in 1924 by Wright who used textile blocks in its design. The Freeman's hosted salons for avant garde artists and politicos including Martha Graham, Edward Weston, Xavier Cugat and many others. Credit for the interior furnishings goes to Rudolf Schindler. The Northridge Earthquake caused extensive damage, and restoration efforts are underway to preserve the structure which remains closed.

CAPITOL RECORDS, *1750 N. Vine Street, Tel. 323/462-6252, Not open to the public*. This landmark building, made to look like a stack of records with a phonographic needle on top, was touted as the world's first circular building. Dedicated in 1956, the tubular silhouette gives definition to the Hollywood skyline and is easily visible from the 101/Hollywood Freeway.

Fun Fact
The **Capitol Records building** rises 150 feet in the air and is crowned with a 90-foot spire. Did you know that the rooftop constantly blinks the letters H-O-L-L-Y-W-O-O-D in Morse Code? It's true!

EGYPTIAN THEATRE, 6712 Hollywood Boulevard, *Tel. 323/461-9737, www.egyptiantheatre.com*. Admission to special events vary. While Sid Grauman is most famous for erecting the landmark Grauman's Chinese Theatre, one of his earlier productions was that of the historic 1922 Egyptian Theatre. This was Hollywood's first movie palace and was the site of the very first movie premiere, *Robin Hood,* starring Douglas Fairbanks. It was modeled

Hollywood
West Hollywood

Pantages Theater
Hollywood Fwy
Doolittle Theater
Hollywood Palladium
Paramount Studios
Vine St.
Cahuenga Blvd.
Melrose Ave.
Beverly Blvd.
Odin St
Franklin Ave.
Hollywood Wax Museum
Ripley's Believe It Or Not!
Hollywood Bowl
Chinese Theater
Santa Monica Blvd.
Highland Ave.
La Brea Ave.
Franklin Ave.
Hollywood Blvd.
Sunset Blvd.
Fountain Ave.
Warner Hollywood Studios
Melrose Shopping
Gardner St.
CBS Television City
Fairfax Ave.
Crescent Heights Blvd.
Melrose Ave.
Beverly Blvd.
Sunset Blvd.
Blvd.
Santa Monica
Pacific Design Center
La Cienega Blvd.
Sunset Plaza Drive
Sunset Plaza
San Vicente Blvd.
Robertson Blvd.
Doheny Dr.

Fun Fact

Leonardo DiCaprio's former home at **1874 Hillhurst Avenue** (in the Los Feliz district at the corner of Franklin) is now one of the city's newest, state-of-the-art libraries. Leo, who spent most of his teen years here, donated $35,000 to the institution's hi-tech computer center.

after the Temple at Thebes, and opened when King Tut's tomb reached public frenzy.

Always the showman, Grauman spared no expense to recreate ancient Egypt in the land of make believe. He adorned the theater with hieroglyphs, sphinx heads and, for the entertainment of boulevard strollers, live caged monkeys.

It originally cost $800,000 to build and was recently renovated to the tune of $12.9 million. Restoration efforts included the original entrance portico, the classic sunburst ceiling, and the installation of a 1922 Wurlitzer theater organ for the use of silent film presentations. The original theater seated more than 2,000 people, but the new Egyptian features two theaters: the 650 seat Lloyd E. Rigler Theatre, and the 83 seat Steven Spielberg Theatre. Contemporary additions include a cafe, publication kiosks and a patio courtyard.

During the day visitors are treated to a documentary about the history of Hollywood beginning with a prologue performed on the 1922 Wurlitzer organ. During the evening, classic films from silent movies to rare film noire are presented. If Sid Grauman were alive today, he would surely applaud the efforts of those responsible for saving this Hollywood relic.

EL CAPITAN THEATRE, 6834 Hollywood Boulevard, *Tel. 323/461-8571, Admission.* Fans of Disney movies, both contemporary and classic varieties, will enjoy the fanfare that takes place inside this historic theater. Crowned with its distinctive tower, this movie palace was where Orson Welles premiered his classic 1939 film *Citizen Cane*. Built in 1925, the lavish interiors were recently restored by the Walt Disney Company and is a venue for Disney animated features. Lavish live stage shows often take place prior to screenings and, in true Disney fashion, an interactive playhouse next door brings the entire experience into full circle.

The El Capitan Theatre is extremely popular, and show times are often sold out days in advance. Now you can purchase E-Tickets online at *http://cms.disney.go.com/disneypictures/el_capitan* and be guaranteed your preferred show time.

GRAUMAN'S CHINESE THEATRE, 6925 Hollywood Boulevard, *Tel. 323/464-8111.* Admission to see a film, no admission to Forecourt of the Stars. An international landmark and movie industry icon this legendary theater was opened by Sid Grauman in May 1927. During construction Grauman saw to it that his Chinese palace would be authentic down to the last detail. Oriental curio shops lined the courtyard as a 30-foot-high dragon peered over the pagoda-like entrance. The crimson colored lobby was graced with expensive works of art, and guests were shown to their seats by costumed ushers.

Over time the legendary theater has undergone a few changes. The interior was remodeled in 1958, and the present owners added two annex theaters to the building's east side. The soaring bronze roof is now a jade hue due to weather elements.

Nearly 200 luminaries have left their indelible marks along Hollywood Boulevard. Today patrons, tourists, starry-eyed dreamers and fans from all walks of life mill about the **Forecourt of the Stars** trying to see if their hand prints are as petit as Marilyn Monroe's or if their footprints measure up to John Wayne's. Movie premieres still take place here, and fans can catch a glimpse of their favorite celebrity from behind the velvet rope. The tourist quota is thick mainly due to the theater's location, which is adjacent to the new Hollywood & Highland shopping complex.

The first cement impressions at Grauman's Chinese Theatre were acciden-tally left by **Norma Talmadge,** who stepped into a block of wet cement at the theater's forecourt. Always one to seize an opportunity, Sid Grauman quickly masked the faux pas by insisting the actress sign her name in the cement. **Mary Pickford** and **Douglas Fairbanks** repeated the gimmick a few weeks later on April 30, 1927, and thus a tradition was born.

HOLLYWOOD SIGN, for an up-close look, follow these directions: take Highland north and turn right on Franklin. Take Franklin to Beechwood and turn left. Stay on Beechwood, passing through the stone gates of Hollywoodland and turn left on Ledgewood. Ledgewood will wind up through the hills, past gracious homes, eventually taking you to the top. When you level out at the top, you'll be right under the sign at Mulholland. As you begin your descent down the other side, you'll see a dirt area to your left that overlooks Lake Hollywood and the city.

This is a great photo opportunity. One of the city's oldest and most famous landmarks is also the easiest to find. Just cast your eyes towards the Hollywood Hills, and you'll immediately see the Hollywood sign. It was unveiled in 1923 as an advertising gimmick to promote a gated housing tract called Hollywoodland.

Harry Chandler, one of the founders of Hollywoodland and then publisher of the Los Angeles Times, is said to have come up with the idea of erecting five-story letters on top of Mount Lee. He also called for the installation of 4,000 light bulbs to ensure the sign would be seen throughout the city, and Chandler financed the entire project to the tune of $21,000.

Each of the 13 letters was 50-feet high and 30-feet wide. The sign was constructed with telegraph poles hauled up the steep and rugged hill by

Parent Tip

Stage your own photo shoot beneath the **Hollywood Sign**. One of the best photo opportunities for capturing this landmark is down below in the flats at the corner of Sunset and Gower in Hollywood.

mules. A team of laborers dug deep holes with pickaxes and shovels to ensure the stability of each letter.

Soon the blinking lights became an annoyance to patrons of the outdoor Hollywood Bowl, and eventually bulbs were stolen or shot out by folks armed with beebee guns. The novelty of the sign slowly wore off, and by 1939 upkeep was sketchy at best. In 1949, the "land" section of the sign tore loose from its base and tumbled down the hillside never to be replaced.

The Hollywood sign has become as infamous as some of the scandals that have taken place in this town. In 1932, Lillian Millicent "Peg" Entwhistle, an aspiring actress, climbed to the top of Mount Lee and jumped to her death from atop the letter "H." The 13-letter sign was soon considered bad luck.

While Entwhistle's death is the only known suicide to have taken place, the sign has played host to a number of practical jokes. During the 1970s counter culture era, two of the sign's letters were altered to reveal "HOLLYWEED." More than a decade later in 1987, when Lt. Col. Oliver North was making headline news for his role in the Iran-Contra scandal, Angelenos awoke to a sign that read "OLLYWOOD."

In 1979, the entertainment community rallied around the idea of building a new sign to replace the dilapidated one that clung to Mount Lee. In a fund-raising coup, chunks of the old Hollywood sign were sold as momentos to the general public. The original sign was replaced with a new and improved one at the cost of $249,300 — nearly 12 times the original price.

KODAK THEATRE, at Hollywood & Highland. *Tel. 323/308-6363.* Hours: Tuesday-Sunday 11am-2pm, closed Monday. Tours run every 15 minutes. Not available during special events. Admission: $15 adults, $10 ages 3-12.

The new Kodak Theatre, where Hollywood's elite pose for the paparazzi on the red carpet, now offers public tours. The tour, which lasts about 35-minutes (about 20 minutes longer than the average Hollywood career), takes you through the process of producing the Academy Awards Show, which is held here every March. Behind-the-scenes tours, conducted by professional, though not famous, actors include the Eastman VIP Lounge where celebs air kiss prior to the start of the awards ceremony. Visitors can also take a trek down the Grand Central Spiral staircase and warm the seats where stars like Warren Beatty and Halle Berry have parked their million-dollar rear ends.

PANTAGES THEATRE, 6233 Hollywood Boulevard, *Tel. 323/480-3232, Admission.* Marion Davies and Al Jolson had the honors of opening the nation's first Art Deco movie palace with the premiere of their 1930 movie *Floradora.* For a decade, the Pantages was the site of the Academy Awards (1949-1959), as well as the backdrop for the Emmy Awards during the 1970s. Howard Hughes even kept offices here at one time. The theater is now used for special events and theatrical productions. The *Lion King* recently ended its two-year run here roaring out of town to make way for *The Producers.*

Time to Eat:
A great way to end a day in Hollywood is with dinner at **Yamashiro,** 1999 N. Sycamore Avenue, *Tel. 323/466-5125, www.yamashiro.com.* Built as a private residence in 1911, the architecture pays homage to the palaces of Japan. Aside from serving authentic Asian cuisine, the restaurant boasts some of the city's most spectacular views. Scenes from the 1957 motion picture *Sayonara,* starring Marlon Brando and Ricardo Montalban, were filmed here. Celebrity noshers include Brad Pitt, Johnny Depp and Ben Affleck.

Fun Fact
If you can't actually star in a film, it is possible to watch one being made from the sidelines. The **Los Angeles Film Permit Office**, located at **7**083 Hollywood Boulevard, 5th Floor, *Tel. 323/957-1000,* supplies "Shoot Sheets" to the public. The Shoot Sheet, which provides daily location filming throughout the streets of Los Angeles, lists the exact addresses of each filming location taking place that day, the name of the movie or television show being produced, and the hours that they have reserved for the shoot. What it doesn't tell you is the name of the actors involved.

Prior to 9/11 you could pick up a Shoot Sheet at the permit office. These days you have to register online at *www.eidc.com.* You might also want to look for the **Star Waggons**, a company owned by former *Carol Burnett Show* regular **Lyle Waggoner ,**which supplies luxury trailers to stars on location.

Long Beach
RANCHO LOS CERRITOS, 4600 Virginia Road, *Tel. 562/570-1755,* Hours: Wednesday-Sunday 1pm-5pm. Free admission. This historic California homestead paints a vivid picture of what life was like in these parts during the 1850s and is one of the few remaining two-story adobes still left in Southern California. Both this rancho and **Rancho Los Alamitos,** located at 6400 Bixby

Hill Road, *Tel. 562/431-3541*, originate from Rancho Santa Gertrudes, the largest land grant ever bestowed in Southern California. Both offer tours, picnics and special events year round. Rancho Los Alamitos features an historic ranch house and six barns situated on four acres of gardens near the Cal State Long Beach campus.

Long Beach is also home to the **world's skinniest house**, according to the Guinness Book of World Records. Located at 708 Gladys Avenue near the corner of 7th Street, the house dates back to 1932 when Nelson Rummond, on a bet, built a house on a lot that measured only 10 feet by 50 feet. The architect hired unemployed craftsmen to construct an Old-English Tudor-style home spanning three stories and 860 square feet. The house, which remains a private residence, was recently on the market for close to $300,000.

Mid-Wilshire/Fairfax District

THE ORIGINAL FARMERS MARKET, 6333 W. 3rd Street. *Tel. 323/933-9211, www.farmersmareketla.com*. Free admission. In 1934, a group of farmers pulled their trucks onto Gilmore Island to display their homegrown wares. Makeshift stalls eventually gave way to more permanent architecture including the landmark Clock Tower. The land was owned by A.F. Gilmore, who made his millions after discovering oil on this former dairy farm. His son, Earl Gilmore, is credited with inventing the first self-serve gas station. The *Gas-A-Teria* was located here in the early 1930s and saved customers five-cents a gallon if they were willing to pump their own petrol.

Farmers Market is an L.A. institution with more than 110 merchants and some 600 employees. More than three-million people pass through the stands and shops each year including such devotees as **Lauren Bacall, Jennifer Aniston, Denzel Washington** and **George Clooney**.

Time to Shop

The Grove, a new streetscape-style shopping complex, is located next door to the Original Farmers Market. Parents will enjoy browsing through Nordstrom, Sur La Table and a selection of specialty shops, while kids will enjoy the spouting fountain and free "Red Car" trolley rides that link the two complexes together. There is also a movie theater and restaurants.

Pasadena

GAMBLE HOUSE, 4 Westmoreland Place, *Tel. 626/793-3334*. Hours: Thursday-Sunday 12pm-3pm, Admission: $8 adults, $5 seniors and students, under 12 free. Built by famed architects Charles and Henry Greene in 1908 for David and Mary Gamble, the other half of the Proctor and Gamble empire, this classic home exemplifies the arts and crafts movement from the early part of the 20th century. Listed on the National Register of Historic Places, the Gamble House offers docent-led tours.

The interiors reflect the craftsmanship of a bygone era with hand-rubbed teak wood, built-in cabinetry, original furnishings, and multi-hued glass windows. The cross ventilation system was ingenious for its time, and provided natural air conditioning before such technology was invented.

You may recognize the Gamble House as belonging to Doc, played by Christopher Lloyd, in the movie *Back to the Future.*

PASADENA CITY HALL, 100 North Garfield Avenue, *Tel. 626/405-4000.* Open during normal business hours. Built in 1927, the regal looking building reflects the style and grace of three famed domed structures: the Church of Santa Maria della Salute in Venice, Italy; the Hotel des Invalides in Paris, France; and St. Paul's Cathedral in London, England.

Many movies and television shows are filmed here, and you are free to walk through this landmark during business hours.

TOURNAMENT HOUSE, 391 South Orange Grove Boulevard. *Tel. 626/449-4100.* Hours: House tours are every Thursday from February to August 2pm-4pm, Rose gardens open year 'round. Closed December 31-January 2. Admission varies, call ahead. If you're traveling with your own little princess, you might be interested to know that each year the Rose Queen for the Tournament of Roses Parade is crowned from this location. This ornate Italian-Renaissance mansion was built between 1908 and 1914 for chewing gum magnate and Chicago Cubs owner William Wrigley, Jr. The Wrigley's enjoyed watching the Rose Parade from their front yard and, when Mrs. Wrigley died in 1958, the estate was given to the Tournament of Roses Association to use as their headquarters. Recently the much admired estate underwent a major renovation.

Fun Fact

George Freeth was the original surfer and was touted as the man who could "walk on water." He was recruited by land baron Henry Huntington to demonstrate the ancient art of surfing to thousands of vacationers who invaded Redondo Beach every year. Huntington, who owned most of the land at the turn-of-the-century, saw the Hawaiian-Irish athlete surfing with other beach boys and thought that Freeth's skills would be such a hit among tourists that he would be able to unload parcels of land for a tidy sum. Freeth became Southern California's first lifeguard and coined many of the surfer phrases that are popular today. Freeth died in 1919 at age 36 from the influenza epidemic that claimed many lives. A bust of Freeth is located on the Redondo Beach pier and is often draped with Hawaiian leis by the many surfers who visit this area from around the globe.

Rancho Palos Verdes
WAYFARER'S CHAPEL, 5755 Palos Verdes Drive South, *Tel. 310/377-7919.* Hours: Daily from 11am-4pm. Free admission. Known as the "glass church," Lloyd Wright, who followed in the footsteps of his famous architect father Frank, designed this transparent chapel as a memorial to Swedish theologian and mystic Emanuel Swedenborg. Constructed of redwood, glass and stone indigenous to this area, its purpose was to provide a place of worship for wayfarers - hence the name.

Built between 1949-1951, its use of triangle shapes and huge, circular glass panes, coupled with the serene grounds, are meant to symbolize spiritual value. The sound of the crashing surf in the distance and the ocean vistas adequately capture the sentiment. Not surprising, it's a popular spot for weddings.

POINT VICENTE LIGHTHOUSE, 31501 Palos Verdes Drive West. Legend has it that the apparition of a young woman, who hurled herself into the same sea that claimed the life of her sailor lover, can be seen walking the tower of this 1926 lighthouse nightly awaiting his return.

Local folklore aside, this tower stands 67-feet and expels one of the brightest lights along the coast of California. Not surprisingly, it no longer has the need for a keeper since it was automated some years back.

Fun Fact

A piece of Americana was nearly lost a few years back when the city of Downey—childhood home of '70s brother/sister pop performers Richard and Karen Carpenter—almost leveled the **Speedee McDonald's Drive-In**. Built in 1953, this is one of the chain's earliest red and white-tile burger stands. Nostalgia reached such a fever pitch in the mid-1990s, even then Governor Pete Wilson urged the company to "preserve for posterity the home of the Golden Arches." The city did, and now you can eat to your heart's content and shop for kitsch souvenirs in the adjoining gift shop. Speedee McDonald's is located at the corner of Lakewood Boulevard and Florence Avenue in the Downey. *Tel. 562/622-9248.*

San Fernando Valley/Mission Hills
MISSION SAN FERNANDO REY DE ESPANA, 15151 San Fernando Mission Boulevard. *Tel. 818/361-0186.* Hours: Open daily 9am-4:30pm, Admission: $4 adults, $3 seniors and ages 7-15, under 7 free. All California school-age children are taught the history of the California Missions. This one is the 17th link in the 21-mission system and was named in honor of King Ferdinand III of Spain by Father Lasuen in 1797. Located 25 miles north of

Downtown Los Angeles, this is the largest free standing adobe in the state and was intended as a hospice for weary travelers.

Today, the buildings, which consist of a church, school, convent and workshops, have all been restored to their original purposes and are available for viewing. The statue of Saint Ferdinand, which is positioned above the church alter, was carried over from Spain more than three centuries ago. A splendid flower-shaped fountain, which stands guard in the old mission plaza, is also an original relic.

L.A.'s other historic mission is located in San Gabriel Valley at 428 South Mission Drive in the city of San Gabriel. *Tel. 626/457-3035, www.sangabrielmission.org.*

San Pedro

KOREAN BELL OF FRIENDSHIP, at Angel's Gate Park, at Gaffey and 37th Streets. Free admission. The people of the Republic of Korea donated this decorative bell to the residents of Los Angeles in 1976 to celebrate America's bi-centennial as well as to honor veterans of the Korean War. The bell is fashioned after the 771 A.D. Bronze Bell of King Songdok, which is still on view in South Korea today. Set in a pagoda-style stone structure, the bell sits atop a bluff offering visitors unsurpassed views of Catalina Island and the harbor below. The bell, sans clapper, is rung from the outside with the strike of a wooden log and can be heard just three times a year: Fourth of July, Korean Independence Day (August 15), and New Year's Eve.

Fun Fact

Visible from the bluffs at San Pedro's Angel's Gate Park is the 1913 **Angel's Gate Lighthouse**. It has marked the entrance to the port for nearly a century, and sits perched on a 44-foot concrete square. The need for a keeper ceased in 1973 when the 73-foot Romanesque tower was automated, but its structure has withstood every treacherous storm that has pounded the coastline. Every 30 seconds its foghorn can be heard. Also located in San Pedro is the wooden **Point Fermin Lighthouse**, constructed in 1874, and one of the oldest lighthouses to grace the west coast.

WAR MEMORIALS, at South Harbor and West 6th Streets. **U.S. Merchant Marine Veterans Memorial** is the first national memorial dedicated to the merchant seamen of the United States, and was erected to honor merchant marine veterans from all wars. The bronze statue is more than 17-feet tall and depicts two merchant seamen climbing Jacob's Ladder after a rescue at sea. The land was donated by the city, but the $700,000 it took to create the project was raised through private donations.

Nearby the main mast of the heavy cruiser CA-135 Los Angeles stands proudly aside her two anchors and capstan. The trio of maritime relics were salvaged to form the **U.S.S. Los Angeles Naval Memorial,** and has been a San Pedro landmark since 1979.

WORLD CRUISE CENTER, in Los Angeles Harbor, Berth 93. Part of the Los Angeles Harbor, also known as Worldport LA, you may recognize this bustling passenger port from the 1970s television series *Love Boat,* where lovelorn passengers were counseled by Captain Stubing and the crew. The port is rarely without a docked cruise ship. On occasion the **Queen Elizabeth II** makes Los Angeles part of her route. Most major cruise lines offer ocean odysseys departing from here en route to the Mexican Riviera, Alaska and other destinations.

Santa Monica

CAMERA OBSCURA, Palisades Park on Ocean Boulevard- access through Senior Center, Call for hours, Free admission. Step inside the revolving turret of this 1889 building, and experience the precursor to the modern-day camera. A mirror reflects the outside scenery onto a table through its convex lens, creating a unique image that even Eastman-Kodak would admire.

Fun Fact
Get your kicks on **Route 66**. The famous and historic highway that stretched across most of America ends on Santa Monica Boulevard at Ocean Avenue.

SANTA MONICA CAROUSEL, at the base of Santa Monica Pier, *Tel. 310/ 458-8867.* Hours: Tuesday-Friday 11am-9pm, opens 10am on weekends, closed Monday. Admission: 50¢ adults, 25¢ children. A timeless treasure, this 1916 carousel was built by the master of merry-go-rounds, Charles Looff. A menagerie of hand-carved animals prance up and down inside the hippodrome building, where countless movies have been filmed including *The Sting, Forrest Gump* and *Ruthless People.* Deservedly, the carousel is on the National Register of Historic Places.

Time to Shop

Santa Monica's Third Street Promenade is a great place to browse and people watch. There are a number of shops and restaurants along this pedestrian-only stretch. At one end is Santa Monica Place, an indoor mall featuring a rather impressive food court with all the usual suspects.

Venice

VENICE RENAISSANCE BUILDING, corner of Main and Rose Avenues. Since its birth in 1989, people can't seem to say enough—good or bad—about the unusual icon that seems to dangle from this building: a 34-foot high sculpture of a male ballerina clown. The upper floors are residential condominiums, while the ground floor is used for retail. Perhaps the ballerina clown, with its mocking smile, would be a bit loud for some cities, but in Venice it looks perfectly normal.

West Hollywood

SCHINDLER HOUSE, 835 N. Kings Road, *Tel. 323/651-1510.* Hours: Wednesday-Sunday 11am-6pm, closed Monday and Tuesday. Admission: $5 adults, children under 12 free. Rudolf Schindler was a project architect and construction supervisor who worked closely with Frank Lloyd Wright on several projects. After Wright was fired by oil heiress Aline Barnsdall, who became frustrated by his lack of enthusiasm for her Hollyhock House, she hired Schindler to complete the project. Aside from a few drawings that Wright made, the Austrian-born designer headed most of the project.

Unlike Wright, Schindler favored Los Angeles and settled here in 1921 with his wife and engineer colleague. The house is a tilt-slab concrete with large vertical glass openings with all rooms facing the courtyard.

Today the house belongs to the Mak Center, which supports projects and ideas pertaining to the fields of art and architecture. Docent-led tours are conducted on Saturdays and Sundays only.

Time to Eat

Hungry? Try lunching at an L.A. landmark - **Tail O' The Pup**, 329 N. San Vicente Boulevard, *Tel. 310/652-4517.* Built in 1946 to look like a giant hot dog, this little roadside stand has been featured in numerous films and television shows including *Ruthless People* and *Beverly Hills 90210.* The hot dogs and burgers ain't bad either.

MUSEUMS & GALLERIES
Beverly Hills

MUSEUM OF TELEVISION AND RADIO, 465 North Beverly Drive, *Tel. 310/786-1025, www.mtr.org.* Hours: Wednesday-Sundays 12pm-5pm, Thursdays till 9pm, closed Monday and Tuesday. Admission: $10 adults, $8 seniors and students w/ID, $5 for children under 14. Beverly Hills is the satellite location for this fascinating New York-based museum, which features a vast collection of more than 75,000 television and radio programs. Designed by renowned architect Richard Meier, who also designed L.A.'s new Getty Center, visitors are able to chronicle 75 years of broadcasting history through permanent and rotating exhibits. Recent displays and exhibits include The Television Work of Sammy Davis, Jr., as well as Sinatra Amidst the Pyramids. Live radio broadcasts are also presented from this site.

The best time to visit the Museum of Television and Radio is on weekends when they offer special screenings that are of interest to children. Saturday mornings are reserved for "Re-creating Radio" workshops, designed especially for families with kids nine years and older.

Downtown

WELLS FARGO MUSEUM, 333 South Grand Avenue, *Tel. 213/253-7166, www.wellsfargohistory.com.* Hours: Monday-Friday 9am-5pm, Free Admission. Besides being a well-known banking institution, the name Wells Fargo also conjures up the image of a stagecoach blazing trails across the new frontier. This museum connects the past with the present with a display of original Concord coaches, banking and express documents, unique artifacts, vintage photos, gold coins, mining tools, working telegraphs and collection of fine western art. In keeping with the tradition, the museum also maintains bankers' hours!

OLD PLAZA FIREHOUSE, 134 Paseo de la Plaza, *Tel. 213/625-3741.* Hours: Call ahead. What kid doesn't love visiting a fire station? This particular one is a California State Historic Landmark and was built in 1884. The brick firehouse was the first building constructed as a fire station in Los Angeles and remained as such until 1897. Since 1960 it has served as a museum with a display of vintage fire fighting equipment, photographs and various exhibitions.

EXPOSITION PARK, bounded by Figueroa, Exposition, Menlo and Martin Luther King Jr. Boulevards.

Neighboring the University of Southern California (USC) is Exposition Park, home to the **California Science Center, California African-American Museum, Natural History Museum of Los Angeles County**, the **Los Angeles Memorial Coliseum** and the **Los Angeles Sports Arena**. The State Exposition Building opened to the public in 1912 and is where the California Science Center is now housed. A year later the Natural History Museum of Los Angeles County made its debut under the moniker The L.A. County Museum. It wasn't until 1923 that The Coliseum was completed with a capacity to seat an astounding 75,000 people; it was eventually enlarged to accommodate 105,000 people for 1932 X Olympiad games In 1959, Exposition Park welcomed the Los Angeles Memorial Sports Arena; and in 1984 both the California African-American Museum was founded and the IMAX Theater opened. This is truly one-stop shopping when it comes to cultural enrichment.

California Science Center, at Exposition Park at 700 State Drive. *Tel. 213/724-3623, www.casciencectr.org.* Hours: Open daily from 10am-5pm. Free admission.This contemporary science and technology museum showcases fascinating exhibits pertaining to aerospace, science, earthquakes, mathematics, chemistry, health and computers. Children will marvel at the interactive presentations designed with them in mind. A seven-story high **IMAX Theatre** is located on the premises, and the overwhelming dimensions of the screen are designed to make you feel as if you're part of the action. Screenings change regularly, and there is an admission charge to view the 2D and 3D classics.

California African-American Museum, in Exposition Park at 600 State Drive, *Tel. 213/744-7432,* Hours: Tuesday-Sunday 10am-5pm, closed Monday. Free admission. Opened during the 1984 Olympic Arts Festival, this museum commemorates the achievements made by those of African descent.

Natural History Museum of Los Angeles County, at Exposition Park at 900 Exposition Boulevard, *Tel. 213/763-DINO, www.nhm.org.* Hours; Tuesday-Sunday 10am-5pm, closed Monday, Admission: $8 adults, $5.50 seniors and students, $2 ages 5-10, under 5 free. Just as the name implies, this museum provides visitors with a wealth of exhibits and displays from nature and human history. Revealed are the history of the Earth, its evolution, and the diversity of life and culture as we know it. The museum is divided into a trio of departments: Life Sciences, Earth Sciences and History. With more than 16 million specimens to view, including the skeletal remains of one of the largest dinosaurs ever discovered, this ranks as the third largest natural history museum in the nation. **The Insect Zoo**, with its exhibit of live giant beetles and oversized cockroaches, may not be endearing to moms, but will definitely be intriguing to children.

The **Los Angeles Memorial Coliseum**, 3939 S. Figueroa, *Tel. 213/748-6136*, offers tours of the field, locker room and the famous Peristyle of the only stadium in the world to host two Olympiad Games, two Super Bowls, a World Series and a papal visit.

JAPANESE AMERICAN NATIONAL MUSEUM, 369 East First Street. *Tel. 213/625-0414, www.janm.org.* Hours: Tuesday-Sunday 10am-5pm, till 8:00pm Thursday, closed Monday. Admission: $6 adults, $5 seniors, $3

Fun Fact

Exposition Park, which contains more than 150 varieties of roses blooming from 17,000 bushes, is home to the **world's largest rose garden**. Blossoms, which can be viewed daily from 8:30am to dusk, are at their peak during April and May, and again in September and October. *Tel. 213/748-4772.*

students with ID and children 6-17, under 5 free. Free admission every Thursday from 5pm-8pm, and all day every third Thursday of the month.

This is the only museum of its kind in the nation dedicated to sharing the experience of Americans of Japanese descent. Housed in a restored Buddhist temple is an impressive collection of Japanese American objects, images and documents which create a timeline connecting the past to the present.

The Japanese American National Museum, Museum of Contemporary Art and Moca at the Geffen Contemporary are free to the public every Thursday from 5 to 8pm. The Autry Museum of Western Heritage offers free admission every Thursday starting at 4pm.

MUSEUM OF CONTEMPORARY ART, 250 South Grand Avenue. *Tel. 213/621-2766, www.moca-la.org.* Hours: Tuesday-Sunday 11am-5pm, till 8pm on Thursday, Admission: $8 adults, $5 seniors and students with ID, under 12 free. Each year the Museum of Contemporary Art (MOCA) showcases more than 20 exhibitions, from historical and thematic to one-person retrospectives. Mediums include painting, sculpture, drawing, video, photography, film, music, dance, performance, design, architecture and new forms combining various disciplines. Permanent collections include masterpieces from abstract expressionist and pop art, as well as works by young, emerging artists.

The Geffen Contemporary at MOCA, is housed a few blocks away in a former municipal warehouse at 152 North Central Avenue in Downtown's **Little Tokyo** district. The museum maintains innovative and popular exhibit space showcasing the city's art scene. One ticket will buy you entrance to both venues.

MUSEUM OF NEON ART, 501 W. Olympic Boulevard. *Tel. 213/489-9918, www.neonmona.org.* Hours: Wednesday-Saturday 11am-5pm, Sunday 12pm-5pm, closed Monday and Tuesday. Admission: $5 adults, seniors and students 13-22 w/ID $3.50, under 12 free. Free admission for all on the second Thursday of every month from 5pm-8pm. Before massive electronic signs littered our nation's highways, there was the glow of neon. The Museum of Neon Art offers a fine collection of electric art and traveling exhibitions in its Downtown gallery.

In addition to this location, MONA also maintains an exhibit of signs from its permanent historic collection on building facades located at the whimsical **CityWalk at Universal Studios.** Narrated evening bus tours of the city's neon signs, movie marquees and permanent installation of contemporary electronic art are conducted by MONA's knowledgeable staff.

Griffith Park/Los Feliz

AUTRY MUSEUM OF WESTERN HERITAGE, in Griffith Park at 4700 Western Heritage Way. *Tel. 323/667-2000, www.autry-museum.org.* Hours: Tuesday-Sunday 10am-5pm, closed Monday. Admission: $7.50 adults, $5 seniors 60+ and students with identification, $3 ages 2-12. Located just north of Downtown near the Los Feliz district, this museum is named for its founder, the legendary Gene Autry. The museum pays homage to the traditions of the American West. Here you'll find one of the most comprehensive collections of western artifacts and artwork within its seven permanent galleries and special exhibitions.

Items on display include historic firearms, tools, clothing, toys and furnishings of both well-known and lesser known folks who helped shape western civilization. For kids there is the **McCormick Tribune Foundation Family Discovery Gallery**, where children and their families get a hands-on look at history through games and exploration. There are also children's workshops, classes and activities.

TRAVEL TOWN, located in Griffith's Park at 5200 Zoo Drive, *Tel. 323/ 662-9678*. Hours: Monday-Friday 10am-4pm, till 5pm Saturday and Sunday, Free admission. This outdoor museum displays an array of vintage railroad cars, trolleys, planes, trains and automobiles. An enclosed area contains a fleet of

Parent Tip

Let's face it: The best things in life are free! Well, they are if you're on a budget. Los Angeles is a town that many visitors might find hard on the wallet, but it doesn't necessarily have to be that way. There are plenty of things to do that don't cost a nickel, you just have to know where to go.

Free tours are available of the Pacific Stock Exchange, *Tel. 213/ 977-4500*, LA Times, *Tel. 213/237-5757*, and the Music Center, *Tel. 213/972-7483*.

Free admission to museums including the California Museum of Science and Industry, *Tel. 213/744-7400*; the Getty Center, *Tel. 310/ 440-7300*; California Afro-American Museum, *Tel. 213/744-7432*; Wells Fargo History Museum, *Tel. 213/253-7166*; and the Travel Town Museum, *Tel. 323/662-9678*.

Free concerts at the California Plaza in Downtown. Call for a schedule of performances at *Tel. 213/687-2159*.

Free TV Tapings allow you to be part of a studio audience at your favorite shows. You may write for tickets in advance or pick them up in person since free tickets are available daily at selected studios. Tickets and seating are on a first-come, first-served basis with many enforcing a minimum age requirement of 14. For information, contact Audiences Unlimited, *Tel. 818/506-0043*. Free tickets are also available outside Grauman's Chinese Theatre in Hollywood, at Universal Studios Hollywood and at the Glendale Galleria shopping mall.

fire trucks plus a circus animal wagon with plenty of opportunity for children to climb aboard and explore. Every Sunday the Los Angeles Live Steamers Club showcases a variety of miniature steam locomotives, with free rides for the kids.

GRIFFITH OBSERVATORY is undergoing a major renovation and expansion, and will reopen to the public in late 2005. You can still learn about the stars at the **Griffith Observatory Satellite** located nearby at 4800 Western Heritage Way. Here you'll find a modest display of astronomy exhibits, an innovative planetarium theater, a lecture and presentation venue, and a high-powered telescope for nighttime stargazing.

Hollywood

HOLLYWOOD BOWL MUSEUM, 2301 N. Highland Avenue. *Tel. 323/850-2058.* Hours: Tuesday-Saturday 10am-4pm, until 8:30pm during the summer. Free admission. The museum, located on the grounds of the famed Hollywood Bowl, includes exhibitions which chronicle the amphitheater's history. Included among the finds is an original drawings of a concert shell by Lloyd Wright, Frank's son. There are also tapes of past performances available for listening as well as traveling exhibitions.

HOLLYWOOD ENTERTAINMENT MUSEUM, 7021 Hollywood Boulevard. *Tel. 323/465-7900, www.hollywoodmuseum.com.* Hours: Tuesday-Sunday 10am-6pm, closed Monday, Admission: $8.75 adults, $5.50 seniors, $4.50 students, $4 ages 5-12, under 5 free. If you can't get tickets to a television taping, this is the next best thing. Get beamed up in the Star Trek transporter or sit on a stool at the Cheers bar where everyone knows your

Parent Tip

If you want to experience some of L.A.'s key attractions, consider the **Hollywood CityPass**. Enjoy seven attractions, including Universal Studios Hollywood, American Cinematheque at the Egyptian Theatre, the Hollywood Entertainment Museum, Starline Tours of Hollywood, the Petersen Automotive Museum, The Museum of Television and Radio, and the Autry Museum of Western Heritage, all for one packaged price. Adults are just $59, kids ages 3-11 just $39. CityPass is good for 30 days from purchase, so you can also go at your own leisure.

You may also purchase the new **Southern California CityPass**, that includes admission to Disneyland Resort, Knott's Berry Farm, SeaWorld San Diego, and the World-Famous San Diego Zoo. This package is just $166 adults, $127 ages 3-9. CityPass is available for purchase at the first attraction you visit or online at *www.citypass.org*.

name. Film and television buffs get a behind-the-scenes look at the history of movies, television, radio and recording.

Actual sets are on display, and visitors can visit hi-tech interactive stations, multimedia exhibits, recreated backlots complete with prop shops and wardrobe exhibits. There is also props from many local studios. There is even an education wing where visitors are transformed into foley artists, helping to create the much-needed sound effects used in films. There is a lot to see and experience at this Tinseltown-style museum.

HOLLYWOOD STUDIO MUSEUM, 2100 N. Highland Avenue. *Tel. 323/ 874-2276*. Hours and prices vary, call for information. This historic building was nearly lost a few years ago as an early morning blaze swept through the facility. Luckily, the building and its many priceless artifacts were salvaged. Film pioneers Cecil B. DeMille, Jesse Laskey and Samuel Goldwyn rented this former 1895 horse barn in 1913, and it had multiple purposes including its use as a set, offices and dressing rooms for the film *The Squaw Man*.

In 1985 it was moved from its original location at Selma and Vine Streets to its present home and was painstakingly restored by the non-profit group Hollywood Heritage. Artifacts found within its confines include the chariot used in the 1926 production of *Ben Hur*, a make-up case belonging to Mary Pickford, and a helmet worn in the 1934 production of *Cleopatra*.

Parent Tip
If your kids are tired of traipsing around to the more cultured venues, take them to the **Hollywood Wax Museum** and the **Guinness World of Records**. These neighboring Hollywood "museums" are what put the "T" in Tinseltown...or was it tacky? At any rate, it's the stuff kids go for. The Hollywood Wax Museum features celebrity wax figures, while the Guinness World of Records, housed in Hollywood's first movie theater, features a slew of oddities. The Hollywood Wax Museum is located at 6767 Hollywood Boulevard, *Tel. 323/462-5991*; the Guinness World of Records is at 6764 Hollywood Boulevard, *Tel. 323/463-6433*.

Long Beach
MUSEUM OF LATIN AMERICAN ART, 628 Alamitos Avenue, *Tel. 562/ 437-1689, www.molaa.com*. Hours: Tuesday-Friday 11:30am-7pm, Saturday 11am-7pm, Sunday 11am-6pm, Admission: $5 adults, $3 seniors and students with ID, 12 and under free. Housed in the former Balboa Studios, once the world's most productive silent film studio MoLAA, as it is more commonly known, it the only museum in the west dedicated exclusively to promoting contemporary art hailing from Mexico, Central and South America as well as

Parent Tip

So you've seen the great works of art at L.A.'s collection of museums, now it's time to visit the **Dark Horse Museum** at 4235 Donald Douglas Drive, Long Beach, *Tel. 562/420-3600*. Hours: Open daily 10am-3pm - closed during motion picture filming, Free admission.

If you enjoy celluloid aviation, then you'll surely want to check out this unusual museum. Housed in a giant hangar owned by Motion Picture Aviation Services, a company providing production assistance to the entertainment industry, you'll see sets from such films as *Top Gun*, *Firebirds* and *Hot Shots* plus a B-2 Stealth Bomber used in the John Travolta film *Broken Arrow*.

the Spanish-speaking Caribbean. On-going education includes Family Art Workshops held every Sunday at noon. The restaurant next door, Viva, is also owned by MoLAA, and features cuisine created to complement current exhibits.

QUEEN MARY, 1126 Queens Highway. *Tel. 562/435-3511, www.queenmary.com.* Hours: Open daily 10am-6pm, till 9pm summer Saturdays, Admission: $24.95 adults, $22.95 seniors, $12.95 ages 5-11, under 5 free. Guided tours are additional. Strolling the decks of this 1936 ocean liner is likened to time travel. After all, these are the same decks Greta Garbo strolled in search of solitude, and this is the ship from which Winston Churchill gave the orders for the D-Day Invasion during World War II. While kids may not be familiar with the legends that traveled on board, they are certainly impressed with the size of this "city afloat."

For those who fell in love with the idea of transatlantic travel following the release of James Cameron's epic film *Titanic,* this is as close as you'll ever come to experiencing such a relic. There are self-guided tours allowing you to walk from the engine room to the wheel house at your own leisure. The Behind-the-Scenes tour, conducted by a guide or ship's office, explores areas not open to the general public such as stateroom suites where passengers such as Mary Pickford, the Duke and Duchess of Windsor, and Marlene Dietrich sequestered themselves during crossings. You'll also tour the magnificent Art Deco swimming pool, and the Grand Salon where dignitaries and movie stars dined on extravagant meals. The Ghosts & Legends tour delves into paranormal activity on board...yes, the Queen Mary is rumored to be haunted, while the World War II Tour reveals how the ship played an instrumental role in the Allied effort.

Stealth also floats next to wealth in the form of a Cold War-era Russian submarine whose code name is Scorpion. Tour the cramped quarters of this

300-foot maritime wander, where dozens of sailors spent months at a time without ever seeing daylight. It's quite a contrast to the elegance and allure that possesses the Queen Mary.

Time to Eat:
Consider visiting the Queen Mary for a weekly Sunday Brunch. Served in the original first-class dining room, the spread is quite impressive as guests meander past a number of themed-buffet tables. A special children's feast makes this most definetly a family event. Included in the price is a complimentary self-guided shipwalk tour.

Malibu
ADAMSON HOUSE, 23200 Pacific Coast Highway. *Tel. 310/456-8432.* Hours: Wednesday-Sunday 11am-3pm, closed Monday and Tuesday, Admission: $3 adults, under 17 free, entrance to the garden is free. This Spanish Revival homes located at Malibu Lagoon State Beach is open for all to enjoy. Flanked with ceramic tiles, the interiors have withstood the test of time showcasing the craftsmanship of beam ceilings and inlaid floors. The gardens, which you can walk through without incurring a fee, thrive with blooming flora due to its beachfront location.

Mid-Wilshire/Museum Row
MUSEUM OF TOLERANCE, 9786 W. Pico Boulevard. *Tel. 310/553-9036, www.wiesenthal.com.* Hours: Open Sunday 11am-7:30pm, Monday-Thursday 11:30am-6:30pm, Fridays till 5; closed Saturdays and major Jewish holidays. Admission: $10 adults, $8 seniors, $6 students. This museum adds an educational element to any family vacation. Chronicling the history of the Holocaust, it also explores the impact of racism and prejudice in America. It's an arena of eight levels featuring high tech and interactive displays, special exhibits, multimedia work stations, artifacts, documents and theaters. Replicated gates of Auschwitz are truly haunting, and the original letters of Anne Frank are of particular interest.

The **Point of View Diner** gives new meaning to the term *food for thought.* Designed to resemble a typical 1950s diner, this slice of Americana serves a menu of controversial topics on video jukeboxes where visitors input their opinions.

Holocaust survivors are on hand Sunday-Thursday afternoons to share their experiences with museum guests. The Survivor Testimonies have been an integral part of the Simon Wiesenthal Center since its opening and are recommended for older children.

PETERSEN AUTOMOTIVE MUSEUM, 6060 Wilshire Boulevard. *Tel. 323/930-CARS, www.petersen.org.* Hours: Tuesday-Sunday 10am-6pm, closed Mondays, Admission: $10 adults, $5 seniors and students, $3 ages 5-12. A taxi used in *Seinfeld*, which many claim is too clean to be an authentic New York cab, is on display here as well as more than 200 vehicles including rare cars and classic automobiles.

The Streetscape gallery takes visitors through five themes of transportation: how people travel, live, consume, have fun, and the public cost of private transportation. Hollywood Star Cars is an exhibit that marries Tinseltown with famous T-Birds and other high-profile vehicles, including Elvis Presley's '71 Pantera, Jean Harlow's '32 Packard and the Batmobile II used in the recent Batman movies. Everything you wanted to know about cars—and then some— is found at the Petersen Automotive Museum.

The **May Family Discovery Center**, located within the Petersen Automotive Museum, features areas of interactive exhibits designed just for children and their families. Children can sit on a giant combustion engine with wheels and be transformed into "human spark plugs" (*kids, don't try this at home!*). The Open Road has little ones dressing up in vintage motoring attire and climbing into a 1910 Model T for an L.A. photo op.

LOS ANGELES COUNTY MUSEUM OF ART, 5905 Wilshire Boulevard. *Tel. 323/857-6000, www.lacma.org*. Hours: Monday, Tuesday and Thursday 12 noon-8pm, till 9pm Friday, weekends 11am-8pm, closed Wednesday. Admission: $7 adults, $5 seniors and students 18+ w/ID, $1 children ages 6-17. Known around town as LACMA, this county museum offers an impressive collection of more than 150,000 works of art. Permanent exhibits include works of American Art, Ancient and Islamic Art, Costumes and Textiles, Decorative Arts, European Paintings and Sculpture, Far Eastern Art, Japanese Art, Modern and Contemporary Art, Photography, South and Southeast Asian Art, and Prints and Drawings. Recent exhibits have included Picasso's Masterworks and Vincent van Gogh paintings borrowed from Amsterdam.

The museum also offers year-round children's art classes, which focus on artworks in the museum's permanent collection or in special exhibitions. Creative problem solving and art-making activities are integrated into each class. Enrollment is on a first come, first-served basis with limited space available.

Parent Tip

Every **Friday night**, April through December from 5:30pm-8:30pm, LACMA presents free jazz concerts on the plaza in the Times Mirror Central Court. **Sundays afternoons**, in the Leo S. Bing Theater, free chamber music concerts are presented by the City of Los Angeles Cultural Affairs Department.

THE PAGE MUSEUM AT THE LA BREA TAR PITS, 5801 Wilshire Boulevard. *Tel. 323/936-2230, www.tarpits.org.* Hours: Monday-Friday 9:30am-5pm, Weekends 10am-5pm. Admission: $6 adults, $3.50 seniors and students with I.D., $2 ages 5-12. A respected research and educational facility, The George C. Page Museum is located at the world-famous La Brea Tar Pits where historic fossils from the Ice Age are located. Visitors to the museum are transported back more than 40,000 years ago, when saber-toothed cats called the Los Angeles basin home. Many of the exhibits cater to children who can test their strength against the pull of asphalt or touch the bone of an extinct animal. The Fossil Preparation Laboratory is exposed so visitors can witness rare bones as they are being cleaned, repaired and reassembled for display.

Kids seem to get a bigger kick out of the actual **La Brea Tar Pits** located beyond the museum's doors. Parents will smile knowing that this experience is free of charge. Geologists discovered in 1906 that the bubbly pits had entrapped more than 200 varieties of mammals, plants, birds, reptiles and insects from prehistoric times.

In 1914, the skeletal remains of a young woman believed to be a Chumash Indian was found in Pit 10. Through research scientists concluded she suffered a blow to the head more than 9,000 years ago. Each day approximately 8-12 gallons of asphalt still ooze and bubble at the tar pits' surface, and manage to still entrap a collection of insects and worms. Replicas of life-sized mammals are strategically placed about to remind us of what once roamed these lands years before. The tar pits have been seen in many films including *Bad Influence* and *Volcano*.

Pasadena/San Gabriel Valley

HUNTINGTON LIBRARY, 1151 Oxford Road, San Marino. *Tel. 626/405-2141, www.huntington.org.* Hours: Tuesday-Friday 12pm-4:30pm, Saturday and Sunday 10:30am-4:30pm, Admission: $10 adults, $8.50 seniors. $7 students, $4 ages 5-11. Located in the affluent neighborhood of San Marino, this is one of the most remarkable settings for a museum and library. The grounds encompass more than 150 acres of breathtaking gardens including a stunning botanical variety.

The estate, which belonged to railroad tycoon Henry Huntington, features three art galleries and a library boasting a priceless collection of rare books and manuscripts, 18th and 19th-century British and French works of art, American art from the 18th century to the early 20th century, and a small impressive collection of Renaissance paintings. Highlights include the Gutenberg Bible circa 1455, as well as masterpieces *The Blue Boy, Pinkie,* and *Madonna and Child.*

In addition to the wondrous art and manuscript collection, the grounds feature a 12-acre desert garden, a secluded Japanese garden, a delightful camellia garden, and other natural wonders.

Parent Tip

You might not associate afternoon tea with Los Angeles; after all, L.A. is more of a "double decaf, non-fat latte" kind of town. But, believe it or not, the **Huntington Library's Rose Garden Tea Room** is one of the most delightful places to enjoy this afternoon ritual. Overlooking three acres of roses, guests enjoy limitless pots of brewed tea and scones with a central buffet providing an array of finger sandwiches, strawberries and cream, fresh fruit, imported cheeses and crackers, and much more. The price is $12.95 per person; children under 7 are just $6.50. If you want to explore the museum, that is an additional cost. In keeping with L.A.'s casual dress code, shorts and t-shirts are perfectly suitable. Reservations are required: *Tel. 626/683-8131.*

KIDSPACE, 390 South El Molino Avenue. *Tel. 626/449-9144, www.kidspacemuseum.org.* Hours: Tuesday-Sunday 1-5pm, till 8pm on Thursday. Admission: $6 ages 3 and up, $3.50 seniors, under 3 $2.50. This participatory museum offers hands-on exhibits designed to make learning fun and enjoyable. Exhibits and programs range from a 17-foot simulated ant hill to a 22-foot tree house that reveals animal and insect habitats and ecosystems both above and below the ground.

NORTON SIMON MUSEUM OF ART, 411 West Colorado Boulevard. *Tel. 626/449-6840, www.nortonsimon.org.* Hours: Wednesday-Monday 12pm to 6pm, closed Monday, Admission: $6 adults, $4 seniors, under 18 and students with ID free. Housed under one roof are masterpieces from the Renaissance age to 20th-century. On display you'll discover works by Raphael, Botticelli, Rubens, Rembrandt and Goya, as well as those by Impressionist and Post-Impressionist artists including Renoir, Monet, Degas, van Gogh and Picasso.

Be sure to stop by the Admission Desk and pick up a free Family Guide. Inside the brochure are fascinating facts about the museum's collection with questions and activities geared towards children.

San Pedro

FORT MACARTHUR MILITARY MUSEUM, 3601 South Gaffey Street. *Tel. 310/548-2631, www.ftmac.org.* Hours: Saturday and Sunday noon-5pm, Admission: Donation encouraged. Military enthusiasts will enjoy one of the most complete coastal defense batteries in the United States with 400 vintage photos and historic memorabilia dating from World War I through the end of the Vietnam War.

LOS ANGELES MARITIME MUSEUM, Berth 84. *Tel. 310/548-7618.* Hours: Tuesday-Sunday 10am-5pm, closed Monday, Admission: Free admission, donations welcome. With the word maritime in the title, it's relatively easy to surmise what this museum contains. Housed in the historic Municipal Ferry Building at the Port of Los Angeles, artifacts, scale models of ships and nautical art are displayed about. Of particular interest is an 18-foot replica of the ill-fated *Titanic* plus a ship's model used to film the treacherous scenes in *The Poseidon Adventure.* There are even working vessels to be found including two 100-foot topsail schooners.

S.S. LANE VICTORY MEMORIAL MUSEUM, Berth 94. *Tel. 310/519-9545.* Hours: Open daily 9am-4pm, Admission: $3 adults, $1 children. This 10,000-ton ship served as an ammunition carrier during three wars: World War II, as well as the Korean and Vietnam Wars. Measuring 455-feet long with a 70-foot beam, it now pays homage to the conflicts in which it was used through exhibits and artifacts.

Santa Monica

ANGELS ATTIC MUSEUM, 516 Colorado Avenue. *Tel. 310/394-8331.* Hours: Thursday-Sunday 12:30pm-4:30pm. Admission: $6.50 adults, $4 seniors and $3.50 children 12 and under. Kids and collectors will take interest at this Queen-Anne Victorian manor which displays an array of antique dolls and houses, miniatures and toys. Exhibits include a miniature copy of Versailles, Noah's Ark and a variety of English, American, French and German dolls.

Simi Valley

RONALD REAGAN PRESIDENTIAL LIBRARY, 40 Presidential Drive. *Tel. 805/522-8444 or 800/410-8354, www.reagan.utexas.edu.* Hours: Open daily 10am-5pm, Admission: $5 adults, $3 seniors, children under 15 free. "The doors of this library are open now and all are welcome. The judgment of history is left to you — the people. I have no fears of that, for we have done our best. And so I say, come and learn from it." Ronald Reagan spoke these words at the November 4, 1991, dedication of his presidential library.

No matter what conclusions you draw from our 40th President and his legacy, there is no doubt that Ronald Reagan has enjoyed a most charmed life. Making the transition from B-movie actor to Governor of California, he did what some considered the impossible by being elected to the nation's highest office.

His presidential library is the nation's largest and most elaborate, providing visitors with a glimpse into both his public and private life. Displays and exhibits include a full-size replica of the Oval Office and a recreated White House State Dinner, as well as a full section of the Berlin Wall presented to President Reagan at the Library on April 12, 1990. Traveling exhibits also make their way to the museum.

THE RICHARD NIXON LIBRARY & BIRTHPLACE, 18001 Yorba Linda Boulevard, Yorba Linda. *Tel. 714/993-3393, www.nixonfoundation.org.* Open daily in nearby Orange County. About 45 minutes from Downtown Los Angeles. This nine-acre complex is the only United States presidential library built and maintained through private funds. Best described as a three-dimensional walk-through memoir, highlights include a 52,000-square-foot museum, 22 high-tech galleries, movie and interactive video theaters, and the graceful First Lady's Garden.

Of special significance are President Nixon's fully restored birthplace, his childhood home built by his father the year before he was born, and the flower-circlet memorial sites of both the President and Mrs. Nixon.

West Los Angeles

GETTY CENTER, 1200 Getty Center Drive. *Tel. 310/440-7300, www.getty.edu.* Hours: Sunday, Tuesday-Thursday 10-6, Friday and Saturday till 9pm, closed Monday. Free admission. Parking is $5 per vehicle, and a reservation must be made ahead of time. No reservation required for those arriving by public bus or taxi. Perched high atop a terraced hillside, the 110-acre Getty Center is often touted as the most magnificent museum to grace the West Coast. Designed by renowned architect Richard Meier at a cost of $1 billion, the center provides a stimulating environment for appreciating art in its purest form. In many ways the modern complex can be likened to a small community, boasting its own full-service restaurant, two cafes, a bookstore, a 450-seat auditorium and tranquil gardens.

Parent Tip

The Getty has some innovative methods to get kids interested in art. The Gallery Games lets families create their own masterpieces by taking an "Art Kit" filled with drawing materials into the gardens. There are also treasure hunts with "The Getty Art Detective." You'll also find a family audio guide with special stops and activities, as well as stories, fun facts and questions about art. Headsets are available for $3 in the Museum Entrance Hall, as well as a list of the family stops.

The experience begins with a scenic five-minute tram ride from the parking area to the top of the complex. Upon arrival, you're ushered into the glass encased Entrance Hall with its stunning rotunda. As you roam through the cluster of buildings that house the artwork, walkways and balconies provide panoramic views of the city. The Central Garden, hidden from view, is a place of contemplation with trees, fountains and reflecting pools.

The many galleries contain rotating exhibitions as well as a stellar collection of pre-20th-century European paintings, drawings, illuminated manuscripts, sculptures, decorative art and photographs. Selected works by such artists as van Gogh, Monet, Renoir and Cezzane are displayed for the first time in history. The **Family Room** is geared towards children with hands-on activities, games and displays, and is a perfect venue for introducing youngsters to art.

Everything you may have heard or read about The Getty Center doesn't do it justice; it is something that must be experienced.

Shopping Districts

Beverly Hills

RODEO DRIVE, between Santa Monica and Wilshire Boulevards. With all the money flowing through these parts, it's surprising Rodeo Drive isn't paved with gold. Luxury cars and chauffeured-driven limousines are spotted every few seconds, and celebrity sightings are common occurrences. You may recognize the streetscape as the place where Julia Roberts goes on a first-class shopping spree in the film *Pretty Woman.*

If you favor such retailers as Tiffany & Co., Van Cleef & Arpels, Harry Winston, Armani, Versace or Bijan, you'll find them all along this affluent stretch. Of course, if you're credit card limit isn't limitless or you're wallet feels a bit thin, don't be shy about browsing. Many of the folks traipsing up and down this street are visiting from other parts and also wish to see how the other half lives.

Located at the southend of Rodeo Drive is a European-style shopping promenade called **2 Rodeo.** Here you're instantly transported to a European village complete with cobblestone sidewalks and plenty of charm. Rodeo's neighboring streets, such as Dayton Way, Brighton Way, Wilshire Boulevard and Little Santa Monica Boulevard, also offer additional shopping and dining excursions.

Downtown

FASHION DISTRICT, located near the California Mart at 9th and Los Angeles Streets. *Tel. 213/488-1153.* This is the hub of Los Angeles' garment district where rolling racks are seen gliding down sidewalks. In this area there are more than 56 blocks of retail stores, wholesale outlets and ethnic marketplaces where bargains abound. Be sure to visit **Santee Alley,** located behind Santee Street and Olympic, where you'll find the real deals if you're willing to dig. Free trolley tours are available for the asking, just call ahead for details.

Hollywood
MELROSE AVENUE, between Fairfax and La Brea Avenues. This street has undergone plenty of changes during its lifetime. In the 1950s, it was mostly lined with furniture showrooms and picture-framing shops, and was merely another thoroughfare for crossing town. During the 1970s, it became a ghetto for punk rockers in search of second-hand clothes and Doc Martens. As the 1980s approached, it become the center for fun and funky as innovative retailers breathed life into the bland, stucco buildings that lined the street. Suddenly Melrose Avenue was in vogue, boasting a bevy of vibrant shops and cafes frequented by an outlandish clientele sporting mile-high mohawks and multi-pierced body parts.

Many of the unique shops have left this high rent district, yet it still remains one of the city's more colorful streets. Melrose Avenue is also a great place to people watch and younger celebrities are known to favor its sidewalks.

Pasadena
OLD TOWN PASADENA, Colorado Boulevard between South Pasadena and South Arroyo Parkway, and neighboring side streets. There was at time you wouldn't even think of venturing to Old Town Pasadena. It was run down with nothing to offer in the way of shopping and dining. Now you can hardly find a place to park within the 20-square-block district, and pedestrian traffic has reached its zenith.

Historic buildings are home to many retailers, restaurants and entertainment venues. Sadly, it's starting to resemble the local shopping mall as national retailers and restaurants move in and individually-owned establishments flee for lower rent districts. This is a really fun place to spend a weekend night, but if you want to avoid the torrential crowds that flood the streets Friday through Sunday, arrive mid-week.

Further up Colorado, at **280 E. Colorado,** is the new **Paseo Colorado**. This outdoor marketplace features a collection of shops, restaurants and movie theaters.

Parent Tip

If you happen to be near the Beverly Center, make it a point to stop into **Storyopolis**, 116 North Roberston, *Tel. 310/358-2500, www.storyopolis.com.* This children's bookstore and performance gallery is jam-packed with an exciting calendar of events including weekly craft and story hours, book signings, in-store concerts, slide and puppet shows, and improv performances.

Santa Monica
MONTANA AVENUE, between 7th and 17th Streets. If you want to see a celebrity or two or three, it's most likely you'll see them along this tony stretch of sidewalk. Amanda Pays, wife of actor Corbin Bernsen, owns a shop here, and retailer **Shabby Chic** made slipcovers fashionable from this very location.
THIRD STREET PROMENADE, Third Street between Broadway and Wilshire Boulevard. This trendy trail, modeled after outdoor European pedestrian malls, features a collection of cafes, restaurants, coffee houses, clubs, cinemas, book shops and boutiques. Among the individual retailers are many familiar names such as Z Gallery, Pottery Barn and Borders Books. It's completely zany on weekend and summer evenings when street entertainers are littered about.

West Hollywood
SUNSET PLAZA, *Sunset Boulevard between La Cienega and San Vicente Boulevards*
A melange of Colonial Revival, Neo-Classical and Regency-style 1930s buildings in West Hollywood create this chic sliver along the famed Sunset Strip. This is where young celebrities can be spotted shopping and dining. An outdoor seat at any one of the sidewalk cafes makes for an idle afternoon of people watching.

Fun Fact
Los Angeles is the birthplace of the "mall rat." But, if you like to shop, the enclosed **Beverly Center**, 8500 Beverly Boulevard, *Tel. 310/854-0070*, and the open-air **Century City Marketplace**, 10250 Santa Monica Boulevard, *Tel. 310/553-5300* are also where you're likely to rub elbows with a celebrity or two.

Studio Tours
San Fernando Valley/Burbank
NBC STUDIO TOUR, 3000 West Alameda Avenue. *Tel. 818/840-3538.* Hours: Call ahead for daily schedule, Admission: $7.50 adults, $5.50 seniors, $4 ages 6-12, Under 6 free. From beautiful Downtown Burbank, it's the Tonight Show...and much more. Get a behind-the-scenes look at television in the making with a 70-minute walking tour of the NBC broadcasting complex.
Though you won't actually go chin-to-chin with Jay Leno, you will get a chance to strut around the stage of *The Tonight Show*, as well as be privy to the wardrobe and make-up departments, video demos, an NBC sports presentation and set construction. Each tour varies a bit, and you never know

who you may encounter while on the lot. Best of all, there is no minimum age requirement; just make sure your kids are up for the trek.

WARNER BROS. STUDIOS, 4000 Warner Boulevard. *Tel. 818/846-1403*. Hours: Monday-Friday, 9am-4pm, Prices: $32 adults, no children under 10 permitted. Children 10 years and older can join their parents on a personalized VIP Tour of this popular studio, which is now home to the fledgling WB Network.

The tour begins with a short film showcasing the movies and television shows created by studio talent throughout the years. Next, it's off on a 12-person mini-cart tour to the studio grounds. Because actual filming is taking place within the compound, no two tours are ever alike. Places you're likely to visit include a live production, recording stages, the actual mill where the sets are constructed, a stop at the prop shop and views of exterior sets. The fun part about this studio tour is that you never know what—or whom— you will encounter: A chance meeting with one of the actors from *Friends* or a stroll down New York Street, originally constructed during the 1930s, and now used for such television dramas as *ER*, are just a few of the possibilities.

You may even be ushered on to Stage 16, which is among the world's tallest stages boasting a concealed tank with the capability to hold up to two-million gallons of water. This Hollywood marvel was most recently used for the action-packed sea adventure scenes in the film *The Perfect Storm* starring George Clooney.

Fun Fact

The studio tour concept dates back to 1915, when film pioneer Carl Laemmle purchased a parcel of rural land near Hollywood. He quickly transformed the chicken ranch into a movie studio and began charging visitors a quarter to tour the lot and witness movie making first hand. In those days, lunch was included and eggs could be purchased upon exiting. Today, it is better known as Universal Studios.

Theme Parks

Hollywood/Universal City

UNIVERSAL STUDIOS HOLLYWOOD, 100 Universal City Plaza. *Tel. 818/777-1000, www.universalstudios.com*. Hours: Vary, call for information, Admission: $47 adults, $34 seniors, $37 ages 3-11, under 3 free. While this remains a working studio, Universal, the birthplace of the studio tour, is predominantly a tourist attraction that just happens to make movies.

This is by far the world's largest movie studio offering an extensive Backlot Tram Tour that transports guests to the land of make-believe, giving each a front row seat and an insider's edge to filmmaking. As the tram meanders about the facades and fabricated cityscapes, guests can view state-of-the-art LCD flat screen video monitors from within the tram displaying many out takes from movies and television shows that were shot on the lot. Celebrity narrators, such as Ron Howard and Jason Alexander, add a bit of anecdotal verve, In fact, Alexander narrates an entertaining film montage titled *Before They Were Stars*, a look at bona fide celebrities before they became household names.

Blurring the line of reality are 11 location sets, from Courthouse Square, one of Hollywood's most frequently used backdrops, to Six Point Texas, the oldest backlot set and site of the first studio tour. You'll also see such familiar Hollywood sets, such as the town square from the *Back to the Future* films, the house where the Cleavers lived on the 1950s television series *Leave it to Beaver*, as well as special effects used in the movies *Earthquake, Jaws,* and *King Kong* .

On the lower lot, which until recently was off limits to visitors, you can be part of the action at *Backdraft, The E.T. Adventure* and *Jurassic Park — The Ride!* In addition, there are plenty of live shows, demonstrations and stunts to keep the whole family entertained. One thing that kids are sure to love is the **Nickelodeon Blast Zone**, where you can meet the Rugrats, dodge flying foam lava balls in The Wild Thornberrys Adventure Temple and soak up the thrills with that lovable sea urchin Sponge Bob Square Pants. There is also **Spider-Man Rocks!**, an entertaining musical, as well as **The Mummy Returns: Chamber of Doom.**

Universal City Walk, which fronts the gates to the attraction, is also on the premises and offers free outdoor shopping, dining and entertainment.

No trip is complete to Universal Studios without a glimpse at the **Psycho House** and neighboring **Bates Motel**. The house, built for the 1960 Hitchcock classic *Psycho* and used in the recent Gus Van Sant remake, was built to a three-quarters scale atop a knoll to give the illusion of greater distance when viewed from Bates Motel, which is actually just a dagger-toss away at the bottom of the hill.

Santa Clarita Valley/Valencia

SIX FLAGS MAGIC MOUNTAIN, 26101 Magic Mountain Parkway. *Tel. 805/255-4111, www.sixflags.com.* Hours: Vary seasonally, call for information; Admission: $45 adults, $30 seniors , $30 children 4-feet-tall and under, under 2 years free. Located about an hour north of Los Angeles, Six Flags Magic Mountain is definitely not for the faint of heart. There are 10-themed areas of adventure which feature fast, winding roller coasters and water adventures.

Signature rides include *Colossus,* one of the largest, dual track wooden roller coasters in the world; *Batman The Ride,* a futuristic thrill-a-minute adventure ride; *Viper*, the largest looping roller coaster; *The Riddler's Revenge*, the world's tallest and fastest stand-up roller coaster; *Freefall*, a unrestricted drop from the top of a 10-story tower, which descends at the speed of 55-miles per hour; and *Psyclone*, a replica of the classic wooden roller coaster.

X is another cutting edge, one-of-a-kind roller coaster that is touted as the world's first 4th dimensional thrill ride. Once securely fastened in their seats, riders race in prototype vehicles which have the capability to spin independently 360-degrees forwards or backwards on separate axis. The park's newest ride is *Scream!*, which combines traditional roller coaster technology with a unique floorless train design. There are also a number of kiddie rides for thrill seekers in training, as well as a petting zoo and roaming Looney Tunes characters.

Hurricane Harbor, a separate attraction (combination tickets are available), is adjacent to Magic Mountain. Just as the name indicates, it's a water park with a dozen tropical-themed attractions with various slides and pools.

While Magic Mountain remains a popular family attraction, it is also overrun with teenagers. Its steep prices are comparable to those at Disneyland, though it offers none of the magic despite its name. Still, if you're a family that loves heart-stopping rides, it's worth a visit.

Parent Tip

If you don't feel like spending an entire day at one of the area's theme parks, you might get a thrill out of **Pacific Park**, located at the end of the Santa Monica Pier in Santa Monica. Recalling L.A.'s vintage beach amusement park days, this family fun zone features a nine-story high Ferris wheel and thrilling roller coaster that juts out over the ocean. There are also countless carnie-style rides, games and snack areas plus a half-dozen kiddy rides.

At the foot of the pier is the historic Santa Monica Carousel created in 1916 by Charles Looff. The classic hippodrome building houses a menagerie of hand-carved animals that prance up and down to the delight of children. Listed on the National Register of Historic Places, the carousel has been cast in countless films including *The Sting, Ruthless People* and *Forrest Gump*.

Chapter 6

f i e l d   t r i p s

San Diego

GETTING THERE

By Air

Though there are flights between Los Angeles and San Diego, this is the least efficient way to get here. First of all, it's expensive. Then, when you consider that you'll need to arrive at least two hours before your plane is scheduled to depart, you could have already arrived via car or train.

However, if you're still determined to fly, **San Diego International Airport**, also known as **Lindbergh Field**, is located three miles from the heart of Downtown. Serving more than 19 commercial airlines, the airport is easily accessible via Interstate 5 or Highway 8. The airport is divided into three terminals: Terminal 1, Terminal 2 and the Commuter Terminal.

To avoid ending up at the wrong terminal when departing, check to see what your four-digit flight number is. If it is 3,000 or above, your flight will depart from the **Commuter Terminal**, which is serviced by commuter service airlines connecting and originating from San Diego. If your four-digit flight number is under 3,000, you'll be departing from either Terminal 1 or Terminal 2. For up-to-date information, *Tel. 619/231-2100 or www.bestflight.com*

By Bus

The **Greyhound Bus** terminal, *Tel. 619/239-3266*, is located in a questionable area of downtown at 120 West

Broadway and 1st Avenue. Buses arrive daily from all parts of the United States and it's wise to be cautious. Passengers can also link from San Diego to two inland areas including **Escondido** and **El Cajon**, and Greyhound also stops in **Oceanside** in North County. For fare and schedule information, *Tel. 800/231-2222.*

By Car
San Diego's freeway system is a web of multi-lane express ways jutting off in various directions. To reach downtown San Diego from Los Angeles, take **Interstate 5 south**. It's about a two-hour drive without traffic.

By Train
Amtrak, *Tel. 800/872-7245*, stops in **North County** at Oceanside and Solana Beach before arriving in downtown San Diego at the Moorish-style **Santa Fe Depot** located at *1050 Kettner Boulevard, Tel. 619/239-9021.* There are eight daily round-trip passenger trains traveling back and forth between San Diego and Los Angeles. The journey is a pleasant one as you cruise along the coast for most of the ride.

A **taxi stand** is located at the Kettner Boulevard entrance just to your left. If you're journey takes you further south, east or inland, the **San Diego Trolley** provides light rail travel to these areas as well as to the Mexican border. The **East Line** will take you southeast and inland, while the **Mission Valley** line ends at the Fashion Valley Transit Center, stopping at points in between.

TOURIST INFORMATION
San Diego Convention and Visitors Bureau, *Tel. 619/232-3101, www.sandiego.org.* There are two **Visitor Information Centers** where you can obtain the most current information on a wide variety of activities, attractions, dining and lodging options. One is located **Downtown** at 11 Horton Plaza at First Avenue & "F" Street, the other is in the **Village of La Jolla** at 7966 Herschel Avenue at Prospect. Both share the same telephone number, *Tel. 619/236-1212.*

WHERE ARE WE GOING NOW?
Like Los Angeles, San Diego, the nation's sixth largest city, is made up of various enclaves and neighborhoods. Though it is a major metropolis, in many ways it still manages to evoke a small-town feel.

The county is made up of two regions, North County and South County. North County is a diverse area that offers both a sandy coast and arid desert. Among its more popular attractions is America's first and, so far, only **LegoLand**, which is about a 30-minute drive from downtown San Diego. The coastal communities include **San Onofre, Oceanside, Carlsbad, Encinitas,**

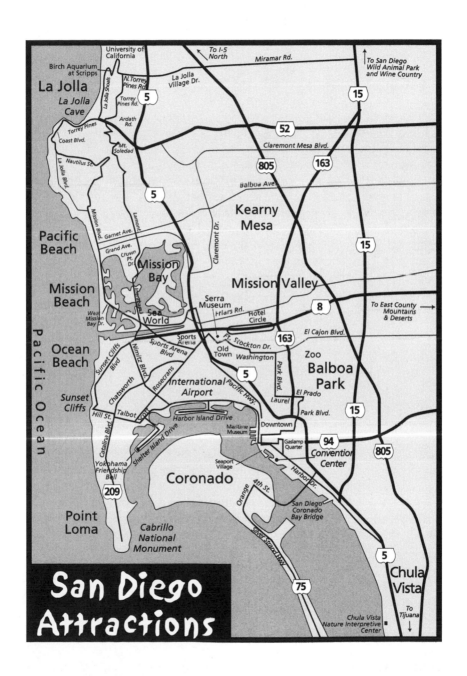

San Diego Attractions

Leucadia, Solana Beach, Del Mar, and **La Jolla**. Not only will you discover some of the best surfing, swimming and skindiving, but many of these communities boast some of the nicest hotels, resorts and shopping. Aside from the beach communities, which San Diego is probably most famous for, this region also features wineries, award-winning golf courses, renowned resorts, rugged terrain and the historic mining town of Julian. San Diego's largest state park, the Anza-Borrego Desert, offers a unique camping experience as well.

The bulk of attractions found in the southern part of the county are located in and around Downtown as well as the Mission Beach area. Downtown San Diego has developed into a thriving urban center with most attractions void of walls and ceilings. **Horton Plaza**, a whimsical shopping and entertainment complex, and nearby **Seaport Village,** are outdoor esplanades. The revival of the **Gaslamp Quarter** in recent years has sparked a harvest of shops, fine dining and plenty of evening atmosphere. A short distance away from Downtown is **Balboa Park** and the **San Diego Zoo**. **Coronado Island**, home to the turreted and gabled **Hotel del Coronado**, is its own hideaway just 10-minutes across the harbor. The beach communities are also just a flip-flop toss away, and this is where you'll find **SeaWorld**, the vintage **Giant Dipper** roller coaster, and Mission Bay.

The following attractions are listed by city or neighborhood.

Balboa Park

BALBOA PARK, located off Interstate 5 at the Park exit. Free Admission. When you think of a city park, you're likely to envision the usual suspects: playground, swimming pool and duck pond. Spanning some 1,200 acres, Balboa Park is more than just a greenbelt and sandbox.

Its development was stimulated with the arrival of two international expositions in 1915 and 1936. This is perhaps the only park of its kind with a kaleidoscope of museums and theaters, flora and fig trees, and lions and tigers. It is home to the world-famous San Diego Zoo, a cornucopia of horticulture, a respected collection of theaters, and a whimsical turn-of-the-century carousel. Spreckles Organ Pavilion is where free concerts are enjoyed each Sunday at 2pm.

Of course, if you're in the mood for nothing more a picnic hamper filled with sandwiches and refreshments, there are plenty of places to relax amid the fragrant blossoms.

Fun Fact
Did you know **Balboa Park** is larger than New York's Central Park and older than San Francisco's Golden Gate Park?

Balboa Park is also an oasis of culture containing more than two dozen museums all within close proximity to one another. While it's impossible to view and enjoy all of them in one day, you will certainly find one or more to your cultural liking.

Among the collections are the **Mingei International Folk Art Museum**, *Tel. 619/239-0003*, dedicated to furthering the understanding of world folk art through a menagerie of displays and exhibits; the **Museum of Photographic Arts**, *Tel. 619/238-7559*, celebrates the union between camera and man, and showcases 20th-century art as illustrated through the lens; the **San Diego Historical Society Museum & Research Archives**, *Tel. 619/232-6203*, offers rotating exhibits from the San Diego Historical Society's collection and archives; located at the **IMAX** theater, *Tel. 619/238-1233*, are more than 50 interactive displays at the **Ruben H. Fleet Space Theatre and Science Center;** the **San Diego Museum of Art**, *Tel. 619/232-7931*, features a collection of European works from the Italian Renaissance and Spanish Baroque periods as well as masterpieces from Asia and the United States.

In addition, kids will especially enjoy the park's three travel-related museums: the **San Diego Aerospace Museum**, *Tel. 619/234-8291*, the **San Diego Automotive Museum**, *Tel. 619/696-0199*, and the **San Diego Model Railroad Museum**, *Tel. 619/696-0199*. Additional museums include the **Museum of Man** and **the Natural History Museum,** just to name a few.

Also located within the parks grounds is a 1910 Herschell-Spillman Company-built **carousel** that has been in operation at Balboa Park since 1922. Located inside the entrance to Zoo Place, near the tiny-tot **Butterfly Rides**, this carousel features a menagerie of prancing animals and is one of the few carousels left that still offers the brass ring. Located adjacent to the carousel is the **Balboa Park Miniature Railroad**, a 48 passenger locomotive that travels through the park. The train is a model G16, which is now a rare antique with only 50 currently in existence. *Tel. 619/231-1515* for hours and information on the Butterfly Rides, Carousel and Miniature Railroad.

Parent Tip
The **Marie Hitchcock Puppet Theater**, located in the Palisades are next to the Automotive Museum, presents year-round puppet performances by a variety of troupes. Show times are Wednesday-Friday at 10am and 11:30am; Saturday and Sunday at 11am, 1pm and 2:30pm. Tickets are $3 adults, $2 children, under 2 years free. *Tel. 619/685-5990.*

SAN DIEGO ZOO, in Balboa Park at Park Boulevard and Zoo Place. *Tel. 619/231-1515, www.sandiegozoo.org.* Hours: Open daily 9am-4pm, extended daily hours till 9pm during the summer, Admission: $19.50 adults, $11.75 ages 3-11, under 2 free. Also located in Balboa Park is the world-famous San Diego Zoo, you'll find some 4,000 inhabitants of rare and endangered animals representing more than 800 species and subspecies. The zoo is also an accredited botanical garden with more than 6,500 species of exotic plants covering some 100 acres. Among the prize collection are orchids, cycads, fig trees, palms and coral trees.

The San Diego Zoo is a must for animal lovers and children, and should be considered by those who want a real workout. The term "sprawling" is an understatement with more than 100 acres of hills, knolls and trails to climb and descend. There is a bus that will take you through the park past the pandas, gorillas and sea otters. If you have younger children in tow I advise that you catch it as early as possible, or you'll be waiting in line for a very long time.

Bai Yun and Hua Mei are the VIPs—Very Important **Pandas**—at the zoo. They hail from the People's Republic of China, and are on loan as part of a 12-year research project. In January 2003 they were joined by 11-year-old Gao Gao, and the trio of giant panda live in an open-moat environment with lush plants and bamboo - much like their native habitat.

A 2.2-acre summer tundra habitat creates a playground for the popular **polar bears, Siberian reindeer, Arctic foxes, yellow-throated martens** and **diving ducks**. A 130,000 gallon, 12-foot-deep chilled pool—known as **The Polar Bear Plunge**—enables the bears to hone their bruin breaststrokes and polar paddles as visitors watch from an underwater viewing area.

Other areas with animal magnetism include Gorilla Tropics, Bonobos, Tiger River, Sun Bear Forest, and a pair of walk-through bird aviaries - the world's largest. New to the zoo is **Ituri Forest**, a complex, multi-species habitat where guests are transported through a mysterious African rain forest. Encountered on this journey are okapis, hippopotamuses, forest buffaloes, spotted-necked otters and a variety of colorful birds and monkeys.

Most of the zoo's animals are from regions outside the United States. The koala colony is the largest outside of Australia, and other residents have been brought here from Indonesia, China, New Guinea, Africa, Vietnam, the Fiji Islands, and many other places.

Throughout the day there are animal shows and strolling characters. Hop aboard the Skyfari aerial tram to travel quickly from one side of the park to the other, or take a guided bus tour. There are several restaurants and eateries located throughout the park.

If you're visiting during the summer, I highly recommend you see the San Diego Zoo at night. From June through September the park remains open till 9pm, and is a completely different experience from the one you'll have during the daylight hours.

If you're considering going to both the San Diego Zoo and Wild Animal Park, then the best bang for your buck is the **Two-Park Ticket**. Included is admission to both venues, which must be used within five days of purchase. The adult fare is $46.80, kids 11 and under are just $31.40.

Carlsbad
LEGOLAND, One Lego Drive. *Tel. 858/918-5346 or 877/LEGOLAND, www.LEGO.com.* Hours: Vary, call for information, Admission: $41.95 adults, $34.95 seniors and ages 3-12. Remember tinkering with those hard plastic building blocks as a kid? Now your childhood can be relived vicariously through your kids at LegoLand, one of only three such theme parks in the world and the only one in the United States. The key target audience is youngsters ranging in age from two to 12, but most kids over 10 may find LegoLand too mild for their adventurous tastes.

This is the first new family theme park to open in Southern California in 25 years, and the first in the nation dedicated to youngsters. LegoLand is a wonderful addition to Southern California's collection of attractions, and the designers have done a first-rate job in creating an exciting place geared exclusively towards younger patrons.

There are seven-themed areas—or "blocks" when using correct Lego lingo—clustered around a two-acre man-made lake. There are more than 40 rides, all designed to be "kid powered" meaning that children are able to push, pull, steer, pedal, squirt, crawl, climb, stomp, program or build their way through the park.

The **Village Green** is for the younger set and features the larger bricks which are easily grasped by tiny clutches. In this block youngsters can navigate a boat ride from a leaf-shaped vessel and search for unlikely variations of well-known fables such as Prince Charming conversing on his cell phone. Most figures are animated and all are entirely crafted from Lego bricks.

Fun Town explores transportation as kids maneuver electric cars, navigate tiny motor boats, and pilot helicopters. Exotic adventures take place at

Parent Tip

If you happen to be visiting LegoLand during the months of March, April or May, take a visit to the **Flower Fields** at Carlsbad Ranch. Located east of the 5 Freeway at Palomar Airport Road, this working farm is blanketed with a spectacular display of giant Tecolote Ranunculus flowers that almost appear surreal from a distance. Bulbs and fresh flowers grown along the hillside are available for purchase. From mid-November through December the ranch hosts a holiday poinsettia event. *Tel. 760/431-0352, www.flowerfields.com.* Admission is $7 adults, $6 seniors, $4 ages 3-10.

the spooky **Adventurers' Club**, where young Indiana Jones types search for clues in such faraway lands as Egypt and its pyramids, the Amazon Rain Forest and to the Artic Tundra. Here parents will be pleased with the well planned family care center with facilities for diapering, warming bottles and food, and privacy for mothers nursing their infants.

Medieval times are relived at **Castle Hill** where jousting astride Lego-made horses and slaying your fears aboard the Dragon Coaster are prime attractions. In this block you'll also find one of the biggest jungle gyms in the world, where kids of all ages seem to gravitate.

Five different geographical regions of the United States are constructed of Lego bricks inside **Miniland**. Here you'll visit California, New England, New Orleans at Mardi Gras, New York City and our nation's capitol, which all soar above tiny roads and trees. The details are amazing with perfect recreations of Grand Central Station's chandeliers and miniature lanterns illuminated and strung across the streets of San Francisco's Chinatown. From this block, the Lions Gate Bridge transports you across The Lake to the base of **The Ridge**, where another block of rides await.

The remaining block is the **Imagination Zone**, where a 15 1/2-foot tall image of Albert Einstein's visage was constructed from more than a million Lego bricks. Here youngsters can toy with Lego Mindstorm robots, a new product with a computer chip imbedded in the plastic bricks. Kids can command these hi-tech robots to sort M&M's by color or have a vacuum cleaner pushed about the room.

LEGO Sports Center, a new 16,000-square-foot themed area launched as this book went to press, makes guests feel as if they're the all-stars. This area features the latest NBA and NHL-themed LEGO Sports Build & Play toys and attractions while offering sports-related activities geared towards youngsters. Kids can also compare the size of their handprints to those of famous athletes, as well as test their skills at football, basketball and soccer.

The park also recently introduced a trio of new attractions. Bionicle Blaster, which just opened in spring 2003, features a dozen individual circular cars that twist and spin on and around a circular platform. LEGO Technic Coaster is among the park's fastest ride, allowing test drivers to maneuver life-sized TECHNIC vehicles through a maze of twists, dips and razor-sharp curves along a high-performance track. LEGO Racers 4D, an interactive movie and multi-sensory experience, is more innovative than a 3-D film as it transports audiences into the wild and out-of-control world of race car driving.

About the only thing not made from Lego bricks is the surprisingly good food, which is prepared to order. The pasta, bread and pizza dough are all made fresh throughout the day, and freezer space is reserved for such things as ice cream.

While LegoLand doesn't possess that magical ambiance found at Disneyland, kids really seem to enjoy it. In fact, our five-year-old can't seem to get enough of it. If you are traveling to the Los Angeles area and have time to head south to LegoLand, I highly recommend it.

Coronado Island
CORONADO WALKING TOURS, departs from Glorietta Bay Inn. *Tel. 619/435-5892.* Hours: Vary, call for a schedule and prices. If you really want to familiarize yourself with Coronado Island, the best way to do it is walk. Now you can exercise, get acclimated and learn all at the same time. The route for this 90-minute slow-paced pedi-tour begins with a stroll through the **Hotel del Coronado**, past the historic Duchess of Windsor cottage, to the restored Crown Manor mansion, and finally to the former home of author L. Frank Baum. What you discover along the way is just an added bonus.

Parent Tip
Coronado Island offers a variety of tours, including the **Vintage Motor Tour,** *Tel. 619/435-0511,* a 40-minute guided historical tour conducted from the confines of a classic '65 deluxe VW Microbus. **Coronado Pedicab Tours,** *Tel. 619/572-4651,* allows you to see the town and its landmarks from a rickshaw-style bicycle. Local arborist Shannon Player hosts a 90-minute historic tree tour at **Spreckles Park** every Saturday at 9am. For Information: *Tel. 619/435-1764.*

HOTEL DEL CORONADO HISTORY GALLERY, at Hotel del Coronado, 1500 Orange Avenue. *Tel. 619/435-6611.* Hours: vary, call for information, Free admission. Much of Coronado's history resides under the turrets of the Hotel del Coronado. Even if you are not a registered guest, a **free self-guided tour** detailing more than a century of history is displayed for all to enjoy. Vintage photos of kings and queens, American presidents, foreign dignitaries and Hollywood idols are mesmerizing.

Displays of guest records and other hotel artifacts demonstrate how fashion, technology and leisurely travel have evolved during the last century. If you want to impress your friends with even more Del-iscious trivia, join a one-hour guided tour with the resident historian and discover some of the behind-the-scenes secrets. A **guided tour,** which lasts about an hour, is $15 for non-hotel guests, $10 for hotel guests.

One-time Coronado resident and acclaimed writer L. Frank Baum used the Hotel del Coronado as the inspiration for the Emerald City in his *Wizard of Oz* series. Baum wrote four of his books while living on the island, which is actually a peninsula, and also designed the signature crown chandeliers of the hotel.

Baum lived in the gabled 1896 Meade House, which is located nearby at 1101 Star Park Circle.

SPRECKLES PARK, located on Orange between Sixth and Seventh Streets. Named for resident sugar mogul J.D. Spreckles, it's hard not to notice this Orange Avenue parcel of greenery. The elevated gazebo takes center stage every summer as bands perform free afternoon concerts every Sunday from Memorial Day to Labor Day.

On the first and third Sunday of every month, undiscovered artists and craftsman display and sell their wares. A perfect setting for family picnics, reunions and other leisurely gatherings. The park offers picnic tables, playground equipment and restrooms.

Downtown

FIREHOUSE MUSEUM, 1572 Columbus Street. *Tel. 619/232-FIRE.* Hours: Wednesday-Friday 10am-2pm, till 4pm Saturday and Sunday, closed Monday and Tuesday. Admission: $2 adults, $1 ages 12-18, under 12 free. Located in San Diego's Little Italy district, this museum pays homage to all fire fighters past and present. On display in the city's oldest firehouse is a large collection of fire fighting equipment and memorabilia from across the country and around the world. A vast selection of photographs and gear enhance the exhibits.

GASLAMP QUARTER, 4th, 5th and 6th Streets between Broadway and the waterfront. When you've had your fill of The Gap, Banana Republic and Victoria's Secret, it's time to discover the eclectic retailers of this funky district. Antique shops, art galleries, restaurants, jazz clubs and coffeehouses vie for attention. Many of the distinguished buildings were constructed between 1867 and the turn-of-the-century, and are illuminated at night by the glow of gaslamps.

This was once San Diego's main area of commerce in the 1800s, but when businesses began their exodus from the waterfront, the area quickly became littered with prostitutes, gamblers and hustlers all looking to make a quick buck. It began to make a significant comeback during the 1980s and is the nerve center for most of Downtown's activity.

Horton Plaza, an open-air shopping center, is also part of this area. Its architectural design, an amalgamation of Spanish Colonial, Mediterranean, Moorish, Gothic and contemporary styles, features 49 mind-altering colors splashed across its various buildings, hidden alcoves, slanted bridges and looming towers, this urban marketplace is often referred to as *The Disneyland of Shopping Centers.* There are seven levels twisted around six and a half city blocks anchored by **Nordstrom, Macy's** and **Mervyns**; inbetween there are more than 140 specialty shops, restaurants and services plus a 14-screen cinema. With a melange of street mimes, musicians and jugglers, Horton Plaza is as entertaining as it is functional.

SAN DIEGO MARITIME MUSEUM, 1306 North Harbor Drive. *Tel. 619/ 234-9153, www.sdmaritime.com.* Hours: Open daily 9am-8pm, Admission: $7 adults; $5 seniors, military with ID, ages 13-17; $4 ages 6-12, under 6 free. The centerpiece at this waterfront attraction is the 1863 Star of India, the oldest ship still able to set sail. The museum's fleet also includes the topsail schooner Californian, as well as an 1898 steamboat ferry and a 1904 steam yacht. The 1940s-era museum features three centuries of historic ships, exhibits and models displayed on board the vessels. Seeing the *Star of India* alone is well worth a visit.

SEAPORT VILLAGE, located along the waterfront on California at Kettner Boulevard and West Harbor Drive, *Tel. 619/235-4013, www.spvillage.com.* Wandering through Seaport Village offers hours of mindless entertainment. The seaside shopping and dining center features 59 one-of-a-kind shops and restaurants, plus various street entertainment. Don't forget to take a whirl on the **Broadway Flying Horses Carousel** built by carousel artisan Charles Looff in 1890.

Escondido
SAN DIEGO WILD ANIMAL PARK, 15500 San Pasqual Valley Road. *Tel. 760/747-8702, www.sandiegozoo.com.* Hours: Open daily 9am-4pm, from 7:30am-8pm June-September, Admission: $26.50 adults, $19.50 ages 3-11, under 2 free. Unlike a traditional zoo where animals are viewed from behind high walls, the San Diego Wild Animal Park is almost like being in the wilds of Africa except with the convenience of a snack bar and restrooms.

Spread across 2,200 acres, this wildlife preserve is home to some of the earth's rarest creatures who roam together in herds and flocks in an open-land sanctuary similar to their native environment. There are more than 3,200 animals represented including 400 species with the largest crash of rhinos found in any zoological park.

Seeing all the park has to offer requires a pair of sturdy shoes and comfortable clothing. You'll hike across an abundance of trails to areas of the park that can only be viewed on foot, including the **Heart of Africa**, a 32-acre pedestrian safari. On this expedition you'll get an up-close and personal look at a menagerie of wildlife including cheetahs, rhinos, colobus monkeys, wattled cranes, warthogs and much more.

Once you begin to huff and puff, hop aboard the **monorail,** a five-mile, 50-minute journey that will take you past the expansive recreated regions of Africa and Asia. These unique exhibits vary from 60 to 100 acres and are home to a variety of birds and mammal species indigenous to those countries.

There are opportunities for you to actually interact with the animals. The cheaper version, which costs only a few dollars for biscuits, allows you to **hand-feed the giraffes.** This takes place at various times during the day, so be sure to ask for a daily schedule when you arrive. The second, and much

Parent Tip

For something a bit out of the ordinary, consider booking the **Roar & Snore** at the Wild Animal Park. Every April through October the public is invited to spend the night in a tent along one of the rugged trails with elephants, rhinos and tigers roaming just a few feet away.

This camping safari includes a tent, campfire dinner, guided walking tour, visits with animal trainers and their four-legged students, a pancake breakfast, a ride on the monorail and admission to enjoy the park the following day. In keeping with the safari theme, you'll have to rough it a bit as there are no shower facilities; just cold, running water.

The Roar & Snore campovers take place Friday and Saturday nights. Children under eight years old are not permitted. Call for a reservation, *Tel. 760/747-8702.*

more expensive option ($70-$94 per person), is the **Photo Caravan Tour.** This is comparable to a real African safari where you're loaded into trucks that transport you to the heart of the animal enclosures where you come eye-to-eye with the free-roaming beasts. The tours are offered seven days a week year 'round, weather permitting, by advanced reservation. If this is something you would be interested in, contact the park to make a reservation.

There are also a number of free shows that take place throughout the day starring elephants, birds and rare creatures. The San Diego Wild Animal Park is a unique alternative to the traditional zoo experience, and well worth the price of admission.

La Jolla

BIRCH AQUARIUM AT SCRIPPS, 2300 Expedition Way - Scripps Institution of Oceanography at the University of California, San Diego. *Tel. 858/534000-3474, http://aquarium.ucsd.edu.* Hours: Open daily 9am-5pm, Admission: $9.50 adults, $8 seniors, $6 ages 3-17, under 3 free. Touted as the largest oceanographic museum in our nation, the Birch Aquarium at Scripps allows you to discover the marine sciences through interactive exhibits. Various marine life can be observed from the cold waters of the Pacific Northwest to tropical species indigent to Mexico and the South Pacific. Kids are sure to be fascinated with the rocky tide pool overlooking the coastline, where underwater habitat and various marine plant life can be observed.

Mission Bay

SEAWORLD, Hours: call for a schedule as hours vary, Admission: $44.95 adults, $34.95 ages 3-11. What can you say about SeaWorld? It's fun, entertaining and kids seem to love it. The admission price is steep—the same ticket will almost buy you a day at Disneyland—but, unlike Disneyland, I don't think SeaWorld is worth the price. Still, if you have your heart set on going, this is what you can expect.

The park covers 150 acres and features, among other things, a dolphin interaction program where you can actually touch and feed dolphins. **Shark Encounter** allows you to walk through a submerged plexi-glass viewing tube where *Jaws*-like creatures prey above you. You'll also get to view penguins, animals from the Arctic, bat rays, manatee, tide pools, and a menagerie of birds. Throughout the day there are shows including Dolphin Discovery and Pets Rule! For a nominal fee, you can go behind the scenes on a guided tour. There are also two rides included in admission price, Shipwreck Rapids and Wild Artic, and two that are not, the Skytower and the Bayside Skyride.

For a little something out of the ordinary why not **Dine With Shamu**, SeaWorld's resident killer whale. This special poolside meal service features a buffet and a just-for-kids menu. Guests dine alongside the park's killer whale habitat, and trainers are known to mingle with guests. Shamu has even been known to slide out on occasion. The cost is $30 adults, $15 kids.

Mission Beach

GIANT DIPPER ROLLER COASTER, at Belmont Park, 3190 Mission Boulevard. *Tel. 858/488-1549, www.giantdipper.com.* Hours: Vary, Admission: $4 a ride. This is only one of two wooden roller coasters left in California; the other is in Santa Cruz. You're heart will plunge as you ascend up and down the rickety rails of this moveable 1925 landmark. The creaking and squeaking alone is enough to get your blood pumping. In addition to the roller coaster, you'll find other seaside amusements such as a Tilt-A-Whirl, bumper cars and an arcade.

PIRATE'S COVE, at Belmont Park, 3190 Mission Boulevard. *Tel. 858/488-1549, www.giantdipper.com.* Hours: Vary, Admission: $6.50 per child, two

Parent Tip

Just like Los Angeles, San Diego has an abundance of hotels. Among my absolute favorites are the **Hotel del Coronado**, *Tel. 619/435-6611 or 800/HOTELDEL*, and **Crystal Pier**, *Tel. 858/483-6983 or 800/748-5894*. **Hotel Circle**, which is very centrally located to both Downtown, Old Town and the beach communities, features a collection of affordably-priced accommodations that are extremely family friendly. Visit *sandiegohotelcirclehotels.com* for a list of the hotels and current rates, or call: *Tel. 800/422-5129*.

adults are admitted free with each paying child. Located in the same center as the Giant Dipper Roller Coaster, this matie-themed play zone is designed just for kids. There are kiddie-sized games in the Cannonball Arcade plus endless hours are spent at the play place where small bodies squeeze through tunnels, scoot down slides, crawl across cargo nets and plunge into colorful ball pits. There is also the Captain's Galley where you can pick up a pizza, snacks and soft drinks.

The Giant Dipper Roller Coaster was marked for demolition in the late 1980s. But, thankfully, a band of concerned citizens formed the *Save the Coaster Committee*. After extensive renovation and upgrades, the Giant Dipper reopened in 1990. Over the years couples have been married on board, and two local disc jockeys once attempted to ride the coaster non-stop for 24-hours. The stunt failed after the pair discovered they had weak stomachs.

Oceanside
MISSION SAN LUIS REY, 4050 Mission Avenue, *Tel. 760/757-3651.* Hours: Open daily 10am-4:30pm, Admission: $4 general admission, $3 students; $12 families. The proper name of California's 18th mission is San Luis Rey de Francia, but over the years it's been shortened to its present moniker. Established June 13, 1798, it was named for the St. Louis IX, King of France, patron of the Secular Franciscan Order.

The largest of all the missions, San Luis Rey is dubbed the *King of the Missions* and is run by Franciscan Friars who host retreats and tours. The museum houses exhibits relating to the colorful history of San Luis Rey with a collection of artifacts from various periods. Of special interest are such sacred treasures as the classical and baroque designs of the church altar; the original baptismal font, made of hand-hammered copper by Indians; the Moorish design of the pulpit; and the 1770 statue of the Immaculate Conception.

The 1798 cemetery is the oldest burial ground in North San Diego County and contains early grave markers, mausoleums, and an 1830 monument erected in honor of the Luiseno Indians who contributed heavily to the building of the mission.

Fun Fact
Ventura, just north of Los Angeles is home to the oldest pier in California. However, **Oceanside** wins the prize for having the state's longest. Stretching nearly 2,000 feet into the ocean, the original pier, located at the end of Pier View Way, was constructed in 1888. The present concrete structure made its debut in 1925 with the wooden portions added during its centennial. On a clear day you can see La Jolla and Catalina Island from the pier's end.

The beginning of summer marks the popular Fiesta event, which com-memorates the mission's founding with arts and crafts booths, games, food, live entertainment and festive rides.

Old Town

OLD TOWN, north of Downtown off Interstate 5 at the Old Town Avenue exit. *Tel. 619/220-5422.* Hours: 10am-5pm, extended hours at restaurants. Free admission. Not only is this historic enclave the birthplace of San Diego, it is the beginning of California's history. After Juan Rodriguez Cabrillo landed in Point Loma in 1542, it opened the door for further exploration by the Spaniards. In 1769, Father Junipero Serra established the very first of the 21 California missions on Presidio Hill in Old Town, and the ruins of the original mission can be seen at Presidio Park. The original mission was replaced in 1774 by **Mission Basilica San Diego De Alcala** located at 10818 San Diego Mission Road, *Tel. 619/281-8449,* which is still a place of worship.

Fun Fact

San Diego is dubbed the *Two Nation Vacation* because you can visit both the United States and Mexico in the same day. U.S. citizens need a passport or birth certificate (original or notorized) with a photo ID. Since 9/11, driving across the border is time consuming. Instead, take the convenient **San Diego Trolley**, also known as the Tijuana Trolley because of its destination to the Mexican border, and then simply walk across. Or you can drive to the border town of San Ysidro, located off Interstate 5 and park at facilities near the border. Once you cross the border into Mexico on foot, you can catch a cab to the center of town or simply follow the crowds heading that direction. The bulk of shops and restaurants are located on **Avenida Revolucion.**

In 1820, the Spanish government sent Gaspar de Portola to establish the first European settlement in California, and much of that early life of Mexican and American pioneers is recaptured daily at Old Town San Diego State Historic Park. Here you'll find a collection of restored buildings with others reconstructed to look like the originals on the same foundation. **La Casa de Estudillo** was built in 1827 by the commander of the presidio, and was one of the town's first adobe houses. The interiors resemble the period of which Señor Estudillo and his family lived.

Other interesting stops include a single-story facade housing a replica of the city's first drugstore with displays of pharmaceutical memorabilia and artifacts. You'll also find a bevy of other historic buildings including the old courthouse. Guided tours of Old Town start daily at 2pm near the park headquarters.

The only commercial aspect of Old Town is the colorful **Bazaar del Mundo**, a collection of shops and restaurants with strolling mariachis and folkloric dancers. Many of the buildings are also historic or replicated, and the entire marketplace is centered around a scenic courtyard.

Point Loma

CABRILLO NATIONAL MONUMENT, 1800 Cabrillo Memorial Drive. *Tel. 619/557-5450, www.nps.gov/cabr.* Hours: Open daily 9am-5pm, till 6pm during the summer, Admission: $2 per person. Juan Rodriguez Cabrillo landed at San Diego Bay on September 28, 1542, marking the first time Europeans had set foot on what was to become the western part of the United States. His arrival dispelled myths about the uncharted territory, and he paved the way for his successors to help colonize the expanded Spanish Empire.

This monument, erected in his honor in 1913, was established almost 400 years after his arrival. This spot was the beginning of California, and today it houses a small museum, excellent views of the San Diego Harbor, the Old Point Loma Lighthouse, remains of a coastal fort and tide pools. During the winter, this is an excellent spot to watch the grey whales pass by on their journey to Baja, Mexico.

Trolley Tours

With so much to see in Downtown San Diego and its surrounding areas, it can be a challenge driving from one location to the next, finding a place to park, and then paying to have your vehicle just sit there.

Old Town Trolley Tours, *Tel. 619/298-8687, www.historictours.com,* has taken the hassle out of seeing many of the major attractions in one fun-filled day. This fully-narrated tour, which is conducted from a motorized trolley-style car, combines interesting anecdotes, humorous stories and a detailed history of the city. Stopping at eight key locations: **Old Town State Park, Cruise Ship Terminal, Seaport Village, Horton Plaza, Coronado Island, Balboa Park's San Diego Zoo, Aerospace Museum, and El Prado**, you are free to tour San Diego at your own pace.

Tours begin at any one of the eight locations, and once you've made a complete loop, your ride is up. Tours operate year 'round and begin at 9:00 a.m. The conductors—cum tour guides—are fun, informative and extremely knowledgeable. Prices are $24 adults, $12 for children 4-12, and kids under three are free. Book on line, and save 10%.

I'm Hungry

The restaurants listed are priced inexpensive to moderate, and all feature children's menus.

CASA DE BANDINI, at *Bazaar del Mundo in Old Town, 2660 Calhoun Street, Tel. 619/297-8211, Internet: www.bazaardelmundo.com*
Sheltered by an original 1829 adobe hacienda, Mexican food is served al fresco under one of the vibrant-colored umbrellas. The strolling mariachis create a festive ambiance.

HENNESSEY'S TAVERN, *708 Fourth Avenue, Gaslamp Quarter, Tel. 619/239-9994*
A neighborhood spot with an Irish twist serving breakfast, lunch and dinner. Menu items include salads, sandwiches, meatloaf, steak and seafood.

ISLAND PASTA, *1202 Orange Avenue, Coronado Island, Tel. 619/435-4545,*
A small, but tempting menu of homemade pastas coupled with a choice of fresh sauces such as pesto, alfredo and other favorites. Other items include hand-tossed thin-crust pizza and torpedo-style sandwiches.

KANSAS CITY BBQ, *610 West Market Street, Downtown, Tel. 619/231-9680,*
This restaurant, in all its shoddy glory, was featured in the 1986 summer blockbuster film *Top Gun*. While it attracts plenty of Tom Cruise fans, it also has a loyal following who drop by for some down home cookin'.

OLD SPAGHETTI FACTORY , *275 Fifth Avenue, Gaslamp Quarter, Tel. 619/233-4323.*
Fun and festive, and located in the heart of the Gaslamp Quarter. And, what kid doesn't love spaghetti?

HORTON PLAZA, located in the Gaslamp Quarter, features a **Food Court** on Level 4. When everyone wants something different, you might want to head here. There is everything from the Boston & Maine Fish Company to Great Gyros to Hot Dog on a Stick. This culinary compound even features Mongolian and Japanese fare alongside such standbys as McDonald's and Ben & Jerry's.

Catalina Island

Italy has its Venice. Greece has its Mykonos. And, would you believe, Los Angeles also has its own island paradise? Just 26-miles off the urban coast and accessible only by boat or helicopter is **Santa Catalina Island**.

Simply stated, this is Southern California's best-kept secret. Rich with history, Catalina Island was first developed by chewing gum mogul William Wrigley during the 1920s. It was here that Wrigley built his palatial white palace—with its sweeping ocean views and commanding post. This is where Wrigley also brought his baseball team—the Chicago Cubs—for spring training. The palisade estate has been transformed into a splendid bed and breakfast inn favored by many celebrities.

Fun Fact

If you venture into the island's interior, it's likely you'll spot a **Bison buffalo**. In 1924 fourteen Bison buffalo were brought to the island for the filming of *The Vanishing of America*, based on author, and Catalina resident, Zane Grey's novel. As Hollywood is apt to do with things that are no longer of use, the buffaloes were "discarded" and left on the island to roam about. In 1934, 11 more buffaloes were purchased to supplement the herd, which had increased to 19. Today, more than 200 buffalo roam the island's interior.

The one and only town on Catalina Island is **Avalon**. A stroll down the town's main drag, Crescent Avenue, is a sure sign that much hasn't changed since the days of Wrigley. The streets are scattered with quaint shops, intimate bistros and small inns. The historic Casino—which once was abuzz with social events and island soirees—still stands at the end of town and houses a museum, movie theater and ballroom. Except for the occasional taxi, automobiles are replaced by the quiet hum of golf carts and tandem bicycles. The vintage pier, which stretches out into the harbor, is still a favorite spot for local fishermen.

Catalina Island is truly a haven for urban dwellers and offers something for everyone. It's no wonder that this magical little island is a favorite destination for honeymooners, weekend warriors and family gatherings. This snug island features lots of activities such as golfing, snorkeling, scuba diving, horseback riding, boating, fishing, hiking, and camping. For the less vigorous there are private companies that offer many tours and excursions including dinner cruises, flying fish expeditions, glass bottom boat adventures and inland motor tours.

On the otherside of the island at the remote isthmus is **Two Harbors**. Except for a restaurant, saloon, general store and lodge, Two Harbors is an ideal location for those who enjoy "roughing it." Easy to reach by boat, Two Harbors is home to the historic **Banning House Lodge**, an 11-room bed and breakfast inn built at the turn-of-the-century.

GETTING TO CATALINA

There are only two ways to reach Catalina Island and that's by boat or helicopter. Bringing a car onto the island is not an option.

Catalina Express, *Tel. 800/805-9201,* the fastest of the fleet, provides round-trip service to Avalon and Two Harbors in about an hour from Long Beach and San Pedro Harbors. Round-trip passage is $42 with discounts for seniors and children. The **Catalina Explorer**, *Tel. 949/492-5308,* also offers daily departures from Long Beach and is $38 round-trip. **Catalina Classic Cruises,** *Tel. 800/641-1004*, takes almost twice as long, but is less expensive at just $31.50 for adults. Departures from San Pedro to the island are limited.

Island Express Helicopter Service, *Tel. 310/510-2525*, the more expensive way to reach the island, departs from both San Pedro and Long Beach Harbors arriving to the island in about 15 minutes. The cost is $127 round trip for all ages. You may also choose to sail your own vessel to the island, in which case you'll need to contact the **Avalon Harbor Department**, *Tel. 310/510-0535*.

Once you arrive, Avalon is easy to see on **foot**, but **bicycles** and **golf carts** are another popular way to get around. As far as motor vehicles, Avalon is the only California city authorized by the State Legislature to regulate the number and size of vehicles allowed to putter about city streets. At present, there is a eight to 10-year waiting list to bring a car on the island, and you won't find a single rental agency in sight. However, you can hail a taxicab, tram or bus if needed.

For tourist information, contact the **Catalina Island Chamber of Commerce & Visitors Bureau**, *Tel. 310/510-7606, www.visitcatalina.org.* Call ahead to request a visitors guide.

Parent Tip

Most first-time passengers en route to Catalina via boat service quickly scurry to the upper decks, which are exposed to the elements. As soon as the vessels are at sea, they quickly retreat back inside once the channel winds start to blow. Instead, drape an article of clothing over an inside seat, then walk to the upper deck. This way you're guaranteed a place inside once things get uncomfortable on the open seas. While the crossings are generally calm, those sensative to motion are advised to pop a dramamine an hour before departure. Be sure to arrive at least 30 minutes before the bon voyage, otherwise there is a possiblity that your ticket can be sold to a stand-by passenger.

Where Are We Going Now?

Visiting the island sites will take all of an hour, but if you want a more in-depth tour of the land, contact **Catalina Adventure Tours**, *Tel. 310/510-2888*. The company offers a number of unique packages including a tour of the island's interiors, a tour of Avalon and glass bottom boat rides, just to name a few.

The 1890 **Holly Hill House**, with its cone-shaped roof, looms above the harbor and is the third oldest home on the island. For more than a century it has been a private estate, and its current owner graciously allows docents from the Catalina Island Museum to conduct tours through the house. For a tour schedule, *Tel. 310/510-2414*. Other noteworthy landmarks include the historic 1929 **Casino**, with its distinguished spherical shape, where many special events occur monthly including a smashing New Year's Eve gala; it is also home to the **Catalina Island Museum**. The **Wrigley Memorial and Botanical Garden**, *Tel. 310/510-2595*, located on Avalon Canyon Road (from Crescent take Catalina north to Tremont and turn right, Avalon Canyon Road is on the left-hand side), was born from the green thumb of Ada Wrigley and is dedicated to the preservation of the island's bountiful plant life.

You can't avoid the **Green Pleasure Pier** when visiting Avalon. Built in 1909, it remains the pulse of activity with restaurants, tour companies and fish markets operating from the wharf. Constructed of broad wooden planks and extending a mere 407 feet in to the harbor, the pier was an official weigh station for such legendary chaps as Zane Grey, Cecil B. DeMille and Charlie Chaplin.

While the handful of sights are interesting, most people come to Catalina for the recreation. Whatever your interests—boating, hiking, kayaking, scuba diving, fishing, snorkeling, tennis, biking or golfing—Catalina Island is the place to enjoy them. There are a number of businesses located in town to accommodate your rental needs including **Joe's Rent-A-Boat**, *Tel. 310/510-0455*, for boating and fishing; and **Island Kayak**, *Tel. 310/510-2229*, for scuba, snorkeling and paddle boats. Bike and golf cart rentals are available from a number of vendors along Crescent Avenue including **Brown's Bikes**, *Tel. 310/510-0986*, located 120 yards from the boat dock. The nine-hole **Catalina Visitors Golf Course** is the only place to putt on the island. The oldest course west of the Rockies, and the former home of the Bobby Jones Tournament, green fees are modest at this 2100 yard, par 32 course, *Tel. 310/510-0530*. The island's only **tennis courts** are also located here.

Two Harbors

Located at the isthmus of Catalina Island is the remote area of **Two Harbors**. Direct boat service from San Pedro and Long Beach will get you there the quickest or, once in Avalon, bus service and seasonal coastal shuttle connections are available.

Most people come to this area wanting to do nothing more than escape civilization. Accommodations are limited to the historic **1910 Banning House Lodge**, *Tel. 310/510-2800*, the comfort of a chartered boat or various nearby campsites. Dining choices are even fewer, but the absence of such conveniences doesn't faze the regular visitors who enjoy this remote area. Activities vary to include backpacking, hiking, kayaking, sportfishing and more. All of these outdoor pleasures can be organized through the **Two Harbors Visitors Information & Reservations**, *Tel. 310/510-0244 or 800/785-8425*.

Let's Spend the Night!
Catalina Island makes for a great day trip, but it's also fun to spend the night in one of Avalon's cozy hotels. The **Inn on Mt. Ada**, *Tel. 310/510-2030*, is by far the island's most luxurious, and each stay includes breakfast and lunch plus your own golf cart. The inn only accepts children 14 years and older. Even if you don't stay here, you might consider taking the inn's daily tour. More suitable family accommodations can be found at either **Snug Harbor Inn**, *Tel. 310/510-8400*, or **Hotel Villa Portofino**, *Tel. 310/510-0839*.

I'm Hungry!
Aside from a Cold Stone Creamery, dining on Catalina Island is made up of individually-owned restaurants. Most restaurants are located along Crescent Avenue, adjoining side streets and the pier.
ANTONIO'S PIZZERIA, *114 Sumner, Tel. 310/510-0060*
Pizza, submarine sandwiches and salads.
ERIC'S ON THE PIER, *Green Pleasure Pier, Tel. 310/510-0894.*
Located on the pier, Eric's has been in the same location for more than 50 years. The well-rounded menu features buffalo burgers, tacos, burritos and fish & chips.
EL GALLEON RESTAURANT & LOUNGE, *411 Crescent, Tel. 310/510-1188*
A menu of live lobster, aged steaks and fresh seafood.

j u s t   o u t s i d e   l. a.

Chapter 7

Orange County & Disneyland

Approximately 30 miles south of Downtown L.A.

Orange County, named for the tangy fruit that once blanketed this region, is considered part of Greater Los Angeles. Located approximately 30-miles south of Downtown L.A., there are 31 cities that are mostly bedroom communities consisting of tract homes and shopping malls. Those who find themselves "behind the Orange Curtain," will sense a more conservative political climate, though that is slowly changing.

The wave of national and international attention paid to Orange County really began in 1955 when Walt Disney opened his magic kingdom in Anaheim. People of all ages were transported to the land of make-believe and fairy tales through Disney's creative imagination. Theme parks are the major commodity in these parts, with both Disneyland and Knott's Berry Farm located within a few miles of each other.

Orange County is also especially kid-friendly, and many places are designed for the tiny traveler. For example, South Coast Plaza, home to Chanel, Armani and other fashion forward designers, has a whimsical carousel as its focal point. The Balboa Peninsula in Newport Beach has a vintage fun zone complete with a bayside Ferris wheel, old-fashioned cotton candy, bumper cars and arcade games.

Anaheim

DISNEYLAND RESORT, 1313 Harbor Boulevard. *Tel. 714/781-4565, www.disneyland.com.* Hours: call ahead.

Prices for admission to either Disneyland or Disney's California Adventure: $47 adults, $37 ages 3-9, under 3 free. Touted as the "Happiest Place on Earth," Disneyland Resort features a trio of amusement venues: the original Disneyland, Disney's California Adventure, and Downtown Disney.

Disneyland, which opened in 1955, is home to eight themed "lands" all suitable for the entire family. As you cross through the gates into the Magic Kingdom, your first encounter will be **Main Street, U.S.A.**, a composite of small-town America depicted at the turn-of-the- century. This is where a bulk of the shops are located and it is always part of the park's parade route. As you reach the end of Main Street, you'll encounter a number of paths jutting in different directions to the various lands.

Parent Tip

There are plenty of places to eat inside both Disneyland and Disney's California Adventure. Most are expensive, fast food joints and the selection leaves little to be desired. Instead of wasting your money at one of these places, seek out the restaurants at either Downtown Disney or at one of the Disneyland Resort Hotels. While the restaurants are a bit more expensive, the food is fresher and the choices much more extensive.

Straight ahead you'll see **Sleeping Beauty's Castle** where storybook characters come to life in **Fantasyland.** Most of the rides here are ideal for smaller children, but the lines are also littered with adults hoping to recapture the essence of their own childhood. Classic rides include **Peter Pan, Dumbo, Mr. Toad's Wild Ride** and the wondrous **Small World.** Just pass Sleeping Beauty's Castle is where King Arthur's sword is embedded in rock. Children— and adults—can try their strength at dislodging it. Should you succeed, you'll be the center of great fanfare.

Adventureland is exotically designed to include elements from Asia, India and the South Pacific. A newer park attraction, the **Indiana Jones Adventure**, is the focal point of this province. **New Orleans Square** is the jazzy home of **Pirates of the Caribbean** as well as the **Haunted Mansion.** The **Bayou Restaurant** is a nice alternative to the fast-food restaurants that dominate the park and the setting, inside the Pirates of the Caribbean, is rather unique. The heritage of the Old West can be relived in **Frontierland**, where you'll find canoe rides and Davey Crockett-style hats. **Splash Mountain** is the main attraction in **Critter Country** where you can also visit the new **Many Adventures of Winnie the Pooh**. The three-dimensional cartoon world of **Mickey's Toontown** is where the big cheese himself resides. There are lots

Fun Fact
Disneyland receives more than seven-million phone calls a year, with the bulk of callers asking to speak to Mickey Mouse.

of interactive attractions to discover, and everyone who visits Mickey Mouse's hometown can also meet the famed mouse vis-a-vis.

The final land, **Tomorrowland**, underwent a multi-million dollar facelift in the late '90s. With new rides such as **Honey, I Shrunk the Audience,** a 3-D misadventure including a series of surprising in-theater effects, and **Rocket Rods,** which features prototype vehicles whizzing by on a sleek, elevated wire-frame, Disneyland has joined the technical revolution. While archaic rides, such as the PeopleMover have been retired, classics such as Space Mountain, Autotopia, and the Disneyland Monorail have been subtly updated.

A unique feature to the new Tomorrowland is **The World's Most Unusual Edible Landscape.** This artistic and palatable landscaping design features fruit-bearing trees (orange, apple, lemon, lime, banana, and persimmon), as well as olive, date palm, pecan, fig, pomegranate and avocado trees. The surrounding shrubs and ground covers are also edible, and harvests change with each season.

Disney's California Adventure hasn't quite drawn the crowds the Disney brass were hoping for since opening in 2001. The one-day admission price is the same at both parks and, if you have to choose between the original park and its newer counterpart, the original, as they say, is always the best.

This park showcases a trio of California themed lands, including the Golden State, Hollywood Pictures and Paradise Pier. The park's rides are not as plentiful or as enchanting as those at Disneyland and most are geared towards adults and older children with the exception of "A Bug's Land." Inspired by Disney/Pixar's "A Bug Life," younger children can ride on a caterpillar, fly on a leaf, spin on a ladybug and splash in a giant sprinkler. The classic **Electrical Parade**, which was retired from the original Disneyland several years ago, has been revived here. There are many other shows and parades hosted throughout the day.

Sandwiched between the theme parks is the free **Downtown Disney**. This pedestrian promenade, which resembles a city streetscape, is lined with shops, restaurants and entertainment. A range of cuisine includes Southern Italian fare, gourmet sandwiches, Cajun cooking and seafood. There is also a multi-screened movie theater and live musical entertainment at the **House of Blues** and **Ralph Brennan's Jazz Kitchen.** As for shopping, the **World of Disney** is basically a mega Disney Store featuring apparel, toys and collectibles. There is also a bookstore, a gallery, a home store and other unique shops. Younger children will enjoy creating their own Teddy bear at the **Build-A-Bear Workshop**, where they can stuff, stitch and fluff their own cuddly bear as well as name and clothe them.

Disneyland Resort features more than 2,000 hotel rooms housed at a trio of properties located on-site. There is the **Disneyland Hotel** complete with a faux white sandy beach and 100-foot waterslide; the more upscale **Disney's Grand Californian,** designed in the classic craftsman style with three swimming pools; and the more contemporary **Paradise Pier**. All the hotels feature dining, recreation and a number of guest services. Kids can dine with their favorite Disney characters at **Goofy's Kitchen,** enjoy a morning buffet at Breakfast with **Chip 'n Dale,** or chow down with **Minnie & Friends** at an all-you-can-eat breakfast buffet.

Parent Tip

These days, with Disney's steep admission prices, families almost have to take out a loan to visit the Magic Kingdom. If you're considering spending a few days here, your best bet is to inquire about **Disneyland Vacation Packages**. Included are accommodations, admission to both parks and various other perks, depending on the vacation option you select. For more information: *Tel. 714/520-5060.*

Balboa Peninsula

BALBOA FUN ZONE, 400 East Bay Street. *Tel. 949/673-0408.* Hours: Open daily 10am-10pm, Free admission with rides priced individually. Shrill screams and hearty laughs will lead you to this 1936 landmark. It's entertainment in the purist form with simple rides such as a Ferris wheel, merry-go-round and bumper cars. There are video games, skeet ball, souvenir shops and other distractions along the boardwalk. At many food kiosks you'll find Balboa Bars listed. This local specialty is a real kid pleaser as ice-cream bars are hand-dipped in chocolate then coated with rainbow sprinkles.

If you happen to be in the neighborhood, **Ruby's Diner** at the end of the Balboa Pier is a fun place to dine. There are several Ruby's locations throughout the United States, however, this is the flagship location. Fashioned after a 1940s diner and housed in what used to be a dilapitated bait shop, the restaurant seats just 45 people and offers a menu of burgers, salads and sandwiches paired with Cherry Cokes and thick malts. For kids there is the Fun Club menu where each meal comes with a toy.

And, as long as you're in the area, hop aboard the Balboa ferry to **Balboa Island.** You can either drive your car on, ride your bicycle or just be a passenger; the ride takes all of five minutes. Once you arrive at the other side, stroll along the harbor until you reach the island's tiny Main Street, which is lined with more shops, restaurants and galleries.

Buena Park
   KNOTT'S BERRY FARM, 8039 Beach Boulevard. *Tel. 714/220-5200, www.knotts.com.* Hours: call ahead. Admission: $42 adults, $32 seniors and ages 3-11, under 3 free - On days when the park is open past 6pm, discount admission is given to those who arrive after 4pm. Knott's Berry Farm is America's first theme park spread out on more than 150 acres. For much of its history, the park was low key, offering simple pleasures from the Old West. This theme park was still family owned until 1997 when it was sold to Cedar Fair, L.P. In recent years Knott's has adopted a "keeping up with the Joneses" mentality by building bigger, faster and more thrilling rides.

   There are six themed areas offering everything from the mild to the wild. **Ghost Town** takes you back to the 1800s with an authentic steam train, a century-old stagecoach, and a water spraying log ride. The newest attraction in these parts is a replicated wooden roller coaster - one of the longest and tallest in the world.

   Paying homage to California's Spanish influence is **Fiesta Village**, featuring a collection of high-energy rides. Here you'll find thrills aboard **Montezooma's Revenge** roller coaster, which takes you from zero to 60 in just three seconds through two giant, seven-story loops. There are similar rides that will turn your stomach, but in the middle of all this chaos is a nice merry-go-round for the less daring.

   The Boardwalk is for the extreme thrill seeker. Rides in this area include **Supreme Scream**, which propels you 245 feet in mid-air and plunges you straight down before you have time to realize what's happening. **Boomerang** is another scream machine that has you cruising mostly upside down frontwards and backwards. There are lots more rides here including Xcelerator, Perilous Plunge and Hammerhead - none designed for the faint of heart.

   For hot California days there is the land of **Wild Water Wilderness,** home to one ride only - **Bigfoot Rapids**. This thrilling, outdoor white water river raft ride bounces and tosses you about until your drenched. You'll maneuver you're way through boulders, water falls, geysers, trees and other obstacles before the fun ends.

   Kids will delight with the rides at **Camp Snoopy**, designed for smaller guests. Featured here are the **Red Baron**, where pint-sized pilots can help Snoopy fight enemy aircraft; **Huff n Puff**, where kids push and pump a mini-mining car all the way around a track; and the **Log Peeler,** a mini scrambler providing just enough thrills for little ones. There are plenty of other rides to keep the kids entertained throughout your visit.

There are no rides to speak of at **Indian Trails,** which celebrates the culture and traditions of Native Americans. Aside from shops, restaurants and entertainment, Indian Trails is also home to the world's largest totem pole.

In addition to all the amusements, you'll also enjoy a number of entertaining shows celebrating California and the Old West. Adjacent to the park are 30 shops and restaurants, an exact replica of Independence Hall, plus **Soak City U.S.A.**, a seasonal water park which requires a separate admission.

If you happen to be visiting the area in October, Knott's Berry Farm hosts the wickedly fun-filled **Halloween Haunt**. Now in its third decade, this Southern California tradition gets scarier and more elaborate with each passing year as the park undergoes a major transformation into **Knott's Scary Farm.** Things get underway after dark, and a separate admission ticket is required. For the younger boos and ghouls, **Camp Spooky** offers daytime fun with friendly trick or treating with Snoopy and the Peanuts Gang.

Fun Fact

While Knott's Berry Farm may seem like a fetching name for a western-themed amusement park, at one time there really was a *Knott's Berry Farm*. During the 1920s my grandmother would buy fresh jams and jellies from a tiny roadside stand operated by Mrs. Knott herself. Her husband Walter is credited with creating the boysenberry during the 1930s by crossing a loganberry and red raspberry with a blackberry. All boysenberries in the entire world can be traced back to his farm.

MOVIELAND WAX MUSEUM, 7711 Beach Boulevard in Buena Park. *Tel. 714/522-1154, www.movielandaxmuseum.com.* Admission: $12.95 adults, $10.55 seniors, and $6.95 ages 4-11 under 4 free. It's absolutely tacky, but kids who visit Movieland Wax Museum don't seem to notice. See the likenesses of more than 275 celebrity wax figures with recent inductees including Robin Williams, Keanu Reeves, Julia Roberts, Britney Spears, Jim Carrey and Ricky Martin.

Garden Grove
CRYSTAL CATHEDRAL, 12141 Lewis Street. *Tel. 714/971-4000, www.crystalcathedral.org.* Tours: Monday-Saturday 9:30am-3:30pm. Free admission. This landmark church is located just a few miles from Disneyland. Some people find this glass cathedral godlike, while others simply find it gaudy. Designed by famed architect Philip Johnson for the Reverend Robert

Schuller, the structure resembles a four-pointed star and boasts 10,000 panes of glass covering the web-like translucent walls and ceilings.

The cathedral is the backdrop for two annual productions: the Glory of Christmas and the Glory of Easter. Each critically-acclaimed pageant features a cast of live animals, flying angels and special effects. Sunday services are also held here weekly.

The Crystal Cathedral opened in 1980, but the Reverend Schuller didn't always preach from such opulent surroundings. The year was 1955 and the mid-Westerner originally conducted his sermons from the roof of the snack shack at the nearby Orange Drive-In Theater. Folks enjoyed their weekly dose of religion from their convertible Chevys and Buicks, and the collection plate was passed by car hops who managed to maneuver between the rows of vehicles on roller skates. Talk about divine intervention!

Orange

VANS SKATE PARK, at The Block at Orange, off the 22/Garden Grove Freeway at the City Drive exit. *Tel. 714/769-4000.* Any kid, male or female, who owns a skateboard will be in their element at this indoor/outdoor skate board arena. There is more than 46,000 square feet of space, as well as an 80-foot vertical ramp, an extensive 20,000 square-foot street course, two in-ground cement pools, an area for kids, and a retail shop. Parents of older children can shop at The Block of Orange's variety of retail and discount outlets to pass the time.

Newport Beach

FASHION ISLAND, Newport Center Drive and Pacific Coast Highway, *Tel. 949/721-2000.* Fashion Island, located near the beach, appeals to both parents and kids. Young children will delight in riding the miniature train and dodging the dancing water that unexpectedly spouts from the various fountains lacing this outdoor center. Teenagers can shop 'til they drop at a number of haute boutiques, as well as a collection of major department stores including Bloomingdale's and Neiman Marcus. The center also features an upscale food court, as well as a number of restaurants including The Cheesecake Factory and P.F. Chang's, just to name a few.

San Juan Capistrano

MISSION SAN JUAN CAPISTRANO, Ortega Highway and Camino Capistrano. *Tel. 949/248-2048, missionsjc.com.* Hours: Open daily from 8:30am-5pm, Admission: $6 adults, $5 seniors, $4 ages 3-11, and under 3 free. The sound of century-old bells resonating through the town of San Juan Capistrano is haunting. Established November 1, 1776, this is the seventh of the 21 California mission founded by Father Junipero Serra.

As with all the missions, it was the Indians who were recruited—not always willingly— to construct the buildings. After Spain lost control of California to Mexico in 1821, the mission was sold to Don Juan Forster for $710. Following Mexico's defeat to the United States after the war, President Abraham Lincoln returned the mission to the Catholic Church.

Visitors to the mission can immerse themselves amid the history and architecture of its fabled arches, Moorish fountains, Indian burial ground, ruins of a stone church, soldier's barracks and a 10-acre garden. If you visit the mission on the second Saturday of the month between 10am and 2pm, you can take part in **Living History Days**, which transports you back to another era with costumed docents and demonstrations of such time forgotten skills as wool spinning and gold panning.

The romance and folklore of the mission is captured each spring with the **return of the swallows**. Legend has it that during the early part of the 20th century a broom-yielding shopkeeper was spotted knocking down swallows' nests from the eaves of his shop. Upon witnessing this, Fr. St. John O'Sullivan, pastor of Mission San Juan Capistrano, took pity on the birds and invited them to nest at his mission. The swallows migrated south that autumn and returned to the mission the following spring on St. Joseph's Day, March 19. Thus a tradition took flight. They continue to return each year to build their mud and saliva-mixed nests along the area's rocky cliffs, caves, or under the eaves of the mission's edifice. The annual Swallows Festival is hosted mid-March, and visitors from all across the world take part in welcoming the flock home.

Santa Ana

CENTENNIAL HERITAGE MUSEUM, 3101 West Harvard Street. *Tel. 714/540-0404.* Hours: Wednesday-Friday 1pm-5pm, Sunday 11am-3pm, closed Monday-Tuesday and Saturday. Admission: $5 all ages. Formerly known as The Discovery Museum of Orange County, this compound of sorts features a fully-restored, turn-of-the-century Victorian home once belonging to the Kellogg family. There is also a gallery, blacksmith, water tower and gardens.

The museum features a fun and interactive learning environment where all ages can journey back to the 19th century. Kids are welcome to tickle the ivories on a pump organ, talk on a hand-cranked telephone, gaze through a stereoscope, dress up in Victorian garb, wash clothes on a scrub board, and explore many other aspects of life from a century past.

The setting all seems authentic, as if you really are living in the distant past, until the sound of someone's cell phone quickly jolts you back to modern times.

DISCOVERY SCIENCE CENTER, 2500 North Main Street. *Tel. 714/542-2823,www.discoverycube.org.* Hours: Open daily 10am-5pm, Admission: $11 adults, $8.50 seniors and children ages 3-17, under 3 free - there is an additional charge of $1 per person to see the 3-D laser show. Kids of all ages can explore eight themed areas with more than 100 hands-on exhibits housed in approximately 59,000 square feet. There are opportunities to engage in live science demonstrations and enjoy a three-dimensional show in a high-tech laser theater.

You'll be able to experience a simulated earthquake in the **Shake Shack,** lounge on a **Bed of Nails,** climb the **Rock Wall,** walk through a **Tornado,** and dance on a **Musical Floor.** The **KidStation** is designated for children up to five years, and there is a "soft play" area for toddlers to hone their motor skills. In addition, there are a number of traveling exhibits and displays, snack areas and a souvenir shop.

SOUTH COAST PLAZA, 3333 Bristol Street. *Tel. 714/435-2000 or 800/782-8888.* Bordering Costa Mesa and just a few miles from the beach is this *übermall.* The mall is actually two buildings joined together by an outdoor overpass. Both shopping arenas feature a **merry-go-round,** designer shops, loads of restaurants and major department stores including Nordstrom.

Stanton
ADVENTURE CITY, 10120 South Beach Boulevard. *Tel. 714/236-9300, www.adventurecity.com.* Hours: Call ahead. Admission: $11.95 children and adults, $8.95 seniors, infants 12 months and younger free. Touted as the little theme park built just for kids, Adventure City is just north of Knott's Berry Farm. It is ideal for pre-schoolers and those just a bit older who can still appreciate puppet shows, a petting farm, and do-it-yourself face painting.

There are also 15 whimsical rides that create ear-to-ear grins such as a tiny train and other kid-friendly and educational attractions. If you're traveling with younger children, this is an ideal place for them to play at their own level.

Parent Tip
If you plan on traveling to Los Angeles in a recreational vehicle, pitch a tent or hunker down in your land yacht for next to nothing. Rates at these **Orange County** beachside parks start at around $15 a night.

DOHENY STATE BEACH, in Dana Point at Dana Point Harbor Drive, *Tel. 800/444-7275*

BOLSA CHICA STATE BEACH, in Huntington Beach along Pacific Coast Highway between Warner Avenue and the Huntington Beach Pier.

NEWPORT DUNES RESORT, in Newport Beach at 1131 Back Bay Drive, *Tel. 949/729-3863*

SAN CLEMENTE STATE BEACH, in San Clemente off Avenida Calafia, *Tel. 949/492-3156*

Chapter 8

Los Angeles may have a shortage of rainfall, but when it comes to hotels it's a virtual downpour. Not surprising, room rates for a decent hotel can be quite expensive and don't expect parking to be part of the package.

Still, L.A. gives you plenty of options, and choosing the right neighborhood is essential in making the most of your vacation. A few things to consider when booking a hotel is where and how you want to spend your time. Do you want to explore the museums? Get a thrill from the theme parks? Work on your tan while the kids build sand castles? Once you decide these things, then it's just a matter of selecting a hotel that meets both your needs and budget.

Location, location, location...

Can't decide what part of town to hunker down at? Well, there are the beach communities filled with great surf, outdoor restaurants and limited attractions. The **Westside**, which includes **West Hollywood, Beverly Hills** and a few other desirable districts, offers a great location and is close to shopping, restaurants, cultural venues and entertainment. **Hollywood**, which is undergoing a much-needed revitalization, is once again attracting starry-eyed visitors.

The **San Fernando Valley** is home to Universal Studios, while **Pasadena** offers both charm and character within its Old Town district. **Downtown Los Angeles**, which typically caters to business travelers Monday through Friday, features hotels that offer value-oriented weekend packages. The Metro has also added convenience with subway service to Hollywood and Universal Studios, as well as train service from Union Station to the Disneyland area.

Hotel Rates & Getting the Most for Your Money

As for rates, the ones listed below are rack rates, an industry term for the maximum rate that a hotel charges for rooms. Consider these to be guidelines and nothing more. Typically you can get a much better rate simply by calling the hotel directly, visiting their website (many offer exclusive bargains via the Internet), or utilizing independent travel websites such as **hotels.com** or **travelocity**. If you prefer to travel first-class all the way, **luxurylink.com** is a website dedicated to the sophisticated traveler with five-star package deals and auction opportunities to only the best hotels and destinations including many L.A. area hotels.

If you're planning on going to one of the area's major attractions, such as Universal Studios or Disneyland, ask if the hotel offers any special packages - most do. Don't be shy about bargaining or requesting a discounted rate if you're a AAA member, senior citizen or active member of the military. You might get a good deal if you book early, but last-minute bargains may also be available if a hotel is not filled to capacity. If you're a family, a suite may be more affordable than booking adjoining rooms. Many of the hotels listed below feature kitchen facilities, allowing you to save money on meals. Also, avoid paying surcharges for your children as many hotels allow kids up to 18 years of age to stay free in the same room as their parents. Also, keep this in mind: The cost to "turn" a room is minimal, basically whatever it costs to clean it.

As a rule of thumb, the Downtown hotels are typically less expensive on the weekends when the streets are void of conventioneers and suits. As for the beach cities, you might snatch a cheaper rate during the weekdays after the "mini-breakers" have checked out on Sunday morning.

Hotels are listed in alphabetical order by area and name, and then arranged by price from most expensive to least expensive.

Beverly Hills

Splurge

BEVERLY HILLS HOTEL & BUNGALOWS, 9641 Sunset Boulevard, Tel. 310/276-2251 or 800/283-8885, Fax 310/887-2887, www.thebeverlyhillshotel.com, Cribs: Complimentary. Babysitting: Yes. 203 rooms, Rates: From $345, Parking: $23 per day.

The Beverly Hills Hotel is more than just a place to rest your head, it's a bona fide L.A. landmark. Full of history and, not suprising, plenty of star power; I especially love this urban hideaway for its lore, location and lavish appointments.

Opened in 1912 along what was once an abandoned stretch of Sunset Boulevard, the "Pink Palace" features 203 guest rooms, suites and swank bungalows. Accommodations range from elegant to extravagant with the least expensive lot of rooms found within the confines of the main hotel. While the bungalows are ideal for families with their garden entrances, living rooms, kitchens and dining areas, they also require a rather thick wallet.

The hotel features an infamous swimming pool manned for the last forty years by Danish native Svend Petersen. There are 21 private cabanas, available at an additional charge, boasting televisions, phones and fax machines. Scattered throughout the grounds are two lighted outdoor tennis courts, a fitness center, spa services, signature shops and complimentary limousine service. While the Polo Lounge is a favorite watering hole for generations of celebrities, kids will get a kick out of 1940s-era **Fountain Coffee Shop**. The informal grill features a classically curved counter and 20 flamingo-pink barstools, where a barely recognizable Jodie Foster, clad in jeans and a baseball cap, was recently spotted. Then menu is simple—another plus with children—consisting mainly of omelettes, burgers, sandwiches and ultra-thick shakes.

Children ages 3-12 staying at the hotel are considered **Special VIP Guests** and receive complimentary beverages from either the Fountain Coffee Shop or Cabana Cafe.

THE REGENT BEVERLY WILSHIRE, *9500 Wilshire Boulevard, Tel. 310/ 275-5200 or 800/421-4354, Fax 310/859-9232, www.regenthotels.com, Cribs: Complimentary. Babysitting: Yes. 395 rooms and suites, Rates: From $405, Parking $21 per day.*

Located at the foot of Rodeo Drive, one of L.A.'s most exclusive shopping districts, The Regent Beverly Wilshire, part of the Four Seasons family, is perhaps best known as the hotel where Richard Gere wooed Julia Roberts in the movie *Pretty Woman*.

The hotel, built in 1928 in the Beaux-Arts style, is divided into a pair of wings: The original Wilshire Wing and the '70s-era Beverly Wing. Accommodations are spacious and sublime, and the hotel features a swimming pool, a spa with a menu of treatments and shops.

There's an old adage in Hollywood: Never work with children or animals. Thankfully, The Regent Beverly Wilshire doesn't mind either. Pets are welcome, and kids enjoy the fun-filled complimentary **Comforts of Home** amenity program. Overnight guests ages 2 through 12 receive a stuffed toy animal and Teddy bear candy bar, a personalized Teddy bear t-shirt, a coloring book and crayons, milk and cookies served on a silver tray, balloons, Teddy bear soap and shampoo, washable crayons with an activity placemat, and practical parent-friendly items such as cribs and strollers. In addition, children have access to a variety of board games and videos and the hotel keeps a resource list of neighborhood attractions and activities suitable for children. Babysitting are also available for an additional charge.

144 L.A. WITH KIDS

As for dining, varied children's menus are available in The Dining Room, Lobby Lounge and via room service. Entrees range from silver dollar pancakes to three-cheese pizza to the tried and true peanut butter and jelly sandwich. The hotel also offers snack packs for all-day family outings.

Expensive

THE BEVERLY HILTON, *9876 Wilshire Boulevard, Tel. 310/274-7777 or 800/HILTONS, Fax 310/285-1369, www.merv.com, Cribs: Complimentary. Babysitting: Yes. 581 rooms and suites, Rates: From $185, Parking: $21 per day.*

The Beverly Hilton, part of Merv Griffin's collection of luxury hotels, looks a little worn from the outside. But, as any aging star will tell you, looks can be deceiving. The interiors are quite fabulous, and the hotel has been the backdrop for countless award ceremonies, including the Golden Globes, Oscar Nominees Luncheon, and the Soap Opera Digest Awards, just to name a few.

The rooms are comfortable and the location, where Wilshire and Santa Monica Boulevards collide, is within walking distance of both Century City and Rodeo Drive. The swimming pool is said to be the largest tiled pool in all of Southern California. Live music is played poolside Fridays and Saturdays throughout the summer months, and a newly remodeled fitness center, also poolside, is open daily from 6am to 10pm. There are spa services and 24-hour concierge service, which provides babysitting referrals.

Dining takes place either indoors or poolside at Griff's amid an amusing jungle-themed area. The restaurant is open for breakfast, lunch and dinner, and a menu for children 12 and under is available. If you want to dine at Trader Vic's, a celebrity and community favorite for more than 40 years, then you'd be wise to grab a few Happy Meals from McDonald's just down the road on Santa Monica Boulevard and enlist the babysitting services available. Pets welcome.

Moderate

BEVERLY TERRACE HOTEL, *469 North Doheny Drive, Tel. 310/274-8141, Fax 310/385-1998. Cribs: No. Babysitting: No. 39 rooms, Rates: From $95, Free parking.*

Not everything in Bevery Hills is coated with platinum, and for that we can be thankful. Here is a hotel that is both comfortable and affordable with a collection of suitable rooms. Located on the fringes of Beverly Hills at the entrance of West Hollywood, children six and under stay free. There is a pool on the premises where an al fresco continental breakfast is served each morning. Located on the premises is Trattoria Amici, an Italian restaurant that attracts a weighty clientele. Just minutes away by car is the Beverly Center, Melrose Avenue, the Sunset Strip and Beverly Hills.

Brentwood

HOLIDAY INN BRENTWOOD, *170 North Church Lane, Tel. 310/476-6411 or 800/HOLIDAY, Fax 310/471-3667, www.holiday-inn.com/brentwood-bel, Cribs: Complimentary. Babysitting: Referrals. 211 rooms, Rates: From $149, Parking: $8 per day.*

As you're heading towards the Sepulveda Pass on the 405 Freeway, you'll notice a circular edifice that many people mistake for an apartment building. Located below the Getty Museum, this Holiday Inn recently underwent a much needed $2 million renovation.

Towering 17 stories, each room offers a private balcony. If at all possible, request a room that doesn't face the noisy 405 freeway. Aside from a king or two double beds, rooms also offer a desk or table with a nearby computer dataport. One nice service this chain hotel now offers is its "Forget Something?" program, which provides complimentary personal items to you such as razors, shaving cream, toothpaste, tooth brushes and combs.

While the hotel features an outdoor pool, coin-op laundry, restaurant, spa and fitness center, it's greatest asset is its location. Hop on the 405 Freeway to Universal Studios or take advantage of the free shuttle service to nearby Westwood Village, Brentwood and the Getty Museum.

Downtown

Expensive

THE MILLENNIUM BILTMORE HOTEL, *506 South Grand, Tel. 213/624-1011 or 800/222-8888, Fax 213/612-1545, www.millenniumhotels.com, Cribs: Complimentary. Babysitting: Yes. 683 rooms and suites, Rates: From $174, Parking: $22 per day.*

The famed Biltmore Hotel, part of Historic Hotels of America, opened on October 1, 1923, and was designed in the Beaux Arts fashion by the same architects who created New York's Waldorf-Astoria. Approaching its 80th anniversary, The Biltmore ranks high among L.A.'s legendary hotels.

Guest rooms are tastefully appointed and comfortable, but it's the public rooms that are really magnificent such as the Crystal Ballroom and the Tiffany Room. There are five casual-to-elegant restaurants on the premises, two lounges, an indoor Roman-style swimming pool and many other amenities, such as a weekly brunch and afternoon tea.

Movie buffs might be interested to learn that during a 1927 luncheon hosted by the Academy of Motion Picture Arts and Sciences that Oscar, the international symbol for the motion picture industry, was first sketched on a napkin. Famous faces still flock here, and the hotel has been used as a backdrop for many films.

HILTON CHECKERS LOS ANGELES, *525 South Grand Avenue, Tel. 213/ 624-0000 or 800/423-5798, Fax 213/626-9906, www.hiltoncheckers. Cribs: Complimentary. Babysitting: Yes. 188 rooms and suites, Rates: From $189, Parking: $23 per day.*

In December 1927, a new stylish hotel opened its doors across the street from the Biltmore. Christened the Mayflower, it boasted a Spanish Renaissance facade with Baroque embellishments adorning its grandiose entrance. While the Biltmore aged graciously through the decades, the Mayflower just seemed to age.

The hotel underwent a major renovation in 1985, which resulted in a new owner and name change. The building was peeled away only to reveal the exterior walls and structural beams, everything else is less than two decades old. The hotel went from 348 rooms to just 188, and the original two-story lobby was reduced to a single level with a mezzanine right above. With all the changes came protests from local preservationists, but even some of the harshest critics can agree that much of the architectural integrity was preserved.

Rooms are elegant, yet understated with rare antiques and fine artwork. Guest amenities include complimentary limo service to the Downtown area, three telephones per room, 24-hour room service, in-room coffee, complimentary shoeshine and plush terry robes for lounging. High atop the roof is a stunning outdoor lap-pool and spa, and an exercise room is available to all guests. A restaurant, simply named Checkers, is located on the premises. Pets welcome.

THE NEW OTANI HOTEL & GARDEN, *120 South Los Angeles Street, Tel. 213/629-1200 or 800/273-2294, Fax 213/622-0980,www.newotani.com, Cribs: Complimentary. Babysitting: Yes. 434 guest rooms and suites, Rates: From $180 per night, Parking $18 per day.*

Located in Downtown's Little Toyko district, the New Otani Hotel and Garden is a unique property. This is a harmonious setting where East meets West beginning with the customary, half-acre rooftop garden where weary guests are invited to reflect, refresh and rejuvenate both mind and spirit.

You'll find traditional Japanese-style accommodations with shoji screens, futons, sunken tubs and saunas, and yukata robes, but there are also plenty of Western-style rooms. If you're open to experiencing new cultures, this is a good opportunity to do so. With five restaurants and bars offering everything from sushi to California cuisine, you'll never go hungry. Other conveniences include a fitness center, business area and a health spa offering Shiatsu massage. The hotel also offers complimentary morning shuttle service within the Downtown area to the Financial, Fashion and Jewelry Districts.

THE WESTIN BONAVENTURE, *409 South Figueroa Street, Tel. 213/ 624-1000 or 800/937-8461, Fax 213/612-4800, www.westin.com, Cribs: Complimentary. Babysitting: Yes. 1356 rooms and suites, Rates: From $189 Parking: $22 per day.*

This hotel has had more starring roles than many members of the Screen Actors Guild. The futuristic structure features a cluster of five glass cylinder-shaped towers, helping to give the Los Angeles skyline its distinct silhouette. The hotel, often touted as a city within a city, features a multi-level lobby larger than most malls. Here you'll find 42 specialty shops, boutiques and services, all surrounding a magnificent indoor lake. Hotel accommodations are modern with all the usual amenities. This urban oasis also features a swimming pool, tennis courts and fitness center.

The **Westin Kids Club** is a program that caters to pint-sized travelers. Children are greeted at check-in with a sports bottle or sippy cup, which is filled with complimentary beverages at mealtime. There is also coloring books and bath toys. At bedtime, let your young one dial the designated four-digit number to listen to an age-appropriate bedtime story. Parents are stock-piled with safety kits containing adhesive bandages, electrical outlet covers, ID bracelets, and a list of local emergency phone numbers. Additional items, such as jogging strollers, are available at no charge. Other conveniences include pre-arrival set up of cribs, high chairs and other appropriate items. You can also request preferred reservations when dining at the hotel, which includes ordering meals ahead of time so they'll be ready when you arrive.

Moderate

FIGUEROA HOTEL AND CONVENTION CENTER, *939 South Figueroa, Street, Tel. 213/627-8971 or 800/421-9092, Fax 213/689-0305, www.figueroahotel.com, Cribs: $15 per day. Babysitting: No. 285 rooms, Rates: From $88, Parking: $8 per day.*

Located within walking distance to the Convention Center, Fashion District, Staples Center and other areas of interest, the 12-story Figueroa Hotel dates back to 1927 and was a former YMCA. The mood, decidedly Moroccan, is unlike anything found in Downtown. The lovely lobby features a hand-painted ceiling and tile floor. An inner courtyard boasts a swimming pool, spa and lounge. The rooms, even the snuggest, are creatively appointed.

Most rooms are ample in size and decently furnished, and guests have the convenience of getting their morning coffee fix from the restaurant below. In recent years the hotel has become a popular spot for Hollywood wrap parties, including the Men in Black II shindig.

HYATT REGENCY LOS ANGELES, *711 South Hope Street, Tel. 213/683-1234 or 800/233-1234, Fax 213/629-3230, www.losangelesregency.hyatt.com, Cribs: Complimentary. Babysitting: Referrals only. 485 rooms and suite, Rates: From $99, Parking $20 per day.*

When traveling on unfamiliar turf, sometimes it's comforting to stay with a well-known establishment. While this chain hotel offers no outrageous surprises, you will find the rooms comfortable, the location ideal, and the staff more than friendly. The hotel features two restaurants, an equal number of lounges, an outdoor whirlpool and a fitness center.

Inexpensive
STILLWELL HOTEL, *838 South Grand Avenue, Tel. 213/627-1151 or 800/553-4774, Fax 213/622-8940, Cribs: No. Babysitting: No. 250 rooms, Rates: From $59, Parking: $3 per day.*

A slice of vintage Downtown, this independent hotel hails from the city's glory days. Consider this the Walmart of accommodations, while neighboring hotels are more in-line with a Tiffany & Co. image. The rooms are basic, but comfortable. You can't beat the price, but do be cautious at night.

Hermosa Beach
Expensive
BEACH HOUSE AT HERMOSA, *14th Street at the Strand, Tel. 310/374-3001 or 888/895-4559, Fax 310/372-2115, www.beach-house.com, Cribs: Complimentary. Babysitting: Not available. 96 rooms, Rates: From $199, Parking: $17.*

This is the ultimate beach house. Casually elegant in design, the inn is geared towards business travelers yet equally appealing to the leisurely sojourner who needs only to take a few steps before collapsing on the beach. Each room is described as an ocean loft and amenities vary depending on the rate you're willing to pay, but may include a separate living room and bedroom, private balcony and ocean vistas, whirlpool baths, wood-burning fireplaces and wet bars. This inn is highly recommended if you want to be able to wake up and roll out on the sand.

Hollywood
Moderate
RENAISSANCE HOLLYWOOD HOTEL, *1755 North Highland Avenue, Tel. 323/856-1200, www.renaissancehollywood.com, Cribs: Complimentary. Babysitting: Yes., 637 Rooms and suites, Rates: From $169, Parking: $10 per night.*

This is the first new hotel to open in Hollywood in years, and its stylish mid-century design certainly adds some elegance to the area. The hotel, which offers dramatic views of L.A. and the Hollywood Hills, is the cornerstone of the new Hollywood & Highland dining and entertainment complex. The rooms all feature CD players, coffeemakers, bathrobes and toiletries packed by Bath & Body Works. In addition, you'll find an inviting rooftop swimming pool and Twist, the hotel's signature restaurant serving breakfast, lunch and dinner. The location is also unbeatable. Nearby is the Metro Stop that heads to Universal Studios and Downtown L.A. with Hollywood's Walk of Fame and Disney's El Capitan Theatre at your doorstep.

HOLLYWOOD ROOSEVELT HOTEL, *7000 Hollywood Boulevard, Tel. 323/466-7000 or 800/252-7466, Fax 323/462-8056, www.hollywoodroosevelt.com, Cribs: Complimentary. Babysitting: Yes. 320 rooms and suites, Rates: From $149, Parking: $12 per day.*

As of this writing, the historic Hollywood Roosevelt Hotel is an affordable place to stay. Currently in the midst of a multi-million dollar reservation, the hotel is repositioning itself to become a haute destination for Hollywood's glitterati. I highly recommend you stay here before it truly goes "Hollywood" and rates rise as a result.

Fun Fact

The stars, both living and deceased, still flock to the Hollywood Roosevelt. Those seen breathing are Jennifer Lopez and Elton John, but guests are more likely to spot **Marilyn Monroe**, who posed for her very first ad on the hotel's diving board. She often stayed in the Cabana Rooms after her ascend to stardom, and perhaps that's why many guests have claimed to see her image in a mirror at the lower level elevator landing. While this may seem like an odd place for her to appear, the mirror was removed from the suite Marilyn occupied and repositioned here. Another famous apparition is **Montgomery Clift** who has been spotted on the ninth floor in **Room 928**. It seems that Monty resided there for three months during the filming of *From Here to Eternity*. During that time he was known to pace the hallway rehearsing lines and blowing a bugle. People claim to still feel his presence.

Many other areas of the hotel are reportedly haunted by non-celebrity spirits. These areas include the ballroom, **Room 1032, Suites 1101 and 1102**, and **Room 1221**. As a result, the Hollywood Roosevelt is often visited by psychics trying to make contact with those from beyond. On another note, if your little ones enjoy watching old **Shirley Temple** movies, they may be interested to know that **Bill "Bojangles" Robinson** first demonstrated to the pint-sized star their famous staircase dance on the tile steps leading from the lobby to the mezzanine.

This 1927 hotel is as much a Hollywood relic as Oscar himself; in fact it was the site of the first Academy Awards presentation. Throngs of glamorous movie stars frequented the hotel during its heyday including Louis B. Mayer, Charlie Chaplin, Douglas Fairbanks and Mary Pickford. Its location across from Graumann's Chinese Theatre made it a convenient place for post-premiere trysts. A statue of Charlie Chaplin's character The Tramp greets guests as they enter the wonderful Art Deco lobby. Above is a mezzanine-cum-museum dedicated to the history of entertainment. I recommend you spend a few moments browsing through the photos and artifacts which chronicle Hollywood's humble beginnings.

Rooms range from standard to stunning with junior suites, cabana rooms with private poolside patios, and specialty suites offering spacious surround-ings and celebrity portraits. There are five restaurants and lounges offering everything from gourmet coffee and muffins to fine dining. Outside the hotel doors is the Hollywood Walk of Fame featuring the stars of Natalie Wood, Gene Autry, Cybill Shepard, Maureen O'Hara and many others. Across the street is the Grauman's Chinese Theatre and Hollywood & Highland. Nearby is the Metro Stop to Universal Studios and Downtown L.A.

RAMADA HOLLYWOOD, *1160 Vermont Avenue, Tel. 323/660-1788 or 800/272-6232, Fax 323/660-8069, www.ramadahollywood.com, Cribs: Com-plimentary. Babysitting: No. 130 rooms, Rates: From $109, Parking: $5 per day.*

This location leaves a bit to be desired, but the Ramada name implies dependability. Rooms are your standard chain variety, and guests are treated to a complimentary continental breakfast each morning. On site are a pool, sauna, fitness room and laundry facilities plus an arcade room to keep the kids busy.

Inexpensive

BEST WESTERN HOLLYWOOD HILLS HOTEL, *6141 Franklin Avenue, Tel. 323/464-5181, Fax 323/962-0535, www.bestwestern.com/ hollywoodhillshotel, Cribs: Complimentary. Babysitting: No. 82 rooms, Rates: From $79, Free parking.*

This cinderblock hotel won't win any awards for its design, but as far as location and price it's a decent choice. The no-frill rooms, which feature refrigerators, coffeemakers, microwaves and free movies, are clean and presentable. The rooms in the back are removed from the noise of Franklin Avenue and overlook the swimming pool. The hotel is also located just off the 101/Hollywood Freeway and is three blocks away from the nearest Metro Stop, which travels between Downtown and Universal Studios. The Holly-wood Hills Coffee Shop, a favorite late-night stop for celebrities, is located on the premises. Pets welcome.

HOLLYWOOD HILLS MAGIC HOTEL *7025 Franklin Avenue, Tel. 323/ 851-0800 or 800/741-4915, Fax 323/851-4926, www.magichotel.com, Cribs: No. Babysitting: No. 41 room and suites, Prices: From $69, Free parking.*

The name sounds so inviting, but there ain't nothing magical about this apartment-style hotel. It comes from its close proximity to the Magic Castle, a private club for magicians and their guests, and features full kitchens, free parking, a swimming pool and coin-op laundry, which is especially appealing to families. The location is also close to Hollywood Boulevard's razzle and dazzle. Though the decor is a bit drab, the price is certainly right for vacationing families.

HOLLYWOOD METROPOLITAN HOTEL, *5825 Sunset Boulevard, Tel. 323/962-5800, Fax 323/466-0646, www.metropolitanhotel.com, Cribs: $15 per day. Babysitting: No. 90 rooms and suites, Rates: From $69, Parking: $5 per stay.*

You can zip to Downtown from here or travel a few minutes north to Universal Studios. What you can't do is be too cautious about your surroundings day or night. The modern high-rise hotel offers limited city views and clean comfortable accommodations along with a free continental breakfast. Other conveniences include in-room refrigerators. Within walking distance are the Spaghetti Factory and Denny's, but not much else.

Long Beach
Moderate

DOCKSIDE BOAT & BREAKFAST, *Dock 5 at the foot of Pine Avenue, Tel. 562/436-3111, Fax 562/436-1181, www.boatandbed.com, Cribs: No. Babysitting: No. Rooms: 5 boats, Rates: From $175. Parking: $7.50-$11 in nearby city lots.*

This is one lodging establishment that will truly dazzle the older kids. With a fleet of five vessels, occupants can enjoy a high-seas adventure without ever leaving the port as guests slumber onboard static luxury yachts. Vessels include 44 to 60-foot sailboats plus the unique and alluring Mei Wen Ti, a 53-foot Chinese Junk. This unusual decade-old vessel features wood stained the color of brown sugar and accented with Asian symbols in shocking hues of red, green and yellow. A grinning tiger, looking fierce, is painted against the bow of the ship and the elevated deck,. Wicker deck chairs provide an excellent observation area for admiring the Queen Mary's silhouette. Below deck, the mood is snug but comfy with a sitting area, bedroom and galley.

The fleet of vessels all boast ample deck space, eating areas, on board restrooms with showers, CD players, televisions with VCRs, and everything else you'd expect to find ashore. The private dock also has a grill for warm weathered barbecues. Also included are complimentary breakfast, snacks and bottled water. You're moored near the Aquarium, Shoreline Village, Downtown shops and restaurants. A complimentary city-operated shuttle stops nearby. Pets welcome.

HYATT REGENCY LONG BEACH, *200 S. Pine Avenue, Tel. 562/491-1234 or 800/233-1234, Fax 562/983-1491, www.longbeach.hyatt.com, Cribs: Complimentary. Babysitting: Not available. 531 Rooms, Rates: From $140, Parking: $9 per day.*

When Hyatt opened its doors in Downtown Long Beach in 1983, it paved the way for other big chains to follow in its corporate footsteps. Nearly two decades later, the Hyatt Regency looks just as contemporary as the day it opened. The 16-story glass complex overlooks the Aquarium of the Pacific and Shoreline Village, with the Queen Mary in the distance. It is also adjacent to the Long Beach Convention Center, making it a favorite pied-a-terre for businessmen. Rooms are large and spacious with most offering views of either the harbor or city, and guest amenities include an outdoor swimming and whirlpool, fitness room and paddle boat rentals for the manmade lagoon. Within walking distance are restaurants, shops and the Aquarium.

MARRIOTT RESIDENCE INN, *4111 E. Willow Street, Tel. 562/595-0909 or 800/331-3131, Fax 562/988-0587, Cribs: Complimentary. Babysitting: Not available. 216 rooms, Rates: From $99, Free Parking.*

I think the Marriott really hit on something with their all-suites concept. An ideal set-up for traveling families, these properties tend to resemble apartment complexes rather than hotels. Each suite is spacious with either one or two bedrooms plus a kitchen. Other amenities include a complimentary breakfast and afternoon drinks, in-room VCR, two outdoor pools and a pair of whirlpools.

This location lacks excitement but makes up for it with convenience. You're close to both the freeway (with easy access to both Los Angeles and Orange County) and the Long Beach Airport. Pets welcome.

THE QUEEN MARY, *1126 Queens Highway, Tel. 562/435-3511 or 800/437-2934, Fax 562/437-4531, www.queenmary.com, Cribs: Complimentary. Babysitting: Not available. 365 rooms, Rates: From $79, Parking: $8 per day.*

Here's your opportunity to relive the elegance of transatlantic travel aboard the last great ocean liner afloat. From 1936-1967, this former Cunard ship ferried passengers across the North Atlantic from Southampton, England, to New York City, and was a troopship during World War II. With a portion of her engines removed, this floating palace and Art Deco masterpiece has been permanently berthed in Long Beach Harbor for more than 30 years.

Each of the Queen Mary's 365 staterooms, which recently underwent a much-needed renovation, are some of the largest ever built aboard a ship and feature original appointments including built-ins, wood paneling, artwork and, of course, portholes for outside cabins. The most extravagant rooms are those named for their famous occupants such as the Churchill and Windsor Suites. These cabins feature foyers, master bedrooms, parlors and maids quarters which now serve as a single bedroom.

The bathrooms feature four bathtub faucets: hot fresh water, cold fresh water, hot salt water, cold salt water. Although the latter two are no longer operable, their presence provides a bit of seafaring ambiance. Each overnight stay includes a self-guided shipwalk tour and, for a nominal fee, guests can take advantage of a Behind-the-Scenes guided tour which goes to areas not open to the public. You might consider coordinating your trip with one of the ship's annual events, such as the Scottish Festival, July 4th Celebration, Shipwreck Halloween fête, or New Year's Eve.

Fun Fact

The Hollywood Roosevelt Hotel is not the only hotel in LA where ghosts hang out! Rumored to be haunted as well, the Queen Mary has been the subject of reported paranormal activity for years. Many guests have claimed to have had a close encounter with another kind in such places as the hotel lobby, the Queen's Salon, the engine room, the 1st Class swimming pool and various staterooms. Experiences range from flickering lights and late-night knocks on cabin doors to guests dressed in 1930s-style garb disappearing into thin air. The ship offers a **Ghosts & Legends Tour** that delves into some of the occurances that have taken place on board throughout the years.

Malibu
Expensive

MALIBU BEACH INN, *22878 Pacific Coast Highway, Tel. 310/456-6444 or 800/462-5428, Fax 310/456-1499, www.malibubeachinn.com, Cribs: Complimentary. Babysitting: No. 47 rooms and suites, Rates: From $209, Free Parking.*

Weary travelers are sure to embrace this small, beachfront hotel. The experience begins as you step into the oceanfront lobby, and things just keep getting better. Each room in this Mediterranean-style inn offers wood-beamed ceilings, fireplaces, private beachfront balconies, and hand-painted tile bathrooms. Begin and end each day watching the sunrise and set from the privacy of your oceanfront balcony.

Perks here include complimentary continental breakfast, 24-hour room service, nightly turn-down service and in-room massage upon request. It's an affordable slice of heaven considering its pretentious location, which some may find to be a bit inconvenient and too out-of-the-way.

Moderate
CASA MALIBU INN ON THE BEACH, *22752 Pacific Coast Highway, Tel. 310/456-2219 or 800/831-0858, Fax 310/456-5418, Cribs: $15. Babysitting: No. 21 rooms, Rates: From $99, Free parking.*
If you were cruising down PCH, you may not even look twice at this small, intimate inn. At first glance, it appears to be nothing more than an old motel past its prime. But those who have stayed here know it's a great little find along the coast.
A pair of transparent doors usher guests from the tiny lobby to the garden setting of this two-story inn. A small deck, surrounded by blooming bougainvillea and other colorful flora, offers prime views of the Pacific Ocean. Guests are privy to a private beach just beyond - a luxury not afforded to other area hotels.
Guest rooms are nicely appointed with various amenities such as private decks, ocean or garden views and fireplaces. **The Catalina Suite** is the former digs of actress Lana Turner, who use to enjoy extended stays. The proprietors, a husband and wife team, are very friendly and helpful.

Manhattan Beach
Expensive
BARNABEY'S HOTEL, *3501 Sepulveda Boulevard, Tel. 310/545-8466 or 800/552-5285, Fax 310/545-5849, Cribs: Complimentary. Babysitting: Not available. 126 rooms, Rates: From $99, Parking: $10 per day.*
Located on a busy thoroughfare which threads together L.A.'s coastal communities, this boutique hotel manages to encapsulate its guests. The olde English motif, complete with dark woods that would make Winston Churchill feel right at home, are a contrast to your typical beach hotel.
The guest rooms are stylish in a vintage kind-of-way with antique furnishings, leaded glass, and canopied beds. There's an exceptionally good restaurant on the premises and a relaxing British pub. An outdoor swimming pool and whirlpool spa are the only modern fixtures to be found at this quaint inn. Across the street is a mall with shops, restaurants and theaters. Just down the road is the beach, and the airport is located just minutes away. The hotel offers a shuttle to and from LAX from 5am to 10pm daily. Pets welcome.

Marina del Rey
Splurge
THE RITZ-CARLTON MARINA DEL REY, *4375 Admiralty Way, Tel. 310/ 823-1700 or 800/241-3333, Fax 310/823-2403, www.ritzcarlton.com, Cribs:*

Complimentary. Babysitting: Yes. 304 rooms and suites, Rates: From $249 Parking: $23 per day.

The Ritz-Carlton is synonymous with luxury. This particular property has the least character compared to some of its sister hotels, but the public interiors are undoubtedly showpieces.

Overlooking the marina, the hotel is situated on five acres with panoramic views of the waterfront. The rooms are, as expected, tastefully appointed and the staff is well trained. Amenities include 24-hour room service, two restaurants, child care, and one of the largest swimming pools in West Los Angeles. There are also tennis courts, bikes and a lighted basketball court.

While there is no arguing that The Ritz-Carlton experience is one of indulgence, this location isn't what I would consider pristine unless you're in town on business. In my humble opinion, in this area the luxury hotels of Santa Monica offer more bang for the buck.

Moderate
MARINA INTERNATIONAL HOTEL AND BUNGALOWS, *4200 Admiralty Way, Tel. 310/301-2000 or 800/882-4000, Fax 310/301-8867, www.marinaintlhotel.com, Cribs: Complimentary. Babysitting: Not available. 134 rooms and bungalows, Rates: From $75, Free parking.*

This seaside compound features 110 oversized guest rooms with patios or balconies plus two-dozen freestanding bungalows. You'll marvel at the breathtaking marina views, and the free shuttle to the airport saves you both time and money. There is also a restaurant on the premises; room service is also available. Close by are shops, eateries and the marina.

Pasadena
Expensive
THE RITZ-CARLTON HUNTINGTON HOTEL, *1401 S. Oak Knoll, Tel. 626/568-3900 or 800/241-3333, Fax 626/568-3700, www.ritzcarlton.com, Cribs: Complimentary. Babysitting: Yes. 392 rooms and cottages, Rates: From $205, Parking: $19 per day.*

Steeped in history, the resort opened as the Hotel Wentworth in 1907. After a dismal beginning, it closed shortly thereafter and remained dormant until railroad tycoon and art connoisseur Henry Huntington purchased the hotel in 1911. He hired a prominent Los Angeles architect to redesign the main building and grounds, and it reopened in 1914 as the Huntington Hotel. In 1985, the hotel was forced to close its doors due to its inability to meet earthquake structural standards. In March 1991, after an extensive renovation, the hotel reopened once again under the Ritz-Carlton banner.

The hotel may seem a bit stuffy for curious children, but plenty of families choose to stay here. The common areas offer superb elegance, but unless your budget allows for a cottage or a suite, you'd be better off staying at a less expensive hotel. While the staff is schooled in the art of hospitality with twice-daily maid service, 24-hour room service, evening turn-down service, a collection of restaurants plus poolside dining, the fact is the superior and deluxe rooms are nice but not over-the-top spectacular. The hotel does, however, offer a limited kids program for ages 6-12 with supervised activities such as arts and crafts, swimming, tennis and soccer. **Kids Night Out** is offered Friday and Saturday evenings from 6-10pm. For a $30 fee (subsequent children are $25) kids enjoy dinner and a movie while mom and dad take to the spa or an adult-style dinner. Extended hours are available until midnight for $10 per hour, per child.

One down side to staying here is that you'll definitely need a car - even if it's just to get to Pasadena's Old Town area or the Lake Street shopping district, as the hotel is located a few miles away. On the other hand, if you treasure seclusion, no other hotel in the area can compete.

Parent Tip

If you're considering a stay at The Ritz-Carlton Huntington Hotel & Spa, you'll rest easy with the hotel's **P.O.L.O. Program**, which stands for Protect Our Little Ones. Designed for children under five years of age, this complimentary program includes a kit containing a night light, tub spout cover, electric outlet plugs, first-aid kit and an emergency safety card with a list of local emergency telephone numbers. A specially-trained bellman will also escort families to their rooms upon check in as well as install the safety features and briefly explain other precautionary measures.

Moderate

WESTIN PASADENA, *191 N. Los Robles Avenue, Tel. 626/792-2727 or 800/222-8733, Fax 626/795-7669, www.starwood.com, Cribs: Complimentary. Babysitting: Yes. 350 rooms, Rates: From $129, Parking $5 per day.*

Until recently this hotel was part of the DoubleTree portfolio. It is ideally situated near Old Town and offers more ambiance than you might expect. Located at the historic Plaza Las Fuentes, a Spanish-Mediterranean courtyard whose name means "Plaza of the Fountains," the hotel is surrounded with graceful fountains, sculptures and hand-painted tiles.

Standard rooms are quite comfortable, while executive suites are spacious in size and offer outdoor patios with city and mountain views. There is also an outdoor heated swimming pool and spa, 24-hour room service, and two full-service restaurants.

Inexpensive
   SAGA MOTOR HOTEL, *1633 East Colorado Boulevard, Tel. 626/795-0431, Fax 626/792-0559, www.thesagamotorhotel.com, Cribs: Complimentary. Babysitting: No. 60 rooms, Rates: From From $74, Free Parking.*
   Located on the Rose Parade route, this mid-century motor lodge is a throwback to the days when Route 66 was heavily traveled. While some may say it's a bit tired, it possesses character. The rooms are nothing fancy and the Astroturf surrounding the swimming pool might be considered a bit tacky, but the price and location are unbeatable. Nearby is the Huntington Library, Rose Bowl and Old Town Pasadena. The Family Room accommodations, the most expensive of the lot, feature a king and two double beds. There is also a courtyard garden, outdoor heated swimming pool and complimentary breakfast buffet.

Playa del Rey
Moderate
   INN AT PLAYA DEL REY, *435 Culver Boulevard, Tel. 310/574-1920, Fax 310/574-9920, www.innatplayadelrey.com, Cribs: Complimentary - one available on a first come, first-served basis. Babysitting: Not available. 21 rooms, Rates: From $145, Free parking.*
   Another one of L.A.'s charming seaside bed and breakfast inns is this Eastern Seaboard-style hideaway. The inn overlooks one of the few remaining wetlands in Southern California, which is constantly in danger of being developed.
   Seemingly somewhat removed from the hustle and bustle of L.A., each room is individually decorated with such refinements as four-poster beds, armoires, fireplaces and pull-out couches for the kids. All rooms feature private baths, televisions and reading chairs.
   I highly recommend this inn if you want comfort and convenience. You'll be treated to a gourmet breakfast each morning and some treats in the afternoon. If you feel like pedaling to the beach, there are bikes to borrow.

Redondo Beach
Expensive
   CROWNE PLAZA REDONDO BEACH & MARINA HOTEL, *300 North Harbor Drive, Tel. 310/318-8888 or 800/368-9760, Fax 310/376-1930, www.crowneplaza.com, Cribs: Complimentary. Babysitting: Yes. 339 rooms, Rates: From $160, Parking: $12 per day.*
   Located across from the popular King Harbor, this five-story property is your typical chain variety with the usual amenities (swimming pool, tennis court, exercise room and spa). The cookie-cutter rooms are comfortable, but nothing extraordinary with mini coolers, coffee makers, hair dryers and the other usual suspects; many feature views of the water. There are two

restaurants on the premises: the highly-acclaimed **Splashes**, and the more casual **Reef**. A courtesy shuttle will chauffeur you around to area malls.

San Pedro
Moderate

HOLIDAY INN, *111 South Gaffey Street, Tel. 310/514-1414 or 800248-3188, Fax 310/831-8262m www.holidayinnsanpedro.com, Cribs: $10 flat fee. Babysitting: Not available. 60 rooms, Rates: From $75, Free parking.*

This Holiday Inn has more character than most, and the architecture actually looks more historic than its 15 years. The rooms have a pseudo-Victorian quality with printed wallpaper and period-style furnishings. Some of the amenities you'll receive are a complimentary buffet breakfast, in-room refrigerator and coffee maker, daily newspaper and free parking. There are also rooms equipped with kitchenettes.

The hotel's location is freeway close. If you're planning on embarking on a family cruise or want to spend the day exploring Catalina Island, the hotel is just a short jaunt from the port where both the World Cruise Center and Catalina Island Terminal are located.

Santa Monica
Splurge

LOEWS SANTA MONICA BEACH HOTEL, *1700 Ocean Avenue, Tel. 310/458-6700 or 800/238-6397, Fax 310/458-0020, www.loewshotels.com, Cribs: Complimentary. Babysitting: Yes. 340 rooms, Rates: From $305, Parking: $18 per day.*

This is a great family-friendly hotel, albiet an expensive one. In 1989 Loews Hotels revolutionized the Santa Monica skyline with the opening of a luxury hotel, surprisingly the first beachfront hotel to be built in Los Angeles County in decades. The view from Ocean Avenue doesn't really do it justice, you must step inside to appreciate all this hotel has to offer.

The soaring four-story glass atrium lobby overlooks the sand and surf beyond. Off the lobby is the swimming pool, which is partially enclosed, plus a sun deck with lounge chairs and tables. Early risers can grab a cappuccino from the lobby coffee cart before beginning their day.

The guest rooms are located on the four floors above, and have recently undergone a multi-million dollar refurbishment. The relaxed surroundings coalesce nicely with the seaside setting. Rooms feature muted hues, roomy beds, oversized bathrooms, contemporary furnishings and convenient in-room fax machines for business travelers. While most rooms overlook the ocean, there are some that only offer views of busy Ocean Avenue. If you plan on spending anytime at all in your room, it's really worth it to pay a bit more for the sound of the surf. There are two restaurants on the premises, **Lavande** (take advantage of the hotel's babysitting services and go this one alone) and

Papillon plus room service, poolside dining, limousine service, bike and skate rentals, and spa services.

Located near the base of the famous Santa Monica Pier, Loews Santa Monica Beach Hotel is within easy walking distance to the Third Street Promenade shops and restaurants as well as Palisades Park. Pets welcome.

SHUTTERS ON THE BEACH, *One Pico Boulevard, Tel. 310/458-0030 or 800/334-9000, Fax 310/458-4589, shuttersonthebeach.com, Cribs: Complimentary. Babysitting: No. 198 rooms and suites, Rates: From $595, Parking: $21 per day.*

Gracious coastal living best describes this Southern California retreat. Built in 1993, its vintage-style architecture emulates the seaside resorts that once dominated the coastline during the 1920s and '30s. The slate-grey shingled siding, vine-covered trellises, white-washed wooden balconies and striped awnings are aestically appealing from all angles.

Situated near the historic Santa Monica Pier, each guest room is its own mini beach house configured to make the most of the oceanfront setting. Shuttered doors slide back to reveal shoreline breezes, and rooms are furnished with comfy chaises and marble baths. Luxury takes on a new meaning in the well-appointed suites where wood parquet floors and fireplaces are a few of the elegant touches. There are three casual-to-elegant restaurants, a swimming pool, spa treatments, 24-hour room service, and twice-daily maid service. Kids can enroll in **Shutters Kid Power**, a program operated by Adventure Fitness. The $85 per child fee includes a myriad of activities, from sandcastle building to kiddie yoga to beach volleyball and more.

Expensive

THE GEORGIAN HOTEL, *1415 Ocean Avenue, Tel. 310/395-9945 or 800/538-8147, Fax 310/451-3374, www.georgianhotel.com, Cribs: Complimentary. Babysitting: Not available. 84 rooms and suites, Rates: From $235, Parking: $14 per day.*

Located across the street from the beach, the Georgian Hotel first opened as the Lady Windemere in 1933. For a brief moment its sweeping verandah doubled as an infamous speakeasy. Its Art Deco elegance attracted the likes of Carole Lombard, Clark Gable, and even gangster Bugsy Siegal. These days you're likely to find Robert DeNiro or Arnold Schwarzenegger mulling about.

Located across the street from the famed Santa Monica Pier, the public rooms are classic Art Deco with arched entryways, geometric marble floors and crown-molded ceilings. The color scheme—pink, green and black—are true to the era, and a vintage elevator complete with an operator ferries guests up and down. Each chamber evokes the casual style found at such seaside lodges, and no two rooms are alike. The best rooms—and most expensive — are those on the higher floors offering ocean views. Each night a yellow rubber ducky, complete with snorkel gear, is placed tubside.

The Georgian Hotel, a member of the prestigious *Historic Hotels of America*, is a unique choice if you seek charm, history and a central location. Ask about special hotel packages offered throughout the year. Pets welcome.

THE FAIRMONT MIRAMAR HOTEL, *101 Wilshire Boulevard, Tel. 310/ 576-7777 or 800/325-3535, Fax 310/458-7912, Cribs: Complimentary. Babysitting: Yes. 302 rooms, suites and bungalows, Rates: From $210, Parking: $21 per day.*

Originally a private residence built in 1889, film buffs may be interested to know that this was the first California hotel Greta Garbo resided at when she made her pilgrimage from her native Sweden to the California coast via New York. In recent years Bill Clinton fancied the compound

Perched atop a coastal bluff overlooking the Pacific Ocean and the historic Santa Monica Pier, this full-service facility features an historic wing, contemporary tower and a smattering of bungalows. Amenities include a spa and health club, swimming pool and convenient beach access. The Miramar, which has a a pair of restaurants plus a morning cart located by its Koi Pond, is also close to Santa Monica's trendy shops, restaurants and entertainment.

Moderate

CHANNEL ROAD INN, *219 West Channel Road, Tel. 310/459-1920, Fax 310/454-9920, www.channelroadinn.com, Cribs: Complimentary. Babysitting: Yes. 14 rooms, Rates: From $145, Free parking*

When it comes to bed and breakfast inns, they are few and far between in Los Angeles - at least any worth writing about. But in Santa Monica Canyon, just a short hike from the beach, is an imposing 1910 Colonial Revival home that could easily rival any four-star hotel. Each of the 14 rooms offer romantic touches with soft down comforters, private bathrooms, soothing color combinations, and large picture windows draped in billowy fabrics. Best of all, with the recent addition of a first-floor children's room in the ground floor junior suite, families are graciously welcome.

Complimentary conveniences include bikes, afternoon tea, plates full of cookies, evening wine and cheese, glasses of ice-cold lemonade and tea, and hearty breakfasts. There is also a garden-enclosed whirpool, and en suite massages can be arranged. The bustle of Santa Monica evaporates once inside this compound, but the excitement of this affluent beach community remains a sandal-toss away.

HOTEL CARMEL, *201 Broadway, Tel. 310/451-2469 or 800/445-8695, Fax 310/393-4180, www. hotelcarmel.com, Cribs: $10 per day. Babysitting: Not available.110 rooms, Rates: From $159, Parking: $8 per day.*

This stylish little inn was built in 1924 and bills itself as a European-style hotel. It's not unusual to hear guests speaking Italian, German, French and other foreign languages inside the tiny lobby.

The decor is comfortable, but hardly plush, with a green and pink paisley motif and basic beds. A continental breakfast of croissants and a cup of strong coffee is included. This hostelry is appealing because of its ideal location near shopping and the beach.

Universal City/San Fernando Valley

UNIVERSAL CITY HILTON & TOWERS, *555 Universal Terrace Parkway, Tel. 818/506-2500 or 800./HILTONS, Fax 818/509-2058, www.universalcity.hilton.com, Cribs: Complimentary. Babysitting: Yes. 483 rooms and suites, Rates: From $225, Parking: $11 per day.*

Overlooking Universal Studios is this luxury chain property. The contemporary rooms offer fantastic views from nearly every angle, and a scattering of amenities, such as a swimming pool, restaurant, two lounges and a fitness room, offer convenience.

The hotel is also within walking distance to Universal CityWalk and, of course, Universal Studios. While this is a favorite resting spot for tourists, it also enjoys a brisk conference business. If you want to stay here, be sure to book a room well in advance.

SHERATON UNIVERSAL, *333 Universal Terrace Parkway, Tel. 818/980-1212 or 800/325-3535, Fax 818/985-4980, Cribs: Complimentary. Babysitting: Yes. 442 rooms and suites, Rates: From $149, Parking: $11 per day.*

If you just have to stay near Universal Studios, this hotel is located right on the lot, which explains the high rates. Conveniences include a location close to Hollywood and the West Side, a Starbucks lobby coffee cart, a restaurant, game room, outdoor pool, and free shuttle service to Universal Studios.

Venice Beach

Moderate

VENICE BEACH HOUSE, *15 30th Avenue, Tel. 310/823-1966, www.venicebeachhouse.com, Cribs: No. Babysitting: Not available. 9 rooms, Rates: From $130, Free parking.*

This is an ideal find if you enjoy bed and breakfast inns and, as I mentioned before, Los Angeles has so very few to offer that for most folks staying in a hotel is a safer bet. This California Craftsman-style home dates back to 1911, when Venice Beach was at its prime. There are four rooms and five suites, with the latter being more suited to families. Guest rooms are furnished with antiques, vintage-style wallpaper and tasteful artwork.

The public areas include a cozy living room, an outdoor patio and a lovely garden. Included with each stay is breakfast and afternoon beverages and snacks. The Venice Boardwalk is just a few blocks away, and after you've spent the day watching body builders, roller skaters and aspiring actors vie for attention, it's nice to return to a bit of normalcy.

West Hollywood

LE PARC SUITE HOTEL, *733 West Knoll Drive, Tel. 310/855-8888 or 800/ 578-4837, Fax 310/659-7812, www.leparcsuites.com, Cribs: Complimentary. Babysitting: Yes. 154 suites, Rates: From $185, Parking: $18 per day.*

This out-of-the-way boutique hotel is tucked in a quiet West Hollywood neighborhood and offers guests a luxe lifestyle minus the pretense. Guests are about as diverse as you'll find with designers, studio types, marrieds with children and gay couples checking in non-stop. Rooms are spacious with studios offering a minimum of 800-square-feet plus kitchenettes featuring microwave ovens and refrigerators. Other homey touches include gas fire places, private baloncies, twice-daily maid service, and CD and VCR players. Amenities you'll enjoy are a fruit basket on arrival, a rooftop terrace with a heated pool, whirlpool spa, and tennis courts, 24-hour room service, and a full-service restaurant reserved mainly for hotel guests.

Nearby is Sunset Boulevard, the Beverly Center, Farmers Market and Beverly Hills. Pets Welcome.

Expensive

CHATEAU MARMONT, *8221 Sunset Boulevard, Tel. 323/656-1010 or 800/242-8328, Fax 323/655-5311, Cribs: Complimentary. Babysitting: Yes. 64 rooms, Rates: From $250, Parking: $21 per day.*

A hotel resembling a gothic castle may seem out of sorts in Hollywood, but then again, this is the land of make believe. Built in 1929, the Chateau Marmont opened as an upscale apartment complex and was quickly converted into a hotel after the stock market crashed the same year. The Chateau Marmont is legendary both for its timeless beauty and Hollywood scandals. It gained notoriety in 1982 after comedian John Belushi took a fatal overdose of drugs behind the door of Bungalow #3.

Since its opening, the turreted hotel, which dangles high above Sunset Boulevard, has had its share of ups and downs. But with a recent facelift, Hollywood heavyweights, such as Keanu Reeves, Ethan Hawke, Madonna and Tim Robbins, are checking in daily to rooms and bungalows adorned with rattan chairs, O'Keefe & Merritt stoves, and other furnishings reminiscent of the era. Almost every unit has a kitchenette or full kitchen.

While the hotel is probably one of the town's most colorful, I wouldn't say it's the most glamorous nor is it for everybody. Those with a craving for Hollywood lore and celebrity spotting will find they're in their element. There is an outdoor heated swimming pool and deck, a restaurant, in-room spa treatments and exercise room. Pets welcome.

HYATT WEST HOLLYWOOD, *8401 Sunset Boulevard, Tel. 323/656-1234 or 800/233-1234, Fax 323/650-7024, www.westhollywood.hyatt.com, Cribs: Complimentary. Babysitting: No. 262 rooms and suites, Rates: From $210, Parking: $15 per day.*

This Sunset Boulevard landmark earned a reputation as the rock n' roll hotel as many rauchous musicians were semi-permanent guests over the years including Little Richard. But, like many of its former guests, this mid-century hotel has matured with age. The boxy structure rises 13 stories and its interiors were recently renovated to resemble a temple of Art Deco design. Standard guest rooms are just that - standard, but the plush junior suites feature VCRs, CD stereos and in-wall fish tanks. There is a rooftop pool with captivating views, an Italian-style bistro, lobby coffee cart, and room service from 6am to midnight. Avoid the lower rooms facing Sunset Boulevard...noisy, noisy, noisy!

LE MONTROSE, *900 Hammond Street, Tel. 310/855-1115 or 800/776-0666, Fax 310/657-9192, www.lemontrose.com, Cribs: Complimentary. Babysitting: Yes. 132 suites, Rates: From $295, Parking: $16 per day.*

Located in a quiet residential neighborhood just south of the curvy Sunset Strip, this swanky hotel caters to a genre of travelers including a heavy dose of celebrities. Reminiscent of a European inn, each suite spoils guests with the comforts of home. Fireplaces, kitchenettes, living rooms, secluded balconies plus plush robes and slippers are standard. There are even laundry facilities on the premises, and fresh fruit and mineral water welcomes arriving guests.

A rooftop swimming pool, spa and tennis court cap the building as guests lounge about under Hollywood-style cabanas. There is also a fitness center, 24-hour room service and an on-site restaurant open solely for hotel guests and their visitors. Pets welcome.

WYNDAM BEL AGE HOTEL, *1020 N. San Vicente Boulevard, Tel. 310/854-1111 0r 800/996-3426, Fax 310/854-0926, www.wyndam.com, Cribs: Complimentary. Babysitting: Yes. 200 suites, Rates: From $199, Parking: $18 per day.*

The Bel Age, now part of the Wyndam family of hotels, may look familiar as it is often used as a backdrop in television and movie productions. Located just off Sunset Boulevard, the hotel doesn't make much of a statement from the outside but once inside you'll find it to be richly appointed with warm woods, sleek marble and crystal chandeliers. The walls are bedecked with an expensive collection of original art, and the rooftop garden and pool affords some rather spectacular city views. The rooms are actually gargantuan-size suites boasting sophistication with more original artwork, private balconies, VCRs and CD players. Kids can amuse themselves with the in-room Sony Playstation.

There are two restaurants: La Brasserie and Diaghilev, the latter has received accolades for its Franco-Russian cuisine. You'll also be spoiled with 24-hour room service and a small shopping arcade. You may or may not be interested to know that Minnie Driver, Sharon Stone, Will Smith and Harry Connick Jr. have all slumbered here at one time or another.

Moderate

BEST WESTERN SUNSET PLAZA HOTEL, *8400 Sunset Boulevard, Tel. 323/654-0750 or 800/421-3652, Fax 323/650-6146, Cribs: Complimentary. Babysitting: Referrals only. 100 rooms, Rates: From $109, Free parking.*

Talk about the most bang for your buck. Not only are you in the heart of the Sunset Strip, this particular Best Western is amazingly stylish and, best of all, affordable. If you can't afford The Argyle next door, you can still see the comings and goings from this neighboring property. Each modern guest room offers in-room refrigerators and safes; some even include a kitchen.

The hotel's only suite, which is two bedrooms and sports a spa, is the most expensive room at $250. Amenities include 24-hour concierge service, complimentary parking (this alone is quite a savings), a complimentary continental breakfast buffet, swimming pool and on-site laundry services. Teenagers will enjoy spending time at the hotel's video arcade. Though the rooms facing Sunset Boulevard can be noisy, the balconies provide front-row seats to some amazing and zany entertainment courtesy of the passersby.

With is trendy location, reasonable rates, and free parking (almost unheard of along the Sunset Strip), this is by far the best deal in town.

RAMADA WEST HOLLYWOOD, *8585 Santa Monica Boulevard, Tel. 310/652-6400 or 800/845-8585, Fax 310/652-2135, www.ramada-wh.com, Cribs: Complimentary. Babysitting: No. 176 rooms, Rates: From $179, Parking: $18 per day.*

Ramada Inns are certainly functional, but rarely fabulous. But when you decide to open in one of L.A.'s most trendiest neighborhoods, you better be able to deliver the goods. Surprisingly, this Ramada Inn does that and more.

The outside is quasi-Art Deco and truly eye catching with balconies jutting from various angles. The rooms are equally whimsical, especially the suites with second-story lofts, wet bars, sitting areas and spiral staircases. Within walking distance are restaurants, shops, coffee houses and the funky happenings taking place along Santa Monica Boulevard. This stretch of Santa Monica Boulevard is a mix of straight and gay, and is one of the town's most colorful districts. The hotel is close to the Beverly Center, Beverly Hills, Century City and Sunset Boulevard. The hotel is home to DuPar's coffeeshop, and Starbucks is also nearby. Also featured is a swimming pool and 24-hour room service.

Westwood
Moderate
HILGARD HOUSE HOTEL, *927 Hilgard Avenue, Tel. 310/208-3945 or 800/826-3924, Fax 310/208-1972, www.hilgardhouse.com, Cribs: Complimentary. Babysitting: No. 48 rooms, Rates: From $144, Free parking.*

Located near the UCLA Campus, this contemporary inn offers affordable accommodations in a comfortable setting. In addition to complimentary parking and continental breakfast, guests rooms are equipped with hair dryers and refrigerators. Rooms with whirlpool spas and kitchenettes are also available upon request. Ask about the hotel's Family Plan, which saves you money on multiple rooms if needed. A daily complimentary breakfast is also available to all guests.

Leave the car parked and take a short stroll to Westwood Village for dining, shopping and entertainment. The new Getty Center is just 10 minutes away by car, and neighboring communities, such as Beverly Hills, West Hollywood and Hollywood, are about the same distance. A great location and inexpensive rate make this hotel worth considering.

Chapter 9

Los Angeles is notorious for its restaurant openings, and even more so for its restaurant closings. While many of the eateries I've included are established, I would still recommend you call ahead to be sure that the hours and address have not changed. Each listing tells you whether or not a restaurant offers a separate child's menu, but all are considered child friendly.

Beverly Hills
ITALIAN
Moderate
   THE STINKING ROSE, *55 N. La Cienega, Tel. 310/652-7673, www.thestinkingrose.com, Hours: 11:30am-11pm daily. No children's menu available.*
   This place stinks...literally. The Stinking Rose is all about garlic. Every item on the menu, from the pasta dishes to the seafood to the salads, is seasoned with the stuff - even the ice cream! If you have an aversion to the pungent bulb, then beware; although, some dishes can be ordered without it or "Vampire Style." While there is no kids menu, there are child pleasing five-inch pizzas. And, don't forget, garlic is reported to have health benefits, too.

AMERICAN
Moderate
   KATE MANTILINI, *9101 Wilshire Boulevard, Tel. 310/278-3699, Hours: Monday-Thursday 7:30am-1am, till 2am Friday, Saturday 11am-2am Saturday, Sunday 10am-midnight. Child portions available.*
   Kate Mantilini was opened in the late '80s by Harry and Marilyn Lewis, founders of the once popular Hamburger

Hamlet restaurant chain. While the menu offers a long list of comfort foods, you'll find each dish is flavored with a bit of Beverly Hills. Chicken sandwiches are served on grilled rosemary bread, and the meatloaf presentation looks nothing like any blue plate special I've ever had. The sleek restaurant, a take-off on a 1940s diner, is also a favorite among celebrities and moguls. While there is no official kids menu, many of the items, like the mac 'n cheese, can be ordered in child-size portions.

RIBS
Moderate
R.J.'S THE RIB JOINT, *252 N. Beverly Boulevard, Tel. 310/274-7427, Hours: Open daily 11:30am-10pm, Kids menu available.*

R.J.'s doesn't have the usual pretense associated with Beverly Hills. Wooden booths set the stage for a relaxed meal with an endless salad bar and heaps of ribs and chicken. Desserts are usually multi-layered and oh-so decadent.

DELI
Moderate
NATE 'N AL'S, *414 N. Beverly Drive, Tel. 310/ 274-0101, Hours: Open daily 7am-9pm. Kids menu available.*

Located in image conscious Beverly Hills, Nate 'n Al's is anything but pretentious. Old-time movie stars are often found here noshing on bagels and lox, cheese blintzes, corned beef sandwiches and other reasonably-priced deli fare. The waitresses seem to be stuck in a time warp, which makes this place all the more appealing. Locals pour into Nate 'N Al's for breakfast, lunch and dinner, so be prepared for a wait.

STEAKHOUSE
Expensive
LAWRY'S, *100 N. La Cienega Boulevard, Tel. 310/652-2827, Hours: Monday-Friday 5pm-10pm, Saturday and Sunday 4:30pm-11pm. Kids menu available.*

Lawry's generous portions of prime rib and steak prompted the creation of the doggie bag back in 1938. The original location was across the street, but a recent move hasn't compromised Lawry's quality or service.

This L.A. institution, located along what's known as Restaurant Row, is where competing teams eat before the big Rose Bowl game; on separate nights of course. The huge slabs of prime rib are juicy with a nice taste and texture, and are served with such tried and true favorites as creamed spinach or mashed potatoes. The children's menu is equally sophisticated and features a 4-ounce prime rib served with a side dish and vegetable, salad, yorkshire pudding, beverage and ice-cream for $12.95.

Downtown

Moderate

ENGINE CO. NO. 28, *644 S. Figueroa Street, Tel. 213/624-6996, Hours: Monday-Friday 11:15am-9pm, Saturday and Sunday 5pm-9pm. Kids menu available.*

Housed in a vintage 1912 firehouse, one of the last to handle horse-drawn trucks, the building has been handsomely restored from the white, pressed-tin ceiling to the last remaining fire pole. The food is good—not spectacular—with a selection of juicy cheeseburgers, fries, thick chili, yummy crab cakes and other satisfying fare. It's really the atmosphere, melodic sounds of 'Ol Blue Eyes piped throughout and the decadent desserts that make this place worth visiting.

THE PACIFIC DINING CAR, *1310 W. 6th Street, Tel. 213/483-6000, Open 24 hours. No children's menu available.*

Since 1921, The Pacific Dining Car has been serving business types in what's now considered an old-fashioned railroad car, but was state-of-the-art for its time. If you're in the mood for a thick, juicy steak or a satisfying breakfast day or night, this 24-hour restaurant can fill the order. While there is no children's menu, siblings can split orders or they can simply share their parents' plates.

A nice clubby atmosphere with crimson wingback chairs and low lighting, The Pacific Dining Car also boasts excellent service and a great wine list. Check out the daily afternoon tea served from 3pm-5pm.

Inexpensive

THE ORIGINAL PANTRY, *877 South Figueroa, Tel. 213/972-9279, Open 24-hours. No children's menu available.*

Since 1924, even when the original location was located just a couple blocks away, long lines have formed day and night down 9th Street as customers wait for the first come, first-served tables and counter stools inside this cramped restaurant. Owned by former L.A. Mayor Richard Riordan, it's strictly a menu of old-fashioned, comfort food.

The Pantry is known for its hearty breakfasts, and the decor hasn't changed much over time. Depending on where you're seated, you can watch the cooks hovering over the flaming grill. The thick, buttery sourdough toast is just perfect for sopping up the runny egg yolk and most of the breakfast entrees include a cup of joe. There is no kids menu, but you can ask for a side of dollar-size pancakes. Cash only.

PHILIPPE'S, THE ORIGINAL, *1001 North Alameda Street, Tel. 213/628-3781, www.philippes.com, Hours: 6am-10pm daily. No children's menu available.*

My Dad has been eating here since he was five-years-old, and he actually brought my Mom to Philippe's on one of their first dates. The sawdust-cloaked floors and communal tables did little to impress her, but the food knocked her off her feet.

Generations of Angelenos have been devouring Philippe's famous French dips for more than nine decades. The trademark sandwich is made with a choice of roast beef (my favorite), pork, leg of lamb, turkey or ham. The meat is then placed between a homemade French roll dipped in au jus (be sure to ask for a "double dip," a service not listed on the menu board) and placed on a sturdy paper plate. The only other condiment worthy of sharing the moist roll is the restaurant's hot mustard, which should be used with caution.

Believe it or not, there is a certain protocol to ordering one of these gems. Behind the deli case, which displays an array of freshly-made salads, dill pickles, pickled eggs and pig feet, are 10 women carvers. Each carver serves a single line, and prepares your meal at the counter as you place your order. She makes your sandwich, prepares any hot dishes, piles on the salads and fetches your drinks. Until 1977, a cup of coffee was just a nickel; today it's a whopping nine cents! Iced tea and lemonade are a mere 70 cents, and beer and wine vary. Although the service takes place at the counter, the usual 15-20% tip rule still applies.

On your way out, be sure to stop by the old-fashioned candy counter or weigh yourself on the actual scale jockey Eddie Arcaro posed on for the famous Norman Rockwell painting which graced the cover of the *Saturday Evening Post*. L.A. dining doesn't get more mainstream than this. Cash only.

Fun Fact

Ever wonder how some foods originated? Take the **French dip**, for instance. By the sound of its name, you might think it was conceived along the streets of Paris - au contrair. It was created, accidentally of course, at Philippe's in Downtown Los Angeles in 1918, a decade after Philippe Mathieu opened his namesake restaurant at its original location on nearby Aliso Street (Philippe's was forced to move to its present location in 1951 when the Hollywood Freeway was constructed). Legend has it that while Mathieu was preparing an order for a police officer, he mistakenly dropped the French roll into the roasting pan of juice. The policeman said he would take the sandwich anyway and left. The next day he returned to Philippe's with friends in tow requesting another "dipped" sandwich.

No one is sure if they name "French Dip" derived from the owner's French lineage, the type of bread used, or the officer's surname.

DIM SUM
Moderate
ABC SEAFOOD, *205 Ord Street, Tel. 213/680-2887, Hours: 8am-10pm daily. No children's menu available.*

Dim sum, which means *delights of the heart*, has always been a popular treat in Los Angeles' Chinese neighborhood. ABC serves dim sum the traditional way with women maneuvering carts around the room, which are displayed with an array of meat dumplings and other little bites.

You order by pointing to whatever you think might be appetizing and hope it's something you'll like. This way of ordering dim sum is authentic and really adds to the dining experience. In recent years a crop of trendy dim sum restaurants has emerged in more fashionable neighborhoods, but the old-fashioned method prevails at ABC Seafood.

JAPANESE
Moderate
SHABU SHABU HOUSE, *127 Japanese Village Plaza (Little Tokyo), Tel. 213/680-3890, Hours: Lunch Tuesday-Sunday 11:30am-2:30pm, dinner 5:30pm-10pm, closed Monday. No children's menu available.*

Here's a place where it's perfectly acceptable to play with your food because you basically cook it yourself. Think of this as the Japanese version of fondue with boiling broth instead of bubbly cheese and high qualities of marbled beef instead of bread cubes. It is worth a try, and the dipping sauces which accompany the meal are savory to say the least. The experience concludes with a round of freshly-brewed iced coffee.

Echo Park
TOMMY'S, *2575 W. Beverly Boulevard, Tel. 213/389-9060, www.originaltommys.com, Open 24 hours. No children's menu available.*

Tommy Koulax, the namesake and founder behind this popular burger shack, opened his first stand at the corner of Beverly Boulevard and Rampart in 1946. People line up at all hours just to savor one of Tommy's messy chili burgers along with an order of equally messy chili cheese fries. You can request plain hamburgers for the kids. The self-service restaurant offers no frills with paper towels instead of napkins and a stand-up counter overlooking the parking lot.

While this is the original location—and an Angeleno favorite—Tommy's are now located throughout Southern California. But be forewarned: others have tried to capitalize on this dive's popularity by using the name *Tommy* somewhere in their title or even ripping off the trademark logo. As the original slogan states...*If You Don't See The Shack, Take It Back!* Cash only.

Encino
ITALIAN
Inexpensive

ROSTI, *16403 Ventura Boulevard, Tel. 818/995-7179 Hours: Daily 11:30am-10pm. Kids menu available.*

This mini-chain of Italian bistros prepares Tuscany-style meals in a casual setting. Everything is good: food, prices, portions and setting. In addition to a nice selection of pastas, risotto and individual pizzas, Rosti's panini sandwiches are superb. Served on thick foccacia bread, fillings include fresh mozzarella, tomato, basil, prosciutto and olive oil; a selection of grilled veggies; roasted turkey and fresh artichoke hearts; or marinated chicken breast with lettuce and tomato.

You'll also find the soup, antipasti and salads quiet tasty, and the wine and desserts aren't too shabby either. Additional locations in Beverly Hills, Santa Monica, Brentwood, and Westlake Village. For an extra charge, you can have your meal delivered to your hotel.

Hermosa Beach
CAJUN
Inexpensive

RAGIN' CAJUN CAFE, *422 Pier Avenue, Tel. 310/376-7878, www.ragincajun.com, open for lunch daily 11am, dinner 5:30pm. Breakfast served Sundays from 8am. Closed Monday. No children's menu available.*

A bit of Bayou cookin' at the beach. Menu items include Po Boys, gumbo, hush puppies and jambalaya. Lots of seafood items to choose from, too. Sunday breakfast features beignets (deep fried chunks of dough) and coffee.

Hollywood
Inexpensive

PINK'S FAMOUS CHILI DOGS, *709 North La Brea Avenue, Tel. 323/931-4223, Hours: Open daily 11am-2am. No children's menu available.*

It may sound silly, but these hot dogs are legendary. You'd probably never even notice the tiny white and red stucco building near Melrose Avenue if it weren't for the perpetual and lingering queue.

The hot dogs, which are traditionally smothered in chili, onions and cheese, literally pop when you bite into them. The menu consists of dozens of ways to top your dog including such unconventional condiments as guacamole. Burgers and tamales are also available, but this place built its reputation on its wieners. While there is no "official" children's menu, what kid doesn't enjoy hot dogs?

The cramped dining room is covered with photos of celebrities also addicted to Pink's. This is a favorite haunt of Roseanne, and legend has it that

Sean Penn proposed marriage to Madonna while here. Paramount Studios is just down the road, so you really never know who you'll spot. A small rear patio offers additional seating at this Hollywood landmark. Cash only.

THAI
Moderate
   TOMMY TANG'S, *7313 Melrose Avenue, Tel. 323/937-5733, Hours: Tuesday-Thursday 11:30am-9:30pm, Saturday noon-10:30pm, Sunday 1pm-9pm. Kids menu available.*
   Eccentric and lively, Tommy Tang's never disappoints. Traditional Thai gives way to trendy dishes such as Tommy's signature duck or spicy mint noodles. To give you an idea how off-beat this place gets. Tuesday night is staffed with female impersonators, which makes what could be just another weeknight anything but a drag.

CHICKEN
   ROSCOE'S CHICKEN N' WAFFLES, *1514 N. Gower Street, Tel. 323/466-7453, Hours: Sunday-Thursday 8:30am-midnight, till 4am Friday and Saturday. No children's menu available.*
   Whatever happened to the traditional pairings of chicken and dumplings or waffles and bacon? Those standing on line will tell you this odd combination is surprisingly good. I myself find this to be an acquired taste, but you be the judge. One thing is for sure - late-night dining has never tasted so incredibly funky.

ITALIAN
Modern
   MICELI'S *1646 N. Las Palmas, Tel. 323/466-3438, Hours: Sunday-Thursday 11:30am-11:30pm, till midnight Friday, and 4pm-midnight Saturday. No children's menu available.*
   Authentic Italian specialties are abundant at this family-owned trattoria, which has been here since 1949. Everything from antipasti and sandwiches to hearty pizzas and pasta dishes are prepared with fresh ingredients and spices. The fettuccini carbonara is one of my favorites, and the tiramisu and Italian ices are a nice way to round out a meal. Kids can order just plain 'ol spaghetti and meatballs.

MEDITERRANEAN
Expensive
   CAMPANILE, *624 S. La Brea Ave., Tel. 323/938-1447, Hours: Monday-Thursday 11am-10pm, till 11pm Friday, Saturday 9:30am-1:30pm and 5:30pm-10pm, Sunday 9:30am-1:30pm. Kids menu available.*

A delightful bistro not far from Melrose Avenue, owner and chef Mark Peel prepares an eclectic menu of pasta, rabbit and seafood all perfectly seasoned. Monday night is Family Dinner night and Thursday night, as strange as it may sound, is when wife and co-owner Nancy Silverton pays homage to the grilled cheese sandwich. Don't expect some grilled white bread with melted American cheese, a pickle spear and parsley garnish to be slung your way. No sir, this is high-class stuff. Using thick slices of country bread, Silverton pairs Gruyere, Manchego and other classy fromage with marinated eggplant, ham and anchovies to create a decadent ensemble.

By the way, Silverton also owns **La Brea Bakery** next door which furnishes Southern California's finer restaurants with her signature crusty loaves of rosemary, Greek olive and walnut breads. Her desserts are some of the most talked about too.

Fun Fact

L.A. is filled with celebrities and, just like you and me, these people have got to eat! So, while there is no guarantee you'll spot one, you can increase your chances by going to some of their favorite places, such as:

Fred 62 in Los Feliz. *Tel. 323/667-0062,* frequented by Cameron Diaz and Leonardo DiCaprio.

Mauro's Cafe inside Fred Segal in Hollywood, *Tel. 323/623-7970,* is where Winona Ryder and Shannen Doherty unwind.

Who's on Third? in Hollywood, *Tel. 323/651-2928,* is where you might find Supermodel Tyra Banks and Courteney Cox-Arquette.

MEXICAN
Moderate

LUCY'S EL ADOBE, *5536 Melrose Avenue, Tel. 323/462-9421, Hours: Monday-Saturday 11:30am-11:30pm, closed Sunday. Kids menu available.*

Located across the street from Paramount Studio's famed iron gates is this Hollywood landmark. Once upon a time Lucy's catered to a wealth of stars who wandered over here after wrapping up a day's filming. A few sit-com stars and production types still enjoy the Mexican food and salty margaritas that made Lucy's famous.

STEAKS & CHOPS
Expensive

MUSSO & FRANK'S GRILL, *6667 Hollywood Boulevard, Tel. 323/467-7788, Hours: Tuesday-Saturday 11am-11pm, closed Sunday and Monday. No children's menu available.*

If you want to experience one of the last remaining institutions from Hollywood's Golden Age, Musso & Frank's is it. Somehow Musso & Frank's, the oldest restaurant in Hollywood, has managed to keep its doors open for more than 80 years. The place looks pretty much the way it did when Jean Harlow, Lana Turner and Clark Gable stopped in for a thick steak and dry martini. Packed with sentimental value, American standards are served at big red-leather banquettes, as well as tables and chairs.

Long Beach

AMERICAN

Inexpensive

HOF'S HUT, *6257 E. Second Street (at the corner of Pacific Coast Highway), Tel. 562/598-4070, Hours: Open daily from 7am. Kids menu available.*

Hof's is a local landmark that first opened in Belmont Shore in 1947. Though the original location was recently transformed into a Lucille's Barbecue, you can still enjoy the vast selection of breakfast, lunch and dinner items at this and other locations. The all- day menu is consistently good, though it has gotten to be a bit steep considering Hof's is nothing more than a coffee shop. House specialties include zucchini sticks, omelets, club sandwiches, meatloaf, chicken fried steak and, of course, burgers. The Chocolate Wipeout Cake, made fresh on the premises, is also a hit. The children's menu features the usual suspects, such as pasta, grilled cheese and corn dog nuggets.

BRUNCH

Expensive

THE QUEEN MARY CHAMPAGNE SUNDAY BRUNCH, *aboard the Queen Mary, 1126 Queens Highway, Tel. 562/435-3511, www.queenmary.com, Hours: Every Sunday from 10am-2pm. Reservations recommended. Kids buffet available.*

For more than 25 years, visitors have been flocking to the Queen Mary every Sunday to enjoy their elegant Champagne Sunday Brunch. I can honestly say that this is one of —if not the best—Sunday brunches I've ever had the pleasure of experiencing. Situated in the historic Grand Salon, where first-class passengers such as Greta Garbo, Elizabeth Taylor, Clark Gable and the Duke and Duchess of Windsor dined during transatlantic crossings, the weekly feast features more than 50 entrees.

Guests wander by a stratum of culinary stations displaying fresh seafood, Asian favorites, Mexican specialties, omelets made to order, layered desserts, pastas and sauces, and everything else imaginable. A harpist is elevated above the tables entertaining diners with classical music, and champagne and fresh orange juice are constantly flowing. Best of all, children are privy to their own buffet, and a self-guided shipwalk tour is included in your meal.

ECLECTIC
Moderate
YARD HOUSE, *401 Shoreline Village Drive, Tel. 562/628-0455, www.yardhouse.com, Hours: Open daily from 11am. Kids menu available.*

This waterfront eatery strikes a nice balance between sophisticated dining and family friendly. It offers a great seaside location and the world's largest draft beer system - a whopping 250 taps. A fusion of American classics and Asian flavorings create a mouthwatering selection of appetizers, sandwiches, seafood, burgers and salads. Some of Chef Carilto's specialties include the crab cake hoagie and the ahi crunch salad.

The Kids Klub features a prix fixe menu that includes entree, French fries or fruit, a kiddie cocktail concoction of soda and fruit flavoring, and a fresh-fruit dessert bar all at a price of just $5.95. The selections are actually the same items found on the adult menu only served in age-appropriate portions. Next door is a carousel and arcade to enjoy before or after your meal, and the Aquarium is within walking distance.

ITALIAN
Moderate/Inexpensive
BUON GUSTO TRATTORIA, *5755 E. Pacific Coast Highway, Tel. 562/494-7591, Hours: Open daily from 11:30am. Kids menu available.*

Sometimes, where you least expect it, a good restaurant is just waiting to be discovered. Take Buon Gusto for example. It's located between a bank and a bagel shop in an average strip mall, but there is nothing average about the authentic Italian cooking taking place inside.

Popular with the locals, this casual bistro features a vast selection of pasta dishes, seafood, veal and poultry as well as Italian-style sandwiches and pizzas. All entrees come with either soup or salad, and there is an endless supply of fresh Italian bread. The decor is simple, but pleasing with booths lining the wall and tables filling the rest of the dining room.

MEXICAN
Inexpensive
SUPER MEX, *4711 East Second Street, Tel. 562/439-4489, www.supermex.com, Hours: Open daily from 11am. Kids menu available.*

What started as a small operation in downtown Long Beach nearly 30 yeas ago, has now morphed into a small mini-chain of restaurants. Still family owned and operated, Super Mex delivers good, flavorful Mexican food at incredibly cheap prices. The decor is basic: white walls, Spanish-tile floors, formica tables and minimal—if any—wall hangings. But that's the charm of Super Mex.

This particular location recently expanded to include a courtyard, an additional dining room and patio. The chips, whole corn tortillas deep fried and served with hair-raising salsa, just keep coming throughout the meal. Burritos come in three sizes: basic, junior and super, and the fresh-made guacamole is chunky and zesty. Cash only.

SPANISH
Moderate
    ALEGRIA, *115 Pine Avenue, Tel. 562/436-3388, Hours: Open daily from 11:30am-10pm. Kids menu available.*
    Located along lively Pine Avenue, Alegria specializes in Spanish cuisine. Order a plateful of tapas, which means little bites. These scrumptious delights are classified as appetizers but can also form an entire meal. The tapas here include little stuffed sandwiches accompanied by various salsas along with other specialties such as paella, roast chicken and refreshing sangria. The breezy patio is ideal for people watching, but at night the real show takes place inside as Flamenco dancers take to the tiny stage.

Malibu/Pacific Palisades
AMERICAN
Inexpensive
    PIERVIEW CAFE, *22718 Pacific Coast Highway, Tel. 310/456-6962, Open daily for breakfast, lunch and dinner. Kids menu available.*
    It's difficult to decide what's better, the view or the food. Located on the beach, this casual Malibu eatery is relatively cheap considering its million-dollar location. The sawdust-covered floors also has an element of unpretentiousness in a most pretentious town. The food is rather tasty with an assortment of sandwiches, burgers, salads and pasta; breakfast is served weekends. Portions are plenty, and the best tables are those on the beachfront patio which, unfortunately for families, can only accommodate up to two guests.

SEAFOOD
Moderate
    GLADSTONE'S 4 FISH, *17300 Pacific Coast Highway, Tel. 310/454-3474, www. gladstones.com, Open daily for lunch and dinner, weekends for breakfast. Kids menu available.*
    Located at the base of Sunset Boulevard along the beach, there is a lot of hype about Gladstone's. The food is average, but the atmosphere is at times over-the-top. The crowds love this place where peanut shells are scattered about the floor, tables overlook the beach and celebrities are known to stop in frequently. While there are a few landlubbing dishes on the menu, you better love seafood or otherwise pass this place up.

HEALTHY
Expensive
   INN OF THE SEVENTH RAY, *128 Old Topanga Road, Tel. 310/455-1311, www.innoftheseventhray.com, Open daily for lunch and dinner plus Sunday for brunch. No children's menu available.*
   This new age, rustic hideaway was rumored to have been evangelist Aimee Semple McPherson's private mountain retreat during the 1930s. Today, it is one of L.A.'s most breathtaking culinary settings. The menu is mostly organic and, while there is no children's menu to speak of, the staff will gladly make concessions to please kids by offering a simple pasta dish or fresh fruit if they don't like what is on the menu. This is a wonderful place for Sunday brunch with tables overlooking a tumbling stream and recorded harp music providing tranquillity, plus children are invited to play in the sandbox and enjoy themselves There's also a fair chance you'll spot a celebrity enjoying the same fare as yourself. The atmosphere at lunch and Sunday brunch is better suited towards families than the dinner crowd - which tends to be mostly couples.

Manhattan Beach
THAI
Inexpensive
   THAI DISHES, *1015 N. Sepulveda, Tel. 310/546-4147, www.thaidishes.com, open daily from 11am. No children's menu available.*
   There are several locations throughout Los Angeles of Thai Dishes, and you'll find that plenty of celebrities congregate at the original Wilshire Boulevard location in Santa Monica - proving that even the fattest of wallets love a good deal. Most dishes are no more than $8 at this family-friendly eatery. The menu features a variety of meat and vegetable dishes, as well as curries, noodles, rice and seafood.

Marina del Rey
ITALIAN
   C&O TRATTORIA, *31 Washington Boulevard, Tel. 310/823-9491, Hours: Monday-Friday from 9am, weekends from 8am. Kids menu available.*
   If you're hungry and broke, head to this Italian dining landmark. This place is such a kick, I don't know anyone who hasn't enjoyed eating here. Nearly every menu item is under $10, and the portions are certainly more than generous. The nightly sing-a-longs and honor wine bar creates a fun and inviting atmosphere.
   You may find it odd that a place known for its pasta lunches and dinners is also open for breakfast. The early morning menu offers a selection of breakfast pastas mixed with scrambled eggs, Italian cheeses and seasonings. A real delicious treat is the sourdough French toast topped with whipped marscapone cheese or the eggs pannini with scrambled eggs, sun-dried

178 L.A. WITH KIDS

tomato and basil piled on top of foccaccia - think of it as an Italian Egg McMuffin. They also have staples such as bagels and cream cheese or eggs and bacon. Great food, lots of fun and extremely easy on the wallet. Full and half orders available.

SOUL FOOD

AUNT KIZZIE'S BACK PORCH, *in the Villa Marina Shopping Center at 4325 Glencoe Avenue, Tel. 310/578-1005, Hours: Open daily from 11am. Kids menu available after 4pm.*

There's some serious southern cookin' taking place in Aunt Kizzie's kitchen. The menu draws from the owners' native Texas and Oklahoma upbringings with down-home favorites such as catfish, hush puppies, fried chicken, collard greens, okra and black-eyed peas. If you can polish off one of the Texas-sized meals, you might want to give the sweet-potato pie a try. Sunday brunch is an all-you-can-eat feast, but be sure to arrive early and a bit famished.

Mid-Wilshire

BREAKFAST
Inexpensive

CAFE LATTE, *6254 Wilshire Boulevard, Tel. 323/936-5213, Hours: Monday-Friday 7am-4pm, Saturday and Sunday 8am-3pm. Kids menu available.*

Located in a non-descript strip mall, this little gem serves a great breakfast of omelets, French toast, thick sausages and great coffee. Nothing fancy, just good food at reasonable prices. Cafe Latte also serves lunch.

MEXICAN
Moderate

EL CHOLO, *1121 S. Western Avenue, Tel. 323/734-2773, Hours: Monday-Thursday 11am-10pm, till 11pm Friday and Saturday, till 9pm Sunday, Kids menu available.*

Since 1927 El Cholo has been serving traditional Mexican food and margaritas along Western Avenue. The neighborhood has gone from good to ghetto, but the food remains just as savory as the day the doors opened.

Over the years, El Cholo has tried to stay contemporary by adding such dishes as crab enchiladas and fajitas, which are about as Mexican as a burrito from Taco Bell. Stick to the basic burritos, enchiladas and tamales, which is what has kept El Cholo alive for so many years. If you're visiting between May and October, try one of the restaurant's seasonal green corn tamales.

Pasadena

AMERICAN

Moderate

BARNEY'S, *93 West Colorado Boulevard, Tel. 626/577-2739, Hours: Sunday-Thursday 11am-10pm, Friday and Saturday till 1am. Kids menu available.*

Barney's opened in 1979, long before Colorado Boulevard was a fashionable esplanade. An array of burgers, meaty sandwiches, omelets, spuds, hot dogs and steaks round out the choices. There is also a nice selection of salads and pastas available; and the fish 'n chips, consisting of hefty chunks of deep-fried Atlantic cod, are exceptional.

DELACEY'S CLUB 41, *41 South DeLacey Street, Tel. 626/795-4141, Hours: Sunday-Thursday 11:30am-10pm, Friday and Saturday 11am-11pm. Kids menu available.*

A popular spot with locals, DeLacey's authentic decor of high-backed wooden booths, tiled floors, starch tablecloths and dark woods is a nice change from the trendy bistros and chain restaurants that have invaded Old Town in recent years. DeLacey's specializes in steaks and chops, but also offers soup, salad, sandwiches, pasta and a nice selection of seafood. DeLacey's is a favorite among location scouts, and has appeared in a number of films including the remake of *Father of the Bride* starring Steve Martin and Diane Keaton.

GORDON BIERSCH, *14 Hugus Alley, Tel. 626/449-0052, Hours: Sunday-Thursday 11am-10pm, Friday and Saturday till 11pm. Kids menu available.*

The courtyard setting at Gordon Biersch is enjoyable, and the American-style menu is both good and consistent. You'll find an array of appetizers, salads, seafood, pizzas, pasta, sandwiches and burgers. While the inside decor is open and airy with brick walls and a slate floor, the tables outside provide a more scenic view.

HOLLY STREET BAR & GRILL, *175 E. Holly Street, Tel. 626/440-1421, Hours: Lunch Monday-Saturday 11am-2:30pm, Dinner Sunday, Tuesday-Thursday 5pm-9:30pm, Friday and Saturday till 10pm, Sunday Brunch 10am-2:30pm. No children's menu available.*

It's not often you can say you dined on the premises of a former mortuary, but this charming brick building, with its steeple and stained-glass, was just that. Located a bit off the beaten path, the restaurant features an extensive a la carte menu of salads, sandwiches, seafood, pasta, game and beef. Sunday brunch features a selection of breakfast favorites such as French toast, lox and bagels, frittatas, omelets, salmon and champagne.

The bi-level courtyard, with its greenery and soothing fountain, by far offers the best tables in the house. If at all possible, request a courtyard table, otherwise you'll be subjected to eating in the cramped dining room. There is no children's menu, but the staff is accommodating by allowing parents to order off-the-menu for their little ones.

GREEK
Moderate

CAFE SANTORINI, 64 W Union Street, Tel. 626/564-4200, Hours: Open daily 11am-11pm. No children's menu available.

Located on the second floor of a brick building, Cafe Santorini overlooks a shopping piazza that really makes you feel as if you're somewhere in the Mediterranean. The menu offers a blend of Greek and Italian favorites such as salads, individual gourmet pizzas, pasta, risotto, kebobs, souvlaki, seafood, beef and poultry.

HEALTHY
Inexpensive

FATHER NATURE'S LAVASH WRAPS, 17 North Delacey Street, Tel. 626/568-9811. Located a 1/2 north of Colorado. Hours: Sunday-Thursday 10am-9pm, Friday and Saturday till 10pm. No children's menu available.

A few years back wraps were all the rage. Though not quite as popular nowadays, they still offer a healthier alternative to fast food. There are three styles of wraps to choose from: vegetarian, specialty and gourmet. Many of the ingredients used are inspired by spices and foods from the Middle East: falafel, humus, tahini, taboule, pilaf and other exotic edibles. Dishes are also void of preservatives, hormones, lard or MSG. There are also salads available, and kids can order bite-size wraps.

STEAK & SEAFOOD
Moderate

CLEARWATER SEAFOOD, 168 W. Colorado Boulevard, Tel. 626/356-0959, Hours: Monday-Thursday, 11:30am-10pm, will 11pm Friday, Saturday and Sunday 9am-11pm. Kids menu available.

Located in a streetside courtyard in the Tanner Market arcade, this restaurant is a seafood mecca with fresh fish flown in daily from Washington, British Columbia, Connecticut and California seaports.

Specialties include succulent oysters on the half shell; cioppino with dungeness crab, shrimp, clams, mussels, calamari and fresh fish; live Maine lobster; swordfish brochette with pico de gallo salsa; and more. Landlubbers would be hard pressed to find a satisfying meal, but there are a few non-seafood items including a selection of sandwiches, garden burgers, pasta and salads.

Clearwater Seafood's ambiance is just as appetizing as the menu with three stylish dining rooms, two courtyards, a modest bar, a lobster and crab tank, and a lively oyster bar. Breakfast is served weekends, but save your appetite for lunch or dinner. The children's menu is quite extensive, and features a selection of chowders, sandwiches, pasta and shrimp dishes.

Redondo Beach
BREAKFAST
Inexpensive
C.J.'s PANTRY, *324 South Catalina Avenue, Tel. 310/318-2411, Hours: Open daily from 7am for breakfast and lunch. No children's menu available.*

This authentic dive is where locals flock for a good, cheap and quick breakfast. Nothing fancy, but getting a table here on weekends can be more challenging than mounting a surf board. All the usual selections are cooked-to-order including eggs, French toast, omelets, pancakes and a bottomless cup of joe.

CALIFORNIA
HENNESSEY'S TAVERN, *1712 South Catalina Avenue, Tel. 310/540-8443, Hours: Open daily from 7am. Kids menu available.*

Noisy and inexpensive, Hennessey's is a pub-style restaurant complete with dark wood and the smell of stale beer. The menu is decent, though nothing award winning, with grilled burgers, salads, club sandwiches, steak and a breakfast that's hard on the arteries.

San Pedro
CALIFORNIA/ECLECTIC
INTERNATIONAL HAMBURGER HUT, *824 South Gaffey Street, Tel. 310/832-4813, Hours: Monday-Thursday from 10am, Friday-Saturday from 6am, Sunday from noon. No children's menu available.*

Not a lot of elbow room to enjoy your eclectic meal of American, Greek and Middle Eastern origins. But I don't come here for the burgers or falafel, I have my favorite spots for those things. I enjoy the gyros made with chicken instead of lamb and topped with yogurt sauce and onions. You'll also find submarine sandwiches and other quick bites. Cash only.

GREEK
Moderate
PAPADAKIS TAVERNA, *301 West Sixth Street, Tel. 310/548-1186, www.papadakistaverna.com, Open daily from 5pm. No children's menu available.*

My big fat Greek dinner was delicious and fun at this wildly popular restaurant. Break plates with the owners/brothers, John and Tom, and take a culinary excursion to the Greek Islands enjoying such authentic dishes as mousaka, souflaki, dolmathes and many other specialties including seafood and pasta.

Established in 1973, John and Tom make you feel as if you're a guest in their home. Guys will enjoy the talents of a belly dancer and, with a little encouragement, the waiters will break into dance. Great selection of domestic and imported Greek wines to complement your meal. If you're in the mood for good food, good fun and the unexpected, grab the kids and go.

Santa Monica

BREAKFAST
Inexpensive

PATRICK'S ROADHOUSE, *106 Entrada Drive, Tel. 310/459-4544, www.patricksroadhouse.com, Open daily for breakfast and lunch. No children's menu available.*

As you're driving down Pacific Coast Highway, you'll see a loud green building with clovers splashed all over it at the intersection of Entrada. This is among L.A.'s best places to fill your plate and people watch as Hollywood heavyweights file in every weekend to enjoy a hearty American breakfast. The menu features lots of omelets, waffles, eggs and sausage delivered in massive portions. Hamburgers are also on the list. Though an official children's menu doesn't exist, the restaurant does produce kids-style meals on demand. In fact, the restaurant is so accommodating that they sent O.J. Simpson banana cream pies while he was in jail awaiting trial. Cash only.

DELI
Moderate

BROADWAY DELI, *1457 Third Street, Tel. 310/451-0616, Hours: Monday-Thursday 7am-midnight, till 1am Friday, Saturday 8am-1am, Sunday 8am-midnight. Kids menu available.*

Broadway Deli is too plain a name for this sleek, contemporary eatery. Set along the Third Street Promenade, the restaurant features everything from meatloaf and mashed potatoes to gourmet pizza and fancy pastas. Sandwiches range from traditional (grilled cheese) to trendy (fresh mozzarella, tomato and basil on a baguette). Near the entrance is a deli and bakery with a cappuccino bar if you want to grab something and go.

FAR EAST
Inexpensive

MONSOON CAFE, *1212 Third Street Promenade, Tel. 310/576-9996, Hours: Open Monday-Saturday from 11:30am for lunch and dinner, 4:30pm on Sunday. No children's menu available.*

It's Tarzan meets Indiana Jones in this jungle-like setting, which is just as appetizing as the food. Forget everything you ever knew about Asian cooking, the tidal wave of food at Monsoon will knock you off your feet. Elements of Korean, Chinese and Vietnamese cooking are found in various dishes such as the Asian tapas, kung pao and spicy mint chicken. No kids menu, but the experience is surely an adventure.

INDIAN
Inexpensive
NAWAB, *1621 Wilshire Boulevard, Tel. 310/829-1106, Hours: Lunch Monday-Friday 11:30am-2:30pm, Dinner Monday-Saturday 5:30pm-10:30pm, weekend brunch served noon-3pm. No children's menu available.*

The food at Nawab is a bit more exotic than most as it specializes in northern Indian Nughalai, a style of food brought to India by Muslim kings. There are some standards on the menu, such as traditional tandoori and kababs, as well as a mildly spicy mulligatawny soup.

ITALIAN
Moderate
FRITTO MISTO, *601 Colorado Avenue, Tel. 310/458-2829, Hours: Open daily at 11:30 a.m. Kids menu available.*

All I can tell you about this place is you'll have to take a number. It's a favorite neighborhood spot, which is always a good indication that both the food and service is worthy of your time. The crowds seem to devour heaping bowls of pasta. Order from the menu or take some creative liberty by designing your own combination of pasta and sauces.

JAPANESE
Inexpensive
NOMA'S, *2031 Wilshire Boulevard, Tel. 310/453-4848, Hours: Lunch daily 11:30am-2:30pm daily, dinner 5pm-10pm daily. No children's menu available.*

Noma's offers Japanese specialties and a traditional sushi bar. The menu won't revolutionize your taste buds, but the selection of seafood, chicken, beef and vegetable dishes are solid. In addition to ordering individual sushi, there are sushi dinners available that are more filling and less expensive. For the healthy minded, there is a tofu steak that many vegetarians and vegans find enjoyable.

MEXICAN
Inexpensive
BORDER GRILL, *1445 Fourth Street, Tel. 310/451-1655, Hours: Lunch Tuesday-Sunday 11:30am-5pm, dinner nightly from 5pm- 11pm. Kids menu available.*

The Food Network's *Too Hot Tamales*, Susan Feniger and Mary Sue Milliken, are the creators of this boisterous, piñata-colored Mexican joint. It's a bit overpriced when you consider many of the staple ingredients consist of beans, tortillas and rice, but it's in a great location and the ambiance is lively.

The food tends to be more trendy than traditional with items like the vegetarian torta made with black beans, guacamole, roasted peppers, cucumber and watercress. The best bet are the griddle tacos made with homemade corn tortillas with various fillings and served in pairs. One nice note: the noise level will certainly disguise the sound of any whining child.

SEAFOOD
Moderate
   THE ENTERPRISE FISH COMPANY, *174 Kinney Street, Tel. 310/392-8366, Hours: Open daily for lunch and dinner from 11:30am. Kids menu available.*

Parent Tip

Sometimes as a parent all you want to find is a decent restaurant where the staff doesn't roll their eyes the minute they see the nuclear family walking through the door. Well, Los Angeles has plenty of places where you can get a decent meal without breaking the bank or having to deal with a snooty waiter. Many of them are national chains; others you may not be familiar with, but are highly recommended and kid-tested by my own five-year-old son. They all offer kids menus as well as multiple locations.
   • Islands - burgers and tacos
   • Joe's Crab Shack - cheap seafood and impromptu entertainment
   • B.J.'s Pizza - Chicago-style pizza plus a lot more
   • Chevy's - sit-down fresh Mex
   • Pick Up Stix - fast-food Chinese
   • Marie Callendars - home-style cooking
   • La Salsa - fresh, Mexican fast-food
   • Baja Fresh - same as above
   • Mimi's Cafe - pseudo French, mostly sandwiches and salads
   • Cheesecake Factory - serving everything but the kitchen sink in massive portions
   • Claim Jumper - an eclectic mix of sandwiches, salads, steak and appetizers also served in massive portions
   • Olive Garden - basic Italian food with an endless supply of breadsticks and salad
   • Rubios - specializing in fish tacos
   • California Pizza Kitchen - the name says it all
   • -Du-pars - filling breakfasts, lunches and dinners

Fresh seafood is the emphasis at this reasonably priced fish house. Mesquite grilled entrees include shrimp, scallops and lobster, plus chicken teriyaki and filet mignon for non-seafood diners. House specialties include crab cakes and a selection of seafood pastas, and the creamy lobster bisque is a meal in itself. The restaurant recently added sushi to its menu repertoire, but it's not what they do best.

Venice
AMERICAN
Inexpensive
FIGTREE'S CAFE, 429 Ocean Front Walk, Tel. 310/392-4937, Hours: Open daily at 9am. Kids menu available.

Since 1978 this friendly eatery with a coffeehouse ambiance has been located along the famed and funky Venice Boardwalk. Breakfast, which is served daily till 1pm, features an array of omelets including a tofu scramble; there's also pancakes and French toast. Lunch and dinner share the same menu of appetizers, sandwiches, salads, pastas, burritos and a smattering of seafood. Breads are delivered from La Brea Bakery, and desserts range from linzer tortes to a chocolate espresso brownie. There is a long list of coffee drinks and teas, and the rich hot cocoa is made with Ghiradelli chocolate.

THE SIDEWALK CAFE, 1401 Ocean Front Walk, Tel. 310/399-5547, Hours: Open daily from 9am. No children's menu available.

I'm not sure which has more flavor, the food or the parade of passersby sashaying, skating, jogging and jiggling along the Venice Boardwalk. It's like a free show with every meal.

While you'll find an endless list of sandwiches, pizza, pasta, burritos and tacos, the basic burger, salad or omelet is your safest bet. The menu also comes with a list of "house rules" such as no special orders or substitutions (don't even think of holding the pickles!) and no separate checks. Though there is no kids menu to speak of, it's likely your little one will find something appealing on the menu.

West Los Angeles
AMERICAN
Moderate
HARD ROCK CAFE, at the Beverly Center, 8600 Beverly Boulevard, Tel. 310/276-7605, Hours: Daily 11:30am-midnight. Kids menu available.

It's hard to find someone who hasn't dined at Hard Rock Cafe. This particular one is located at the Beverly Center and features burgers, sandwiches and salads. There always seems to be a line, so don't arrive famished as it's likely you'll have to wait for a table. Believe it or not, many celebrities dine at this location. In fact, years ago I waited more than an hour for a table—and was still waiting—when Howie Mandel and his family breezed in and were shown to a booth right away.

Most people think New York was home to the first American Hard Rock Cafe, but Los Angeles actually spoiled the Big Apple's debut by opening 24-hours earlier.

Inexpensive
THE APPLE PAN, *10801 W. Pico Boulevard, Tel. 310/475-3585, Hours: Sunday, Tuesday-Thursday 11am-midnight, till 1am Friday and Saturday. No children's menu available.*

Since the late 1940s, The Apple Pan has been serving juicy hamburgers and slabs of apple pie to hoards of Angelenos. The horseshoe counter only offers about 10 or so stools, so lingering isn't looked highly upon by those vying for a seat. If you have toddlers, I don't recommend The Apple Pan simply because the stools are a bit ackward for little ones to sit on. Cash only.

DELI
Moderate
CANTER'S, *419 N. Fairfax Avenue, Tel. 323/651-2030, Open 24 hours. Kids menu available.*

As far as delicatessens go, this is probably the city's most famous. But it's not the food that has put this place on the map, it's the after-hours celebrity watching and the fact that you can get brisket at 2am. The people watching is just as appetizing as the menu.

JERRY'S FAMOUS DELI, *8701 Beverly Boulevard, Tel. 310/289-1811, Open 24 hours. Kids menu available.*

Jerry's claim to fame is an endless menu, huge portions and the convenience of being open 24 hours a day. My advice is that you share a meal because it's nearly impossible to finish an entire entree solo. This particular location has telephones at most every booth and table (very L.A.) so publicists, agents and moguls can do business while noshing.

Moderate
JUNIOR'S, *2379 Westwood Boulevard, Tel. 310/475-5771, Hours: Sunday-Thursday 6am-11pm, till midnight Friday and Saturday. Kids menu available.*

Monica Lewinsky's family is said to be regulars at this pricey deli where generous portions are served morning, noon and night. A few years back Junior's received a facelift, and the contemporary interior seems a bit out of wack for this aged L.A. establishment. The selection of deli fare is good, and the loyal clientele will tell you Junior's is the best delicatessen in all of Los Angeles.

West Hollywood

BRUNCH
Expensive

HOUSE OF BLUES, *9225 West Sunset Boulevard, Tel. 323/848-5100m Hours: three seatings every Sunday from 9:30am-2:30pm. Kids menu available.*

Lord have mercy on the Sunset Strip. This is the first Sunday brunch that is more than a meal, it's a happening. Between the eggs and the bacon, you'll be clapping and stomping while screaming "hallelujah!" as the rousing choir performs. Sunday Gospel Brunch at the House of Blues is a popular feast among locals and tourists alike who come to dine on a buffet of bacon, sausages, barbecue chicken, oysters, fresh fruit, omelets and other heavenly fare.

AMERICAN
Inexpensive

BARNEY'S BEANERY, *8447 Santa Monica Boulevard, Tel. 323/654-2287, Hours: Open daily 10am-2am. No children's menu available.*

President John F. Kennedy is said to have enjoyed the food and atmosphere at the place that claims to have the "2nd Best Chili in Los Angeles." If your indecisively challenged, Barney's may just send you over the top with its vast selection of burgers, hot dogs, sandwiches, omelets and endless variations of chili.

I would guess, although I've never actually counted, there is more than 400 items on the menu. This is another L.A. landmark that should be

---

Parent Tip

Kids taking a longer nap than expected? Too lazy to venture out for a meal? No problem, just give **Pink Dot** a call and they'll be at your door in 30-minutes or less. Serving the cities of Hollywood, West Hollywood, Van Nuys, Burbank, Century City, Venice and Glendale, Pink Dot makes delicious sandwiches, pastas and salads. You can also order groceries, video rentals, bakery goods, aspirin and anything else to be delivered to your doorstep. Best of all, there is never a minimum order or delivery charge; but prices are a bit higher than if you did the schlepping yourself. Delivery available from 9am-3am. In the West Los Angeles area, *Tel. 323/656-6060* or visit Pink Dot on the Internet at *www.pinkdot.com.*

experienced - even if you only stop in for an appetizer. If you're stopping by with the kids, do so before 8pm as it gets a little loud and rowdy as the evening lingers on.

CARNEY'S EXPRESS, LTD., *8351 Sunset Boulevard, Tel. 323/654-8300, Hours: Open daily 11am-midnight,. No children's menu available.*
Take a drive down Sunset Boulevard and you're likely to see just about anything. From a statue of Bullwinkle to an assembly of billboards hocking the latest film release. When you spot a bona fide train car sans tracks, you've arrived at Carney's.
The restaurant's founder selected a vintage rail car to house Carney's because he claimed he could always move it and open elsewhere if he had to. Kids love it here because of its rail car setting and for the menu of chili cheeseburgers, chicken sandwiches, frozen bananas and other simple fare.

DUKE'S, *8909 W. Sunset Boulevard, Tel. 310/652-9411, Hours: Monday-Friday 7:30am-8:45pm, Saturday and Sunday 8am-3:45pm. No children's menu available.*
Duke's was legendary when it reigned supreme along Santa Monica Boulevard during the 1970s. All the famous rock 'n roll artists frequented the place, and wannabes with tight leather pants considered it home.
Now Duke's is located along Sunset Boulevard just a few doors from the Whiskey A Go Go, so the clientele is pretty much the same. The food is your basic American standards: sandwiches, omelets, pancakes, soup and salad. *Friends* **Jennifer Aniston** and **David Schwimmer** have been spotted here as well as many other well-known faces.

MEL'S DRIVE-IN, *8585 Sunset Boulevard, Tel. 310/854-7200, Open 24 hours. Kids menu available.*
Diner food never tasted so hip at this 24-hour virtual sock hop where Tom and Nicole once use to dine when they were Hollywood's power couple. The look is reminiscent of *American Graffiti* with old-fashioned food to match: burgers, fries, milkshakes and other greasy grub. The clientele is young, hip and full of aspiring actors.

CRAVINGS, *8653 Sunset Boulevard, Tel. 310/652-6104, Hours: Monday-Friday 8am-midnight, Saturday and Sunday 9am-midnight, No children's menu available.*
Located smack in the middle of Sunset Plaza, this eclectic bistro is really the quintessential outdoor cafe. An assembly of umbrella-covered tables are positioned along the sidewalk for both the diners' enjoyment and the passersby. Cravings offers a little bit of everything, from Italian to Japanese to even some German favorites.

CANTONESE
Moderate

FORMOSA CAFE, *7156 Santa Monica Boulevard, Tel. 323/850-9050, Hours: Sunday-Thursday 4pm-10pm, Friday and Saturday 6pm-1am. No children's menu available.*

The crimson colored building and Confucius-style lettering has been turning heads since 1934. Here you'll find some tasty Cantonese cooking taking place in the kitchen, and it's still possible to spot a famous face at this Hollywood landmark. Some may recognize the restaurant from its cameo appearance in *L.A. Confidential.* This was once a favorite haunt of gangsters Mickey Cohen and Bugsy Siegal, as well as more law abiding citizens such as Lana Turner. Families should plan on dining here before 8pm.

DESSERTS
Inexpensive

SWEET LADY JANE, *8360 Melrose Avenue, Tel. 323/653-7145, Hours: Monday-Saturday 8:30am-11:30pm, closed Sunday. No children's menu available.*

A savvy little sweet shop where Angelenos go for a sugar fix. Homemade desserts include silky tarts, moist cheesecake and cookies you could cut with a knife. Cakes are indeed a work of art worthy of any gallery. A selection of teas are available, and coffee drinks are a specialty.

Westwood
CALIFORNIA
Moderate

GARDENS ON GLENDON, *1139 Glendon Avenue, Tel. 310/824-1818, Hours: Lunch 11:30am-3pm daily, dinner 5:30pm-11pm Monday-Thursday, till midnight Friday and Saturday, till 10pm Sunday. No children's menu available.*

Located close to the UCLA campus, dining takes place under a towering ficus tree, and the sounds of a pianist on selected evenings is definitely mood enhancing. With a selection of grilled chicken, crab cakes, steak au poivre, fresh seafood, veggie dishes, burgers and chopped salads, there seems to be something for everyone. This is one of the few restaurants where the guacamole is prepared tableside. Kids can order off the bar menu, which features less sophisticated fare.

MIDDLE EASTERN
Moderate

SHAHRZAD, *1442 Westwood, Tel.310/470-9131, Hours: Open daily noon-midnight.No children's menu available.*

Iranians who know a thing or two about marinated lamb, kabobs, chicken stews and other traditional dishes from this part of the world dine here often. You'll find very generous portions at prices that will amaze you.

Inexpensive

FALAFEL KING, *1059 Broxton Avenue, Tel. 310/208-4444, Hours: Sunday-Thursday 10:30am-midnight, Friday and Saturday 11am-1:30am. No children's menu available.*

Just like the name says, Falafel King rules when it comes to falafel. This Middle Eastern specialty consists of deep-fried meat balls served solo or inside pita bread and accompanied by yogurt sauce. UCLA co-eds arrive in droves because of its close proximity to campus and, more importantly, it's cheap! Cash only.

PIZZA

Inexpensive

LAMONICA'S N.Y. PIZZA, *1066 Gayley Avenue, Tel. 310/208-8671, Hours: Open daily 10:30am-midnight. No children's menu available.*

The thin crusted New York-style pizza is really tasty topped with traditional pepperoni, sausage, onions or whatever else you may have in mind. When you and your brood can't agree on a topping, it's just as easy to order by the slice. The New York subway setting makes you feel like you're in the Big Apple, but the sunny weather outside dictates otherwise. Cash only.

l.a. with kids

index

Things Change!

Phone numbers, prices, addresses, quality of food, etc, all change. If you come across any new information, we'd appreciate hearing from you. No item is too small! Drop us an email note at: Jopenroad@aol.com, or write us at:

L.A. with Kids
Open Road Publishing, P.O. Box 284
Cold Spring Harbor, NY 11724

Open Road Publishing
Catalog of Titles

U.S.

America's Cheap Sleeps, $17.95
America's Most Charming Towns & Villages, $17.95
Arizona Guide, $16.95
Boston Guide, $13.95
California Wine Country Guide, $12.95
California's Best B&Bs, $14.95
Colorado Guide, $17.95
Florida Guide, $16.95
Hawaii Guide, $18.95
Las Vegas Guide, $14.95
New Mexico Guide, $16.95
San Francisco Guide, $16.95
Southern California Guide, $18.95
Spa Guide, $14.95
Texas Guide, $16.95
Utah Guide, $16.95
Vermont Guide, $16.95

Family Travel Guides

Caribbean with Kids, $14.95
Disneyworld with Kids, $14.95
Italy with Kids, $14.95
L.A. with Kids, $14.95
Las Vegas with Kids, $12.95
National Parks with Kids, $14.95
Washington DC with Kids, $14.95

Eating & Drinking on the Open Road

Eating & Drinking in Paris, $9.95
Eating & Drinking in Italy, $9.95
Eating & Drinking in Spain, $9.95
Eating & Drinking in Latin America, $9.95

Middle East/Africa

Egypt Guide, $17.95
Kenya Guide, $18.95

Latin America & Caribbean
Bahamas Guide, $13.95
Belize Guide, $16.95
Bermuda Guide, $14.95
Caribbean Guide, $21.95
Chile Guide, $18.95
Costa Rica Guide, $17.95
Ecuador & Galapagos Islands Guide, $17.95
Guatemala Guide, $18.95
Honduras Guide, $16.95

Europe
Czech & Slovak Republics Guide, $18.95
Greek Islands Guide, $16.95
Holland Guide, $17.95
Ireland Guide, $17.95
Italy Guide, $19.95

To order, send us a check or money order for the price of the book(s) plus $4.00 shipping and handling for domestic orders, to:
Open Road Publishing
PO Box 284
Cold Spring Harbor, NY 11724

London Guide, $14.95
Moscow Guide, $16.95
Paris Guide, $13.95
Prague Guide, $14.95
Rome Guide, $14.95
Scotland Guide, $17.95
Spain Guide, $18.95
Turkey Guide, $19.95

Asia
China Guide, $21.95
Japan Guide, $21.95
Philippines Guide, $18.95
Tahiti & French Polynesia Guide, $18.95
Tokyo Guide, $14.95
Thailand Guide, $18.95